Fan CULTure

GW00383271

Fan CULTure

*Essays on Participatory
Fandom in the 21st Century*

Edited by Kristin M. Barton *and*
Jonathan Malcolm Lampley

Foreword by Stephen J. Sansweet

McFarland & Company, Inc., Publishers
Jefferson, North Carolina, and London

LIBRARY OF CONGRESS CATALOGUING-IN-PUBLICATION DATA

Fan CULTure : essays on participatory fandom in the 21st century / edited by Kristin M. Barton and Jonathan Malcolm Lampley ; foreword by Stephen J. Sansweet.
    p.   cm.
Includes bibliographical references and index.

ISBN 978-0-7864-7418-9
softcover : acid free paper ∞

1. Subculture.   2. Fans (Persons)   3. Mass media—Social aspects.   I. Barton, Kristin Michael, 1977– editor of compilation.   II. Lampley, Jonathan Malcolm, 1967– editor of compilation.
HM646.F34 2014
306'.1—dc23   2013038906

BRITISH LIBRARY CATALOGUING DATA ARE AVAILABLE

On the cover: Adam Baldwin, Alan Tudyk, Nathan Fillion and Gina Torres on the set of the 2002 television series *Firefly* (Fox/Photofest)

Manufactured in the United States of America

McFarland & Company, Inc., Publishers
  Box 611, Jefferson, North Carolina 28640
    www.mcfarlandpub.com

For Joss Whedon, George Lucas, R.A. Salvatore,
Gene Roddenberry, Matt Groening, Mitch Hurwitz,
and everyone else who has created something
that I've obsessed over at one point or another.
And Gina, who I'm also a fan of.

— KMB

For Forrest J Ackerman (1916–2012), Uncle Forry
to generations of Monster Kids and an inspiration
for fans and collectors everywhere.

— JML

Table of Contents

Section 3: Fan-Influenced Content

Foreword

Stephen J. Sansweet

Before geek culture conquered the world, we fans were a misunderstood lot. It wasn't that long ago that — after having been a journalist for 30 years — I sat through interviews around the world where I was called a nerd, fanatic, loony, cultist, nutter, or even "anorak," British slang that turned the typical hooded parka worn by trainspotters into a somewhat derogatory term for obsessive fans. (Granted, folks who spend hours on windy train platforms to jot down the times and details of passing trains might seem a bit compulsive to some.) My response was usually to compare myself to the most ardent fans of whatever the top sport was in that particular country.

Fandom today is all about popular culture, mass media, and the ability to instantly connect with like-minded others — something that couldn't have been imagined when science-fiction and comic book fans first started small get-togethers in the 1930s. Fandom got a brief moment in the media spotlight in the late 1960s due to a letter-writing campaign to NBC by *Star Trek* fans, acting on rumors that the series would be killed after just two seasons on air.

But I'd make a strong case that it was the 1977 release of *Star Wars* that jump-started geek culture in the last decades of the 20th century. You'd probably expect me to say that since I was head of fan relations for Lucasfilm Ltd. for 15 years starting in 1996, and remain fan relations adviser. I've seen geeks reclaim that word as proud affirmation of their strength (and buying power) after decades of being sneered at and kept on the sidelines.

I'm proud to have been on the forward edge of this new fandom. I grew up at the dawn of the Space Age, and my fascination with that combined with my life-long love of science fiction (from authors such as Asimov and Heinlein to cheesy TV shows like *Tom Corbett, Space Cadet*) seems to have made my path somewhat predictable. In late 1976, I was a reporter in the Los Angeles bureau of *The Wall Street Journal* when I started collecting space toys like 1960s Japanese battery-operated robots and versions of real-world rockets and space capsules. With the exception of three seasons of *Star Trek* on TV and *2001: A Space Odyssey*, neither considered financially successful, there had been little in the mass media to get me excited.

And then along came George Lucas and his space opera, a Western set amidst the stars, a fantasy that didn't obey the rules and restrictions of hard science fiction. And I was hooked. I got to see it—10 days before the movie opened and the hype exploded—in a theater on the back lot of 20th Century–Fox; it was filled with local journalists and their kids.

Unlike today's "tent-pole" movies, there wasn't much merchandise in advance of the film or even for months after as its popularity swept the U.S. and then overseas. It was truly a case of products chasing pent-up demand as *Star Wars* basically launched the business of licensing motion pictures. The strong desire to take something *Star Wars* home with you, and having to wait, seemed to make what was available even dearer. When small action figures and vehicles finally started appearing more than nine months later, kids finally had a way to recreate scenes from the film and make up new ones. Home video was still several years in the future. I started buying the merchandise as part of my growing space toy collection; eventually, it became my sole focus.

While *Star Wars* had been below the radar for most, including those who booked movies into theaters, a fan community starved for something unique and cool had already been let in on the secret. Out of desperation and inspiration Charley Lippincott, Lucasfilm's head of marketing, publicity, and merchandising, and a comic book and sci-fi geek himself, brought photos and even props and costumes to several fan conventions the year before the movie's release. A paperback novelization of the story, released in November 1976, sold out all 500,000 copies. And Marvel comics had released the first three of its six movie adaptation issues prior to the May 25, 1977, opening. The target audience knew, and those early lines around the block ignited a media firestorm.

That outreach to, and inclusion of, the fan community became part of Lucasfilm's DNA decades before Hollywood studios caught on. There was an internally-run fan club and newsletter, giveaways and contests, and active communications between company representatives and fans. Soon after *Return of the Jedi* was released in 1983, that all faded away. It wasn't until Lucasfilm was getting ready to release the Special Editions of the original trilogy before launching the prequel movies that the fan machinery kicked into gear again.

I had a head start. Besides the continuing growth of my *Star Wars* collection, I had interviewed George Lucas for a column in the *Journal* on the 10th anniversary of the first movie's release. In the early 1990s, Lucasfilm started a publishing unit and I heard that it planned to do a collectibles price guide. I made a cold call and basically said that if anyone were to do such a book, it should be me. "And you are...?" I was asked. But that call led to my first *Star Wars* book; to date there have been fifteen more. The QVC home shopping network had me as a guest on one of its *Star Wars* collectibles shows, and I ended up as co-host for the next six years — more than 60 hours live.

I'd been Los Angeles bureau chief at the *Journal* for nearly nine years, and it was time to move on. So when I got a call from Lucasfilm soliciting advice as to who they could hire for a guaranteed one-year-only job at minimal pay to go to a bunch of fan conventions and let fans in on some of the secrets of the Special Editions, *naturally* I took the plunge. I took mythologist Joseph Campbell's advice: "Follow your bliss." I never left the payroll.

I looked at myself as being Lucasfilm's representative to fans — but just as important, fandom's representative inside Lucasfilm. This wasn't a once a year, let's set up a booth and have a celebrity panel at San Diego Comic-Con International kind of thing. Rather it was let's make our fans as happy as possible, and if we can't do something or there's a bothersome issue, let's explain why. Getting corporate buy-in on a newly formed group wearing *Star Wars* costumes called the 501st Legion is just one example of how understanding fans and their motives can pay huge dividends in the long run.

For me, working inside Lucasfilm while three new *Star Wars* films were being made and marketed was an incredibly exciting second career. But honestly the best part of the job was traveling around the world, speaking before tens of thousands of fans, and getting to become close friends with hundreds of them. The sense of community, of sharing, of caring — in one year two different members of the 501st received kidneys from other members they had never met before — has been truly life-changing.

Now I find myself chief executive of Rancho Obi-Wan, a nonprofit museum that displays my personal collection, estimated at more than 300,000 pieces. Giving personal two-to-three hour tours to small groups lets me share so many stories that have built up over the years, and also leads to new friendships. And George Lucas created a large enough sandbox for millions to play in. How exciting to know that the *Star Wars* gene is going to be passed along to future generations as new movies are made and more fans get to share that far-away galaxy with their children and grandchildren.

And that bodes well for fans of every stripe. Seeing a largely female audience in the thousands lined up outside for a day to see and hear a Comic-Con panel with stars from the Twilight films finally shattered Hollywood's delusion that there weren't any girl geeks. Superhero comics soon will be entering their eighth decade and the high-grossing — and usually pretty good — movies being made from them provide hope for their continued longevity. Some attempts are finally being undertaken to make genre projects include more diverse characters to match the diversity of the audience, although there's still a lot of work to be done there.

It's not so difficult to understand why all of this is happening. Yes, instant communications and sharing go a long way. But underlying that is that the first generations of fans — often the shy, quiet ones who kept to themselves — now control the bully pulpit. They are the writers and directors and Hollywood executives who are making the movies and television series that *they* want to see. They are the storytellers and scripters and artists who have helped break through the comic book/graphic novel demographics barrier. And, quite importantly, they are the journalists and bloggers and social media hounds who keep the fans pumped up and wanting more — of practically everything. Fandom may start with the property, but it ends up being all about the people.

Stephen J. Sansweet is president of Rancho Obi-Wan Inc., a museum in northern California that houses the world's largest private collection of Star Wars *memorabilia. For 15 years, he was head of fan relations and director of content management at Lucasfilm Ltd. and remains a consultant. He has written 18 books, 16 on* Star Wars.

Introduction

Kristin M. Barton

My first experience with the phenomenon known as "fandom" occurred in 1989. I was twelve years old and I had just met Davy Jones. In the late 1980s, MTV began airing reruns of the old NBC series *The Monkees* (1966–1968), and something about the likeable bandmates, their wacky adventures, and the pop soundtrack spoke to my prepubescent self. So you can imagine my excitement when, in the fall of 1989, I discovered that lead singer Davy Jones was signing autographs at the local J.C. Penney (he was in town playing Fagin in a production of *Oliver!*, and my parents readily agreed to take me down to meet him). An hour early and about twentieth in line, my sister and I waited while my parents looked on. As my mother tells it, when I reached the table where Jones was sitting I very loudly said, "Hi!" as he signed a t-shirt for me. His easy smile and genuine excitement to see such a young fan made me aware that the person I'd watched and idolized on screen was some-one who was a real person, and it only served to intensify my need to surround myself with everything Monkees. Afterward I began watching the episodes in earnest, buying up old Monkees albums on tapes (and making a few of my own by holding my parents' tape recorder next to the TV). I was — and to a degree still am — a fan.

As Tanya R. Cochran notes, the term "fan" originally derives from the Latin *fanaticus*, meaning insane, mad, or possessed by the gods (239–240). While not terms most of us would willingly choose to describe our obsessions with popular culture or the like, I'm willing to bet that all of us can acknowl-edge that at some point we've acted that way. But defining what a "fan" is in contemporary terms (especially as it applies to media) has been attempted by dozens of authors on the subject. Beyond the struggle of defining what a fan is, many scholars have compounded the issue by attempting to distinguish one type of fan from another. For example, Matt Hills suggests that the terms "fans" and "cult fans" are largely synonymous terms, but notes that the term cult fans, "*relates not to the intensity, social organization or semiotic/material productivity of the fandom concerned, but rather to its duration, especially in the absence of 'new' or official material in the originating medium*" (x; italics in original). Thus, fans only become "cult fans" once the original artifact has left mainstream culture. So fans of the original *Star Trek* television series became cult fans once the series ended but fan organizations and conventions continued to proliferate.

Rather than trying to define what a fan *is*, this book explores what a fan *does*. That is to say, how do fans show their love for a film franchise? What do fans do when their favorite television series is cancelled? How do fans interact with cultural icons that have had a part in shaping who they are? The reasons we become fans are varied and personal: being a fan allows us to express ourselves, it helps us connect to like minded people, and it allows us to escape into a world devoid of the pressures of life, even if only for 30 minutes at a time. But more than anything, being a fan means being in love. Joss Whedon may have said it best in describing his perspective on his fans and their devotion: "I'm a fan, and it's a huge part of who I am. It's a huge part of why I do this. It's not to make things people like. It's never to make things people like. It's only to make things that they love" ("Re-Lighting the Firefly").

I don't think it's a stretch to say that I, my co-editor, and all the contributors to this volume are all fans of our respective topics, among numerous other facets of popular culture. If we weren't, this project wouldn't have been nearly as enjoyable as it was (early in the writing process I convinced my wife that I needed to re-watch the entire run of *Firefly* episodes under the auspices of "research"). Contained within the following pages are essays exploring how that love and enjoyment manifests itself. The scholars who have contributed their talents to this book have provided thoughtful and inspired analyses into the notion of fandom, and it is through their sagacity that a better understanding of the participatory nature of fandom in the twenty-first century has emerged. To that end, the essays in this book have been divided into three sections, providing thematic cohesion among and between the topics under discussion.

The essays included in Section 1 look at how fans produce new narratives and artifacts for their respective topics. In "Can't Stop the Sequel: How the *Serenity*-Inspired *Browncoats: Redemption* Is Changing the Future of Fan Films" I use the 2010 fan film (which follows events that took place in the 2005 film *Serenity*) as an example of the direction that fan productions might be headed in the future. Having gotten approval for the film from *Serenity*'s creator Joss Whedon and Universal, the fans behind *Browncoats: Redemption* have raised more than $100,000 in charity through DVD sales and merchandising, suggesting a new model for studio/fan partnerships. Jeff Thompson's essay on *Dark Shadows* titled "*Dark Shadows* Fandom, Then and Now (1966–2013)" goes inside fan productions as a means of maintaining interest and discussion of a cultural artifact after it has stopped being produced. Thompson specifically explores how fan-published magazines ("fanzines") and conventions kept the fan community alive, to the point that enough interest remained for a film to be released in 2012 by acclaimed director Tim Burton. Don Tresca, in "Spellbound: An Analysis of Adult-Oriented Harry Potter Fanfiction," reviews how some fans of the Harry Potter series have taken to producing very dark and dystopic tales set in the mythical realm of J. K. Rowling's characters. Tresca delves into the deeper psychological meanings of these drastic interpretations to better understand what this suggests about the authors and their connection to the world of Harry Potter. Concluding Section 1 is Kathleen Williams' essay "Recut Film Trailers, Nostalgia and the Teen Film." In it, Williams looks at the phenomenon of "recutting" trailers, where fans splice together clips from popular films in order to re-imagine the film as they would have liked it or emphasize certain storylines and elements over others.

Section 2 explores social media and its use in attracting, maintaining, and building fan communities. To begin, in "Bringing Piety Back: Tim Tebow, Sports and American Culture" author Susan Orenstein moves the discussion of fan participation away from media vehicles and into the realm of sports. Tebow, a quarterback in the NFL, has had an immense cultural impact in proportion to his impact within the game of football. Orensetin looks at Tebow's impact on his fans, not just in the popular craze of "Tebowing," but also in the context of the impact his religious beliefs have had on motivating his fans to become more religious themselves. "Fan Made Time: *The Lord of the Rings* and *The Hobbit*" by Owain Gwynne (a New Zealand scholar, nonetheless!) explores how fans interact and communicate in the periods that have lead up the releases of the original *Lord of the Rings* trilogy (2001–2003) and *The Hobbit* trilogy (2012–2014). Using the examples from the popular fan site TheOneRing.net, Gwynne dissects how fans use the site as a means to pass time between films and how that interactivity with other fans has become part of their daily routine. Bethan Jones' essay "The Fandom Is Out There: Social Media and *The X-Files* Online" is an examination of the ways fans of the popular series *The X-Files* have taken to fansites like XFN (XFilesNews. com) to rally support for further stories to be produced. Jones specifically cites the "XF3 Army" campaign, which was launched in an effort to encourage producers of the series to make a third film in the franchise. Section 2 is capped off with "Alternate Reality Games, Narrative Disbursement and Canon: *The Lost Experience*," the first of two essays that deal with the highly popular series *Lost*. Kent Aardse explains how multiple media outlets were used in order to maintain fan interest during the show's hiatus and how clues about upcoming storylines were revealed that would entice viewers to tune in when it returned. Through books, online videos, and even puzzles, fans were kept entertained unraveling *Lost*'s mysteries even during the months when new episodes were unavailable.

Section 3 explores the influence fans have on content over various entertainment properties and how producers integrate their input into the final product. This section begins with Jennifer C. Garlen's revealing look into the adult fans of LEGO (AFOL) in "Block Party: A Look at Adult Fans of LEGO." In this essay Garlen discusses how the AFOL communities interact and display their creations, but perhaps most importantly she reveals the influence this group has on determining what products LEGO will release based on their levels of interest. In "A New Kind of Pandering: *Supernatural* and the World of Fanfiction," Anissa M. Graham looks at how fan communities for the CW series *Supernatural* have been directly incorporated into the show. She specifically explores several episodes of the series as examples of how the show's fans have influenced episodes and storylines. Similarly, while not looking at a specific film or television series, Meyrav Koren-Kuik instead focuses on the participatory fandom of a location: Disneyland. In "Desiring the Tangible: Disneyland, Fandom and Spatial Immersion" Koren-Kuik looks at how the entertainment giant produces films based on rides, rides based on films, and touring musicals based on interests and positive receptions received from fans. Following that, I provide my second look at fandom with the essay "Chuck Versus the Advertiser: How Fan Activism and Footlong Subway Sandwiches Saved a Television Series," which looks at how fans of the NBC series *Chuck* came together to save their beloved show from cancellations for three successive seasons. Through their "Finale & Footlong" campaign, fans not only saved the show, but also influenced the show's content and may have reshaped the way fan communities rally support for their favorite shows in the future. The final essay and the second *Lost* entry comes from Michael Graves and is titled "'Guys, where are we?' Podcasts, Online Video and *Lost*'s Participatory Culture." Graves has combed through hours of *The Official Lost Podcast* as well as fan podcasts to understand how fans influenced the directions and storylines that evolved within the series. Graves quotes *Lost*'s executive producers and showrunners Damon Lindelof and Carlton Cuse as they reveal how fan reactions served to shape the show and dictate what storylines were cut short because of almost universal negative reaction.

Works Cited

Cochran, Tanya R. "The Browncoats Are Coming! *Firefly*, *Serenity*, and Fan Activism." *Investigating* Firefly and Serenity: *Science Fiction on the Frontier*. eds. Rhonda V. Wilcox and Tanya R. Cochran. London: I.B. Tauris, 2008. 239–249.

Hills, Matt. *Fan Culture*. New York: Routledge, 2002.

"Re-Lighting the Firefly." *Serenity*. Writ. and dir. Joss Whedon. Universal, 2005.

SECTION 1: FAN PRODUCTIONS

Can't Stop the Sequel

How the *Serenity*-Inspired *Browncoats: Redemption* Is Changing the Future of Fan Films

KRISTIN M. BARTON

"A thriving fan culture can ensure a high public profile for a series that might otherwise quickly vanish into the wastes of television history."—
Sara Gwenllian Jones, "Web Wars: Resistance, Online Fandom and Studio Censorship," 166.

When media scholar Sara Gwenllian Jones wrote the preceding, she was writing at the time of the *Star Trek* franchise and the ancillary revenue that has been generated as a result of its loyal fan following. However, there exists one television series that it may pertain to more directly, having one of the largest and most active fan followings in proportion to the total number of episodes produced. That series is Joss Whedon's *Firefly* (2002), which aired only eleven episodes (many out of their intended order) amid numerous scheduling changes to accommodate baseball playoff games before being cancelled by Fox in December 2002. Despite these setbacks, more than a decade later Whedon's creation enjoys a thriving and involved fan community that continues to maintain a visible profile for the show and raise money for charity through raffles, auctions, and screenings of the show's motion picture continuation, *Serenity* (2005).

Not satisfied to merely sit back and dwell on the show's early cancellation and a lack of film sequels, *Firefly* fan and amateur filmmaker Michael Dougherty sought out a way to continue telling stories in Whedon's imperfect version of the future. Knowing that Fox and Universal (the studios that own the rights to *Firefly* and *Serenity*, respectively) would have lawyers on call ready to pounce at the first sign of copyright infringement, Dougherty and his fellow fans began work on a film that would take place in the same universe as Whedon's stories, but purposely avoided incorporating characters owned by the studios. But most importantly, the film would be made as a means of raising money for charity, something that has become a calling card for fans of the series. Hence, the fan film *Browncoats: Redemption* was born.

The term "Browncoats" is used in the television series as a nickname for the Independent forces (think: the Civil War Confederacy) that fought the better equipped Alliance during their war for independence. The nickname was adopted by fans of *Firefly/Serenity* because, like the Independents, they identified as outsiders: a small group who have stood up against a much more formidable opponents (the Fox Network) to fight a war that was seen by most to be unwinnable (keeping the series on the air). With that "never give up" attitude behind them, the makers of *Browncoats: Redemption* began preproduction in late 2008 and commenced shooting the film in early 2009. The concept Dougherty conceived of for the film was to set it three months after the events in *Serenity* and explore how those events may have affected other ships and crews that might possibly populate Whedon's universe.

In order to produce a large-scale, high-quality fan film, it can be argued that there are two elements vital for any production to succeed: an understanding of the source material and an involved, networked fan community to provide support. Both of these elements have been described and defined as requiring some sort of "capital," which is to say an investment either on the part of the individual or the community as a whole. The first element, an innate understanding of the source material, is necessary for accurate incorporation of a fan film into the large narrative on which it is based. This type of knowledge about a fictional narrative is referred to by Fiske as "fan cultural capital" and is defined as an investment by fans into accumulating knowledge pertaining to a particular object of fandom. This investment in knowledge certainly takes the form of a familiarity with original works produced (television episodes, films in a series, and so on), but in many cases goes on to include expanded knowledge not incorporated into the original artifacts. In addition to *Firefly/Serenity*'s episodes and feature film, this includes canonical supplements such as the Dark Horse comics and the visual companions from Titan Books. This type of expanded understanding of the mythology can also be obtained from several scholarly collections of essays on the topic as well as officially licensed products such as screen-quality replica props and a map of the fictionalized *Firefly* universe produced by the company Quantum Mechanix (QMx). This increased familiarity with a cultural artifact is typical of many fan communities, and as Jones notes, "fans seek to reinforce and expand the fictional cosmology by continually gathering new information about its characters, geographies, backstories, plots and themes" (167).

The second element necessary for fan film production is "fan social capital," which Hills describes as "the network of fan friends and acquaintances that a fan possesses as well as their access to media producers and professional personnel linked to their object of fandom" (57). This builds on the need for fan cultural capital in that fan social capital brings together like-minded fans that, in most cases, already have an extensive working knowledge of a particular fan object. *Browncoats: Redemption* was inundated with fan social capital, as Browncoats from around the globe volunteered to help out, as did professionals involved with the original series and film, including *Firefly* composer Greg Edmonson, who created and donated an original musical track to the fan production. In a letter sent out to fans and supporters of *Browncoats: Redemption* in June of 2012, producer-writer-director Michael Dougherty commented on what he felt was perceived by many to be an impossible task for a group of fans to accomplish:

> I had friends, family, other Browncoats, strangers, and people who work in the industry tell me to my face sometimes in not so nice ways, that Browncoats: Redemption would never be allowed OR get made at all. The fact that it was completed is due, in large part, to you and your support. Thanks to you, the film shipped to every continent on the globe, played in conventions around the world, fully paid for itself, and raised over $117,000 for charity.

The exceptional nature of *Browncoats: Redemption*, with its mission statement of donating all proceeds from the film to charity, is that it can be seen as the template for a "win-win" endeavor, where both fans and the studios benefit from its production. Fans received the satisfaction of furthering the narrative established by Whedon in the *Firefly/Serenity* universe. The studios can rest assured that the content of the fan film doesn't infringe on their copyrighted material and that no one else is profiting from their property. Additionally, for non-profit and charitable organizations, the film raised a significant amount of money that traditional campaigning and fundraising would be hard-pressed to achieve. With this in mind, what follows is a breakdown of how each of these entities specifically benefits from *Browncoats: Redemption* and what this means for the future of fan films.

A Brief History of Fan Films

Before jumping into a detailed examination of *Browncoats: Redemption*, it's worth taking a brief look at the evolution of fan films up to this point. While certainly not comprehensive, the following consists of what many consider to be some of the seminal moments in the field. Clive Young, author of *Homemade Hollywood*, defines the modern fan film as "an unauthorized amateur or semi-pro film, based on pop culture characters or situations, created for noncommercial viewing" (4). He goes on to specifically note that in order to avoid issues of copyright infringement these films can in no way result in financial gain for the filmmakers, saying, "they can't sell copies of their movies, nor can they charge admission to see the flicks" (5). For a vast majority of fan films, financial profit isn't a concern (or an option) as many are made on tight budgets are rarely viewed beyond the filmmaker's immediate circle of friends and family. However, there are exceptions where fans with either the technical skill or financial resources to make a high-quality production have managed to get their product out into the viewing public.

Young suggests that the first fan film may have been produced in 1926 by two con men looking to make money at the expense of the townspeople of Anderson, South Carolina (9). The men (a director and a cameraman) claimed to be from Hollywood and said they were looking to produce an "Our Gang" film (more commonly known today as The Little Rascals). The week-long shoot cast local children in all of the roles (prompting parents to buy tickets en masse), and the finished product was screened at the local theater by the end of the week. While *Anderson "Our Gang"* was an illegal venture perpetrated by charlatans, the end result remains the first known film made about pop cultures figures outside of a studio.

With film equipment being prohibitively expensive for most people in the first half of the 20th century, newer technology and an increase in availability made fan films a more common endeavor post–World War II. While many fan films were created featuring legendary movie monsters and comic book heroes, it was not until 1978 that the potential for what fan films could be was realized. The previous year *Star Wars* (1977) had taken the world by storm, and Ernie Fosselius and Michael Wises set out to parody the blockbuster in their fan film *Hardware Wars* (1978). Featuring the characters Fluke Starbucker, Ham Salad, and Chewchilla the Wookie Monster (a tongue-in-cheek reference to the Cookie Monster doll that was dyed brown for the part), the twelve-minute faux-trailer/film depicted all of the seminal moments from *Star Wars* using noticeably (and intentionally) low-tech effects, including common household appliances such as toasters and a waffle iron in place of spaceships. Young notes that this was "the first high-profile harbinger of today's fan film movement" and inspired countless others to follow in its footsteps (73).

While proficiency and expertise with fan filmmaking would mature in the following decades, what many consider to be the first modern fan film was released nineteen years later. *Troops* (1997) was a fan film created by Kevin Rubio that once again took characters from the Star Wars universe, but this time placed them in a ten-minute parody of the television series *Cops* (1989– present). The film was the first to use what were, at the time, state-of-the-art computer generated graphics to create realistic effects that many amateur filmmakers had struggled with for so long. In defense of previous fan films, Rubio (who had been working in television production for a number of years) enlisted a number of friends who worked in the television and film industries to provide the effects that would make *Troops* so revolutionary. It is estimated that the cost for all of the technical services that were provided free of charge to make the film would have been around $279,000 (Young 155).

It is worth noting here that the two of the major milestones in the history of fan filmmaking coincide directly with major events in the Star Wars franchise. *Hardware Wars* emerged after the blockbuster success of the original *Star Wars* in theaters, and *Troops* was produced during the same summer that the *Star Wars* Special Edition was being re-released in theaters, and when talk of the upcoming *Star Wars: Episode I—The Phantom Menace* (1999) was creating a frenzied environment within the general population. In a way, this connection to *Star Wars* is serendipitous since fan films are famous for being overly ambitious on a limited budget (which *Star Wars* was) and drawing inspiration from iconic characters and classic films (which Lucas acknowledges he did, as his galaxy far, far away was heavily influenced by television serials like *Flash Gordon* [1954–1955] and the films of Akira Kurosawa). In essence, Lucas may not have just made one of the most popular films of all time, but from a certain point of view, he also made the first financially successful fan film.

Following the technical proficiency and expertise demonstrated with *Troops*, fan films became increasingly more polished as digital film equipment and editing software advanced. Following the highly criticized Joel Schumacher film *Batman & Robin* (1997), Hollywood effects artist Sandy Collora put together the eight-minute fan film *Batman: Dead End* (2003) as a demo reel for a Hollywood directing job. The film presented a darker version of Batman, something fans clamored for following Schumacher's overly-cartoony version of the Dark Knight. Premiered at Comic-Con to rave reviews, *Batman: Dead End* led to numerous other fan films that blended do-it-yourself approach with Hollywood quality production. Numerous superhero films followed, including Collera's quasi-sequel *World's Finest* (2004) and the highly stylized trailer/fan film *Grayson* (2004). More recently, actor Thomas Jane produced the fan film *Dirty Laundry*, a ten-minute short where Jane reprises his role as Frank Castle, better known as the ultra-violent comic book vigilante The Punisher (which he'd previously played in the 2004 film *The Punisher*). Co-starring Ron Perlman, Jane said of his return to the role, "I wanted to make a fan film for a character I've always loved and believed in — a love letter to Frank Castle & his fans" (Kit). As this example shows, the line between amateur and professional production continues to be blurred. This may best be exemplified by the homemade Star Trek series *Star Trek: Phase II* (2004–present) which features a $100,000 replica of the original Enterprise bridge and a budget of around $40,000 per episode (Suellentrop). This level of devotion, dedication, and financial investment can only come from a group who, above all else, consider themselves fans.

Fans

One of the most obvious (and sometimes overlooked) benefits fan filmmaking provides is a reminder to the networks and studios that there is an active fan base still longing for continuing stories to be told. Being vocal about their enthusiasm for a product and making their presence known is one way fan communities indirectly influence what film and television projects go into production. While fan films are only one of the many ways fans show their support and love for a television or film series, it could be argued that these projects provide one of the most concrete ways of measuring a communities' dedication, through the number of fans involved in a production, number of views online, and the quality with which it is crafted. But there exist other means of measuring or tracking fans' activity and involvement, especially in the age of the Internet.

When the website io9.com held their March Movie Madness competition in 2011, it asked readers to choose the best science fiction film of all time by voting for films in a series of head-to-head match-ups that were arranged in a format similar to the bracketed NCAA basketball tournament that, through elimination rounds, ultimately determines a national champion. After weeks of voting, *Serenity* (an "eighth seed" in bracketology terms) defeated #2 seed *The Empire Strikes Back* (1980) in the finals to be crowned the winner with 55.72 percent of the votes (Wilkins and Woerner). There can be no doubt that in terms of raw numbers, there are more people who have seen and enjoyed *Empire* than *Serenity*, and this statement can be backed up in almost every way possible: through ticket sales, DVD sales, critics' reviews, award nominations and wins, merchandising, and the like ... but what *Serenity* lacks in volume of fans, it more than makes up for in the dedication of its fans. Fans of *Serenity* take this type of competition as an opportunity to make their presence known and continue an advertising campaign they started for the film almost six years earlier when the film was first released. While many of the site's readers objected to the results in the website's comments section, Browncoats view each of these tiny victories as a way to show their love for Whedon's creation and make their voices heard among the din of larger fan communities.

One of the main factors that has inspired such devotion and dedication within the *Firefly/Serenity* fan community is series creator and all-around mastermind Joss Whedon. His involvement in every aspect of the series and film, from writing scripts to directing episodes to writing the show's opening theme song, has inspired fans who appreciate the care and attention to detail he has demonstrated and every level of production. This hyphenate approach ensures that his vision and unique approach to storytelling are felt within each moment on screen. The term *hyphenate* has been used to describe creators who function in several capacities within a given media vehicle (for example, Whedon was the writer-director-producer of *Firefly*). Milson extends this line of thinking, citing Browncoats as "audience-marketers" or "audience-producers" due to their direct involvement in getting *Serenity* made (277). As Abbott notes, "In the case of *Serenity*, discourses around the film's production have, however, blurred the distinction between creator and fan by positioning them as working together to bring their shared vision to the screen" (236). Even Whedon himself noted this in his recorded introduction to early test screenings of the film, saying, "[*Serenity*] is, in an unprecedented sense, your [the fans'] movie" ("Joss Whedon Introduction").

With box office totals lower than hoped and the possibility of a sequel not looking likely, fans of *Serenity* took the initiative to start creating their own content to keep the franchise alive. In this way, fans moved from the "fan-producer" hyphenate to the much more involved "fan-producer-writer-director." In 2005, just prior to *Serenity*'s theatrical debut, the *Firefly* fan-film parody *Mosquito* was released on the Internet. Writer-director-star Nathan Town says he created the film because "I'm not really an autograph collecting kind of fan. I'm the kind of fan that wants to actually make something concrete to show, like, 'Look, I'm a fan. Here's my proof. Look at this'" (*Done the Impossible*). In saying this, Town expresses the feelings of many fans that look to be more than just passive consumers of the product, but instead seek to actively participate in promoting the shared culture within the fan community. Shot in little over a month on a shoestring budget, Town released the film on the Internet for free because, as he notes above, the ultimate goal of the film was to participate in and show appreciation for Whedon's creation, not seek any sort of monetary benefits. The following year the fan-made documentary *Done the Impossible* (2006) was released, which explored the phenomenon of *Firefly*'s quickly formed fan community, the show's cancellation, and the making of *Serenity* from the fans' point of view. Featured in the documentary are interviews with dozens of fans as well as creator Joss Whedon, six of the nine principal cast members, *Firefly* showrunner Tim Minear, and Universal executive Mary Parent.

But parody films and documentaries can only sustain a fan base for so long; new, original content must be injected into the fan base in order to maintain heightened levels of enthusiasm. With a distinct lack of new episodes or film sequels on the horizon, the task of sustaining the story falls on those that most want it to continue: the fans. This isn't to say that Whedon and the cast wouldn't reunite for a *Serenity* sequel, but with so many of the actors now appearing in popular television series (Nathan Fillion's *Castle*, Alan Tudyk's *Suburgatory*, Morena Baccarin's *Homeland*, to name only a few), that prospect seems less and less likely. To his credit, Whedon has made efforts to keep the fan community happy with new content, most of which comes from the various Dark Horse comics that have been sporadically published since the show's cancellation. But this means that it is up to the fans to create new content, or at least keep the original content somehow fresh. In May 2012, The Institution Theater in Austin, Texas, put on a musical adaptation of the *Firefly* episode "Our Mrs. Reynolds," complete with original songs and music to compliment the story. Jones states that this type of work of fans of cult shows (including *Browncoats: Redemption*) is known as "cult fiction," which she defines as "fiction that fans engage interactively with when they write stories of their own based on characters, events and topographies drawn from the series" (167). It is, however, this type of fiction, based on characters owned film and television companies, which most commonly causes a rift between fans and the studios.

Studios

One of the major areas of contention the studios have with fan films is the perception of fans as "poachers," whereby they pilfer the ideas, characters, and imagery of media properties that the studios own (Jenkins). The problem with this, as Jones notes, is that in the past, "fans produced their own texts only to share them with other fans; their distribution was too small and *their quality too poor to merit any censorious response from the studios* that held copyright on the original works from which they derived" (166, italics added). Jones continues by noting that today "digital and internet technologies facilitate the production and dissemination of high-quality fan-produced texts and 'steals' from source texts in ways that were previously unimaginable" (168). For example, before computer technology was widely available, Star Wars fan films had to rely on shoddy visual effects and homemade sound effects to complete their films. But with libraries of sounds and visual effects widely available via the Internet, even novice auteurs can replicate the glow of a lightsaber or reproduce R2-D2's chirps and chimes with relative ease. Fans have become what Abercrombie and Longhurst refer to as "petty producers" (141) who, according to Hills, "use their finely-honed skills to produce material professionally which can then be marketed back to their own fan culture" (29). *Browncoats: Redemption* has, to a degree, solved this problem by seeing the two groups work together to ensure that the finished product meets the legal standards for avoiding the use of copyrighted characters and ideas while at the same time fully capturing the universe that Joss Whedon created.

The way studios can allow fan films like *Browncoats: Redemption* to be made without dealing with issues of copyright infringement is through the exploration of hyperdiegesis, which, according to Hills, is "the creation of a vast and detailed narrative space, only a fraction of which is ever directly seen or encountered within the text, but which nevertheless appears to operate according to the principles of internal logic and extension" (137). For example, the Star Wars movies showed only the tip of the metaphorical iceberg when it came to the galaxy George Lucas created for his characters to inhabit. Beyond the six films, hundreds of additional stories have taken place on television, in books, and across the pages of comics for decades. In a mythology made up of thousands of races and species, there are almost limitless numbers of Jedi, smugglers, Wookies and droids that could potentially fill out the volumes of fan-created content. What this means for fans is that "hyperdiegesis provides audiences with constant trustworthy, supportive environments for productive practices like discussion, speculation, and fan fiction" (Johnson 286). So despite the fact that fans only saw a small portion of the future as depicted in *Firefly* and *Serenity*, they can rest assured that there are rules and established parameters that allow them to extrapolate how other stories might evolve or play out in the same landscape. The Alliance (the central form of government) that Serenity's crew so desperately sought to avoid is still the authority for others who live in that distant future, so it makes sense that the crews of other ships would experience similar troubles dealing with a corrupt and tyrannical bureaucracy. It is here that the narrative for *Browncoats: Redemption* begins, directly following the events that took place in *Serenity*.

The writers of *Browncoats: Redemption* also managed to cleverly situate themselves in the world of *Serenity* by featuring a number of familiar faces from *Firefly* and *Serenity* without ever directly referencing the characters by name. Series star Adam Baldwin makes a brief appearance in the film as "Alliance Alert Guard," thus giving fans the excitement of seeing one of the franchise's stars on screen without worry from the studio about using Baldwin's iconic character Jayne. One of the notable villains that appeared during *Firefly*'s short run was ruthless businessman Adelai Niska (played by Michael Fairman), whose brief cameo in the film is cited in the credits as "Space Station Owner." Featuring the same cadence of speech and Czech accent that made Niska such a memorable antagonist in the series, Fairman's limited role lends an air of credibility to the production and provides a more fully-developed atmosphere that makes the film feel familiar to fans. Similarly, brothers Yan and Rafael Feldman reprise their roles from *Serenity* as criminal middlemen Fanty and Mingo, who again go unnamed in *Browncoats: Redemption* and are each credited simply as "Business Dealer."

Although these cameos added to the credibility of the production, it should be noted that incorporating the actors from the original source material into a fan film certainly isn't unprecedented. Original *Star Trek* (1966–1969) cast members Walter Koenig and George Takei (Chekov and Sulu, respectively) have each appeared as their iconic characters in episodes of the highly polished fan series *Star Trek: Phase II*, and Australian actor Peter Sumner, who appeared as the character Lt. Pol Treidum in *Star Wars* (famous for delivering the line, "TK–421, why aren't you at your post?"), reprised his role 22 years later for the fan film *Star Wars: The Dark Redemption* (1999). While all of these examples feature actors reprising their roles in fan films, the makers of *Browncoats: Redemption* did so without the worry of copyright infringement or studio reprisal. At various points in time, lawyers for both the Star Trek (Granick) and Star Wars (Borland) franchises have given legal notice to fan producers whom they felt were coming close to (or were blatantly) infringing on licensed property. While none of the projects mentioned above have been the focus of legal actions due to the use of licensed characters appearing in their films, *Browncoats: Redemption* not only made a concerted effort to avoid actionable situations by creatively side-stepping the use of characters' names, the producers also cleared the project with key decision makers before filming began. As the film's website states, *Browncoats: Redemption* prevented any legal issues in this regard as they were able to obtain "20th Century–Fox's nod of approval" and "Whedon's blessing" because "[the film's] focus was on raising money for charities" (*Browncoats: Redemption Official Website*).

The more lenient approach on the part of the studios may be the beginning of a new trend in Hollywood as studios have begun to see the benefits fan films can have for their bottom lines. In many cases, studios have become more accepting of fan films, saving the cease-and-desist letter for those fan filmmakers who would look to profit off of their (the studios') licensed properties. Paramount has taken a laissez faire attitude toward new Star Trek fan films, including high quality productions like *Star Trek: Phase II*. *Phase II*'s executive producer and director Jack Marshall obtained "a basic verbal agreement" with Star Trek's lawyers to continue production under the conditions that they would in no way profit from the production (Young 245). Even Lucasfilm (and more importantly, George Lucas himself) endorsed the fan film community by starting the Official Star Wars Fan Film Awards in 2002 (later renamed the Star Wars Fan Movie Challenge). With a top prize of $2,000, the annual event has been televised on the Sci-Fi Channel and Spike, and many of the winning entries have spawned sequels of their own. As Young notes of early Star Trek fan films, these films were beneficial to television studios and networks because "the new stories [in the fan films] were keeping the hardcore faithful interested in what was otherwise a dead TV show" (83). With no new *Firefly* episodes or Star Trek series on the horizon, one of the best ways for studios to keep their products relevant to audiences is to allow fans to continue making fan films as a means to keep their ardor for the property alive. In fact, fan films have a tendency to *increase* profits for studios by cultivating new fans and maintaining enthusiasm among existing fans. Jones notes, "fans do not profit from fan fiction and neither does fan fiction seem to detract from the sales of broadly similar official spinoffs such as novels" (172). While Jones is referencing written fan fiction, it stands to reason that this model can be applied to fan films as well. So not only do these fan films end up costing money to make, the filmmakers are also most likely buying officially licensed merchandise, which ultimately means more profit for the studio.

A Fan Film for a Cause

As Dougherty mentioned above in his letter to supporters of *Browncoats: Redemption*, the film was produced not just for the pleasure of continuing the story of Whedon's futuristic tale, but also with the specific goal of raising money for charitable organizations. Focusing their energies towards civic engagement, many fan organizations have been extremely vocal and influential in enacting change. Fans of numerous popular culture vehicles have banded together to organize charitable endeavors on behalf of their respective properties. The Harry Potter Alliance (HPA) is an organization of Harry Potter fans who "work with partner NGOs in alerting the world to the dangers of global warming, poverty, and genocide" and "work with our partners for equal rights regardless of race, gender, and sexuality" among other efforts (thehpalliance.org). But what fans undertaking these types of endeavors have lacked is the ability (or permission) to produce artifacts or stories that would supplement the canonical storylines told through the franchise's primary narratives as a means of raising money for charitable causes. Some original content producers have attempted to expand their franchises for charitable causes with great success, as evidenced by Stephanie Meyer's *Twilight* tie-in novella *The Short Second Life of Bree Tanner* (2010), which donated one dollar for each book sold to Red Cross relief efforts in Haiti and Chile, and J.K. Rowling's *The Tales of Beedle the Bard* (2008), a collection of short stories set in the world of Harry Potter that raised over $17 million for Lumos, a children's charity chaired by Rowling (Lumos.org.uk). But these types of cultural products are rarely left to the control of fans, both to maintain quality control of highly profitable properties as well as prevent conflicts over ownership or copyright.

This inability to produce original content on the part of the fans for the purposes of raising money was overcome by the producers of *Browncoats: Redemption* through the "win-win" scenario described at length above. With a product completed and an eager fanbase ready to purchase the supplemental tale from Whedon's universe, the remaining detail was to determine what organizations would benefit from these efforts. The creators of the film decided to channel the proceeds to organizations that helped those in need while simultaneously giving thanks to the cast and crew of *Firefly* and *Serenity* for all their efforts in creating such beloved stories. To that end, money raised from the film went to Equality Now (a human rights organization championed by Joss Whedon), Kids Need to Read (a literacy program co-founded by cast member Nathan Fillion), the Dyslexia Foundation (supported by cast member Jewel Staite), the Al Wooten Jr. Heritage Center (which has been chaired by cast member Ron Glass), and the Marine Corps Law Enforcement Foundation (supported by cast member Adam Baldwin).

Although the $117,000 raised by the film represents one of the largest charitable endeavor Browncoats have undertaken, it is indicative of a building philosophy within the Browncoat community (as well as other fan organizations). Cochran notes that this new approach to fan activism goes beyond "doing something" and has subsequently evolved into "doing something *for humanity*" ("Past the brink," emphasis in original). Since 2006, worldwide screenings of the film *Serenity* have been put on as part of the "Can't Stop the Serenity" campaign, raising money for Equality Now. The screenings (which are typically held in honor of Whedon's birthday) have taken place in dozens of cities across three continents, and have, through 2012, raised over $600,000. Although Browncoats are loyal to charities championed by Whedon and the cast, they have also made efforts to support a diverse range of global issues as well. In 2008, for example, Browncoats were active in raising money for the tsunami in Asia, victims of Hurricane Katrina, and Freedom From Hunger, among numerous others (Cochran, "The Browncoats are Coming!" 242). More than a partition of active fans, Browncoats have become recognized as a social movement, determined to make a difference. Using their fan film as a vehicle for philanthropic efforts, *Browncoats: Redemption* serves as a paradigm for what fan films can someday become.

At the time of writing, the makers of *Browncoats: Redemption* have determined that their next fan film will be called *Z*Con*, focusing on a zombie outbreak that takes place at a science fiction convention. The film, dubbed

"A Zombie Film for Charity," has set the goal of raising even more money than their first effort and has given registered users on their website the opportunity to vote for a charity that will receive part of the proceeds from the film. If this becomes the model for fan films, where the studios and fans can work together to create quality productions that benefit more than just the parties involved, the future for fan creations may be brighter than most could have imagined.

Works Cited

Abercrombie, Nick, and Brian Longhurst. *Audiences: A Sociological Theory of Performance and Imagination.* London: Sage, 1998. Print.

Borland, John. "Homegrown Star Wars, with Big-Screen Magic Intact." CNet.com. 21 Apr. 2005. Web. 24 Jul. 2012. http://news.cnet.com/Homegrown-Star-Wars%2C-with-big-screen-magic-intact/2100-1026_3-5678819.html.

Browncoats: Redemption Official Website. "*Browncoats: Redemption* homepage." 24 Jul. 2012. http://browncoatsmovie.com/.

Cochran, Tanya R. "The Browncoats Are Coming! *Firefly, Serenity,* and Fan Activism." *Investigating* Firefly *and* Serenity: *Science Fiction on the Frontier.* Eds. Rhonda V. Wilcox and Tanya R. Cochran. London: I.B. Tauris, 2008. 239–249. Print.

_____. "'Past the Brink of Tacit Support': Fan Activism and the Whedonverses." *Transformative Works and Fan Activism.* Spec. issue of *Transformative Works and Cultures* 10 (2012). Web. 11 Jan. 2013. http://journal.transformativeworks.org/index.php/twc/article/view/331.

Done the Impossible: The Fans' Tale of Firefly *and* Serenity. Dir. Tony Hadlock, Jason Heppler, Jeremy Neish, Jared Nelson, Brian Wiser. Done the Impossible LLC, 2006. DVD.

"FAQs About the Tales of Beedle the Bard." Lumos.org.uk. 11 Jan. 2012. Web. 30 Jun. 2012. http://www.lumos.org.uk/news.php/336/faqs-about-the-tales-of-beedle-the-bard.

Fiske, John. "The Cultural Economy of Fandom." *The Adoring Audience: Fan Culture and Popular Media.* Ed. Lisa A. Lewis. New York: Routledge, 1992. 30–49. Print.

Granick, Jennifer. "Cyber Rights Now: 'Scotty, Beam Down the Lawyers!'" *Wired* October 1997: 86. Print.

Hills, Matt. *Fan Cultures.* New York: Routledge, 2002. Print.

Jenkins, Henry. *Textual Poachers: Television Fans and Participatory Culture.* New York: Routledge, 1992. Print.

Johnson, Derek. "Fan-tagonism: Factions, Institutions, and Constitutive Hegemonies of Fandom." *Fandom: Identities and Communities in a Mediated World.* Eds. Jonathan Gray, Cornel Sandvoss, and C. Lee Harrington. New York: New York University Press, 2007. 285–300. Print.

Jones, Sara Gwemllian. "Web Wars: Resistance, Online Fandom and Studio Censorship." *Quality Popular Television.* Eds. Mark Jancovish and James Lyons. London: British Film Institute, 2003. 163–177. Print.

"Joss Whedon Introduction." *Serenity.* Writ. and dir. Joss Whedon. Universal, 2005. DVD.

Kit, Borys. "Thomas Jane Makes a 'Punisher' Fan Film." *The Hollywood Reporter.* 16 Jul. 2012. Web. 20 Jul. 2012. http://www.hollywoodreporter.com/heat-vision/thomas-jane-punisher-video-comic-con-349732.

Milson, Jack. "The Powers of Fandom in the Whedonverse." *Joss Whedon: The Complete Companion: The TV Series, the Movies, the Comic Books and More.* Ed. Mary Alice Money. London: Titan, 2012. 270–284. Print.

Suellentrop, Chris. "To Boldly Go Where No Fan Has Gone Before." *Wired* December 2005: 248–255. Print.

Wilkins, Alasdair, and Meredith Woerner. "io9 March Movie Madness the Final Showdown: *Empire* Vs. *Serenity.*" io9.com. 6 Apr. 2011. Web. 26 Jul. 2012. http://io9.com/5789509/io9-march-movie-madness-the-final-showdown-empire-vs-serenity.

Dark Shadows Fandom, Then and Now (1966–2013)

JEFF THOMPSON

The year 1966 saw the television debuts of *Batman* (1966–1968), *Mission: Impossible* (1966–1973), *The Monkees* (1966–1968), and *Star Trek* (1966–1969), among other series that would become cult classics. One such show was ABC's *Dark Shadows* (1966–1971), the daytime serial that introduced Gothic mystery and ghosts to soap opera viewers. The offbeat series *really* took off after the April 1967 introduction of the vampire character Barnabas Collins, played by Shakespearean actor Jonathan Frid. By 1969, when *Dark Shadows* was featuring not only vampires but also werewolves, witches, and time travel, the monster hit was commanding 20 million viewers of all ages (Scott and Pierson 104). In addition to the typical *As the World Turns* (1956–2010) and *Days of Our Lives* (1965–present) demographic, *Dark Shadows* was attracting millions of children, teenagers, and college students who went on to form the first wave of the *Dark Shadows* cult of fans.

Dark Shadows was the brainchild of Dan Curtis, who in the mid–1960s was the executive producer of *The CBS Golf Classic* (1963–1973), a show that he co-owned with CBS. Years before his triumphs with *The Night Stalker* (1972), *Trilogy of Terror* (1975), *The Winds of War* (1983), and *War and Remembrance* (1988/1989), Curtis yearned to try his hand at dramatic television. One night in the summer of 1965, he went to sleep and had a dream that changed the course of television popular culture and the fortunes of third-place ABC. In his dream, Curtis saw a dark-haired young woman riding a train toward her destiny in a house of dark shadows by the sea. She was a present-day Jane Eyre, soon to become a governess caught up in the intrigues and deceptions of a wealthy, eccentric family and its secrets (Thompson, *Television Horrors* 20).

Curtis pitched his Gothic idea to ABC executives Brandon Stoddard and Leonard Goldberg. He was originally meeting with them to discuss a different idea for a series, but his dream of the girl on the train would not leave his mind. After briefly considering *Dark Shadows* as a nighttime program, Curtis and ABC decided to present *Dark Shadows* as a daytime soap opera. Its stars included Hollywood film actress Joan Bennett, New York stage actor Louis Edmonds, and newcomer Alexandra Moltke as Victoria Winters, the girl on the train. In the wake of the November 1965 premiere of NBC's *Days of Our Lives,* with classic Hollywood star MacDonald Carey heading the cast, Curtis decided on Bennett, an even more celebrated movie star, for the anchor role of Elizabeth Collins Stoddard. Edmonds played her brother, Roger Collins. *Dark Shadows,* set at the Collinwood mansion in Collinsport, Maine, debuted on Monday, June 27, 1966.

However, after ten months of low-rated episodes which ABC publicity had unsuccessfully promoted as "a modern tale told in the classic tradition of the Gothic novel" (qtd. in Thompson, *Television Horrors* 21), *Dark Shadows* was in danger of cancellation. After Curtis's three young daughters urged their father to make it scarier, Curtis resolved to introduce the kind of creature that scared *him* the most, a vampire, named Barnabas Collins. The ratings skyrocketed for the next three years (until 1970) and saved the show from a premature cancellation as it told arcane tales of vampires, witches, werewolves, and time travel. Curtis even brought the *Dark Shadows* cast to the big screen when he directed *House of Dark Shadows* (1970), which he filmed in Tarrytown, New York, with half of the cast while the other half continued to tape the daily TV series at the studio on West 53rd Street in Manhattan.

The convoluted storyline of *Dark Shadows* can be easily divided into segments that fans refer to as "pre–Barnabas," "1795," "1897," etc. Henry Jenkins, author of *Textual Poachers: Television Fans and Participatory Culture,* points out that each segment of the storyline of *Dark Shadows* or *Beauty and the Beast* (1987–1990) "is reduced to a brief phrase, evoked for an audience which has already absorbed its local significance and fit it into the larger sense of the series' development" (137). *Dark Shadows* fans definitely need such key words, for the Byzantine storyline of the Gothic serial is not chronological by any means. Characters find themselves first in the 20th century, then suddenly in the 18th, then back in the 20th, then in the 19th, and later even in future and parallel timelines.

The 1966–1967 pre–Barnabas episodes concern the orphaned governess Victoria Winter's exploration of the secrets of her past and their possible link to the Collins family, as well as the mysterious return of Laura Collins (Diana Millay), who was presumed dead. In April 1967, Barnabas Collins rises from his chained coffin, kidnaps Maggie Evans (Kathryn Leigh Scott), and tries to make her over as his lost Josette in the TV show's first highly-rated storyline. The show's ratings continued to rise as the 1795 time period (late 1967–early 1968) revealed Barnabas's life as a mortal and dramatized the witch's curse that caused his vampirism. The 1968 time period, which fans remember fondly, involves the witch's Dream Curse, the *Frankenstein*-like creations of Adam (Robert Rodan) and Eve (Marie Wallace), Barnabas's temporary cure, and the introduction of the werewolf Chris Jennings (Don Briscoe). The extremely popular and highest-rated 1897 time period (March–November 1969) takes Barnabas (a vampire again) back in time to try to save the life of the werewolf Quentin Collins (David Selby), whose curse is linked to that of Chris Jennings in the present time.

Dark Shadows takes a sci-fi turn with the Leviathan storyline (late 1969–early 1970), in which shapeless, prehistoric, Lovecraftian entities possess Barnabas and other members of the Collins family in order to regain their dominion over the earth. A dip in ratings occurs because many fans dislike this storyline, which robs the usually strong Barnabas and others of their free will as they become slaves to the Leviathans. Next (April–July 1970), Barnabas and later Dr. Julia Hoffman (Grayson Hall) enter the world of 1970 Parallel Time, an alternate universe in which the people of Collinsport look the same but lead vastly different lives because they have made different choices. Escaping a burning Collinwood in Parallel Time, Barnabas and Julia find themselves back in their own time band but in the future year of 1995 when Collinwood is in ruins and the Collins family is dead except for Quentin and Carolyn (Nancy Barrett), who are insane. These two weeks of so-called "1995 episodes" in July 1970 are particular favorites among fans, many of whom, in the actual year of 1995, would attend a *Dark Shadows* convention and meet the stars. Next, Barnabas and Julia return to the summer of 1970 and attempt to prevent the future destruction of Collinwood. In the autumn of 1970, their quest again leads them and later Professor Stokes (Thayer David) through time to 1840, when the present-day threat to Collinwood originated with the powerful warlock Judah Zachery (Michael McGuire) and his possession of Gerard Stiles (James Storm), whose evil ghost haunts Collinwood in 1970 and has destroyed the house by 1995. Barnabas, Julia, and Stokes succeed in defeating Judah Zachery, and they return to the present time and find a peaceful, happy Collinwood.

Beginning in January 1971, the final three months of *Dark Shadows* divorce themselves completely from the regular characters' time band and tell a Gothic love story between Bramwell Collins (Jonathan Frid) and Catherine Harridge (Lara Parker) in 1841 Parallel Time. A Frid/Parker romantic pairing was something that many *Dark Shadows* fans had wanted to see for years. The story ends happily for Bramwell and Catherine and this alternate Collins family when *Dark Shadows* aired its 1225th and final episode on Friday, April 2, 1971. While the ratings for *Dark Shadows* were still respectable in the final year of the series, they never rebounded after the Leviathan storyline.

Dark Shadows may have ended its five-year run on ABC, but neither it nor its fans ever really went away. *Dark Shadows* paperback novels and comic books continued into the 1970s, a *Dark Shadows* newspaper comic strip ran from March 1971 to March 1972, and a second *Dark Shadows* movie, *Night of Dark Shadows,* also directed by Dan Curtis, was released by MGM in August 1971. The 1967–1968 year of episodes of the television series itself even returned, in syndication, to TV screens in 1975 and had moderate success for a few years (Scott and Pierson 107–108). The second half of the 1970s also saw the births of the three most significant *Dark Shadows* fanzines: Kathy Resch's *The World of Dark Shadows* (1975–present), Dale Clark's *Inside the Old House* (1978–present), and Marcy Robin's *Shadowgram* (1979–present). The former two were published regularly for decades and still resurface occasionally, and *Shadowgram* continues to deliver official breaking news about all things *Dark Shadows* to hundreds of fans (and to the TV series stars themselves) in both print and electronic editions (Thompson, *Television Horrors* 168–169). Subsequent and notable regional or national *Dark Shadows* fanzines included *The Collinsport Call, Collinwood Revisited, Lone Star Shadows, The Parallel Times,* and *Shadows of the Night* (Thompson, *Television Horrors* 169).

The late 1970s and early 1980s also saw more and more *Dark Shadows* programming and guests at the Shadowcon, Starcon, and Timecon sci-fi conventions on the West Coast. Finally, in 1982–1983, the television series returned in syndication, very successfully this time, on New York-area TV stations and then on the New Jersey Network of PBS television stations. At the same time (mid–1983), the Dark Shadows Festival, the official, all–*Dark Shadows* fan convention, began holding one or two gatherings each year in the New York and Los Angeles areas (and occasionally in Texas and Nevada). Jonathan Frid and two dozen other stars of the Gothic serial began attending the Festivals, which have attracted between 800 and 3000 fans every year for 30 years — six times longer than *Dark Shadows* itself ran on television (Scott and Pierson 108–110, 207–209; Thompson, *Television Horrors* 172–177). Since the mid–1980s, the Dark Shadows Festival has been chaired by Jim Pierson, who also works for Dan Curtis Productions, MPI Home Video, and PBS. Pierson is the author of *Produced and Directed by Dan Curtis* and several other books about *Dark Shadows.*

Writer and filmmaker Jeffrey Arsenault (*Night Owl, Passing Time*) remembers attending, and helping to organize, the first East Coast Dark

Shadows Festival in Newark, New Jersey, in September–October 1983. "I met a great deal of *Dark Shadows* fans, many with whom I had corresponded," Arsenault remembers (e-mail). He adds:

> I also participated in some of the Collinsport Players' skits and met many of the stars of the original series. I remember being impressed with how good they looked, nearly 20 years later. Kathryn Leigh Scott [Maggie] and Lara Parker [Angelique] appeared to be ageless. I loved meeting Joan Bennett [Elizabeth]. She was so gracious and was happy to sign autographs and pose for pictures. Diana Millay [Laura] was also wonderful with her fans, and it was a pleasure to have the opportunity to speak with her. I had arranged for producer Robert Costello to attend the Festival. He had been one of my professors at New York University [Arsenault e-mail].

Dark Shadows fandom in the 1990s was propelled by MPI Home Video's release of all 1225 episodes on VHS videotape, the airing of two episodes each weekday on the Sci-Fi Channel, the ever-growing Festivals, and Dan Curtis's short-lived, Emmy Award-winning revival of *Dark Shadows* as a weekly nighttime series on NBC. The new *Dark Shadows,* which was a remake of both the ABC daytime series and Curtis's 1970 motion picture *House of Dark Shadows,* was filmed in and around Los Angeles from March to December 1990. Curtis directed the first five of the show's thirteen hours, as well as some reshoots for the twelfth and thirteenth. Original *Dark Shadows* writer Sam Hall and music composer Robert Cobert resumed their former duties. NBC's *Dark Shadows* aired on Friday nights in January, February, and March of 1991. For years, *Dark Shadows* fans had been writing to Dan Curtis and all three networks (ABC, CBS, and NBC) begging for a new series. At last, NBC was interested, and the fans were ready to support the show.

This time, the Hollywood star playing Elizabeth Collins Stoddard was Jean Simmons, with Roy Thinnes as her brother Roger Collins and Joanna Going as Victoria Winters. Once again, Curtis's 1965 dream was put on film as the pilot episode began with Victoria's train journey to Collinsport, Maine. Barnabas Collins's release from the chained coffin occurred in that same episode. The new Barnabas was the distinguished British film actor Ben Cross, who played the vampire with more menace and danger than Jonathan Frid had exhibited. However, Cross's Barnabas also had his tortured, vulnerable side. Curtis's *Winds of War* producer and former 1960s "scream queen" Barbara Steele revisited her horror movie roots by portraying Dr. Julia Hoffman, a key role that Sam Hall's wife Grayson Hall had played on *Dark Shadows* and in *House of Dark Shadows.* Despite garnering respectable ratings and positive reviews, the 1991 series was eclipsed by the Persian Gulf War, which occupied viewers' minds and TV sets, and by a change in management at NBC. When *Dark Shadows* was on the verge of cancellation, fans across the country mobilized and declared May 8, 1991, "Save *Dark Shadows* Day." They staged rallies in New York, Nashville, Los Angeles, and several other cities, but NBC cancelled the show anyway (Thompson, *Television Horrors* 70–71).

Like the original show, the 1991 *Dark Shadows* inspired a comic-book series (from Innovation Comics) and other merchandise, such as wristwatches and model kits, and has been rerun on the Chiller Channel from time to time, including on Thanksgiving Day 2012. Meanwhile, the fan conventions continued to grow, and the 1997 Dark Shadows Festival in New York City in August welcomed a record-setting 3,000 fans (Thompson, *Television Horrors* 176). Lifelong fan Helen Samaras, a Dark Shadows Festival Committee member who owns a travel agency, observes, "I am meeting more mainstream people at the Festivals" (e-mail). She explains:

> In the 1980s and 1990s, the people I met were really fanatics. They ate, breathed, and slept *Dark Shadows*. Now, I am meeting more people where this is just *a part* of their lives with happy memories. We socialize more. We get together a lot more over the course of a year.... I lost my only sister in 1988, and it was the fans and the actors from the show who stood by me. They are a second family to me. [Samaras e-mail].

Fellow fan Phil Myers, who works as a chief of building operations, adds, "The fans have matured as well as the actors. I don't see too many fans asking actors about the plotlines anymore" (e-mail). Indeed, the fans' questions at the Festival Q&As have become more substantial. "How did you feel when Barnabas bit you?" has given way to "What is your favorite stage role?" or "How did *Dark Shadows* prepare you for your later acting career?"

Fandom in the 2000s continued to expand because of new generations of fans' discovering *Dark Shadows* through the MPI videotapes and then DVDs, the Sci-Fi Channel's weekday episodes, and the airing of the series on the European Sci-Fi Channel. Now, British fans were joining American baby boomers and much younger fans at the Dark Shadows Festivals (Thompson, *Television Horrors* 176). *Dark Shadows* fandom has always attracted an equal number of women and men, fans of all ages (from schoolchildren to octogenarians), classic-horror devotees, soap-opera enthusiasts, and gay fans who say that they identify with the TV characters' difference and uniqueness.

Also in the 2000s, the stars themselves, especially Kathryn Leigh Scott (who played Maggie Evans and Josette DuPres), began writing books about their experiences and established Internet websites devoted to their careers and their current activities. Many of the stars of the 1966–1971 and 1991 TV series also began recording *Dark Shadows* CD dramas produced by Big Finish Productions of Great Britain (Benshoff 116–118; Thompson, *House* 172). Some of the best Big Finish audio dramas are *The Crimson Pearl,* starring Nancy Barrett, Roger Davis, Jerry Lacy, Lara Parker, Christopher Pennock, Kathryn Leigh Scott, David Selby, and Roy Thinnes; *The Death Mask,* starring Lacy and Parker; *The Night Whispers,* starring Jonathan Frid, John Karlen, and Barbara Steele; *Operation Victor,* starring Selby and *Doctor Who*'s Terry Molloy; *The Voodoo Amulet,* starring Lacy and Parker; and *The Wicked and the Dead,* starring Karlen and Lacy. The Big Finish CDs tell stories placing the *Dark Shadows* characters, as well as new characters, in other time periods, worlds, and situations.

For example, James Goss and Joseph Lidster's *Crimson Pearl,* a fan favorite celebrating the 45th anniversary of *Dark Shadows,* weaves a magical gem through almost all of the time periods depicted or even mentioned on the television series. Mark Thomas Passmore's *Death Mask* and *Voodoo Amulet* dramas cleverly combine Lacy and Parker's lawyer and witch characters in first an Agatha Christie-esque mystery and then a *noir* quest through the supernatural underbelly of New Orleans. *The Night Whispers,* written by Stuart Manning, fulfills fans' most fervent wish by bringing Jonathan Frid back to his signature role of Barnabas Collins for the first (and only) time since 1971. Jonathan Morris's *Operation Victor* is the most exciting of all the more than forty Big Finish CD dramas as it pits the immortal Quentin Collins against a mad Axis vivisectionist during World War II. *The Wicked and the Dead,* written by Eric Wallace, expands on the TV show's popular 1897 storyline by continuing the stories of Carl Collins and the Reverend Gregory Trask.

The Big Finish dramas meet a basic need within most fans, that of creatively filling in countless blanks in the lives of the fictitious characters who, because of the dual allure of horror and soap opera, seem more real to them than many living persons. The Big Finish dramas are fan fiction elevated to a professional, nearly perfect level and made authentic and almost canonical because the actual *Dark Shadows* stars themselves are voicing their original characters. How can *The Night Whispers* not be almost as "real" as a *Dark Shadows* episode itself when Jonathan Frid and John Karlen are playing their Barnabas and Willie characters? Classic horror and the 1991 *Dark Shadows* are even validated, as well, because of the guest appearance of Barbara Steele in *The Night Whispers.* The Big Finish CD dramas, produced regularly since 2006, enjoy robust sales and show no sign of waning because they are giving fans what they want — and fans themselves are influencing the casting of the dramas because of their frequent online requests to bring this character back or bring that actor back to *Dark Shadows* through the audio dramas. Big Finish Productions has a strong presence, both in Q&As and in the dealers' rooms, at every Dark Shadows Festival.

College mathematics professor Patrick Murphy is active not only with the Festivals but also with the Central Florida *Dark Shadows* Fan Club (CFDSFC), which, he says, "has been around for more than 20 years" (e-mail 16 Aug.), and states:

Through the club, I have been exposed to rare collectibles, heard tales of fans' encounters with celebrities, participated in ghost tours, traveled to *Dark Shadows* filming locations, attended club costume parties, and made some great friends. The Central Florida *Dark Shadows* Fan Club even creates its own *Dark Shadows*-themed T-shirts and glow-in-the-dark mugs! [Murphy e-mail 16 Aug.].

A new CFDSFC glow-in-the-dark mug premiered at the Central Florida fan organization's Halloween party in Orlando on Saturday, November 10, 2012. Activities included a two-round trivia game built around facts about *Dark Shadows* actors and actresses, a photo-caption contest, a screening of the 2012 *Dark Shadows* movie, the cutting of a huge cake with the faces of Barnabas Collins (Jonathan Frid and Johnny Depp) decorated into the frosting, and an elaborate costume contest. The female and male winners of the contest were club members dressed as Magda Rakosi and Count Petofi, both characters from the 1897 storyline seen on *Dark Shadows* in 1969 (Murphy e-mail 11 Nov.).

While both official and fan-made *Dark Shadows* merchandise continues to flourish in the 2010s, printed fanzines, a mainstay of almost all fandoms for decades, have diminished considerably in favor of Internet websites. Some of the new e-zines are *Blog of Dark Shadows, Collins Mausoleum, Collinsport Historical Society, Dark Shadows Journal, Dark Shadows Online,* and *Shadows of the Night* (Thompson, *Television Horrors* 169–170). The Dark Shadows Festival has its own website, as does *Shadowgram.* Yearly convention attendee Phil Myers remarks that *Dark Shadows* "awakened my creativity like my website *Phil's Stairway Through Time*" (e-mail). Lifelong fan Mark Booher, who works in the legal field, adds, "Technology has made a major difference. The many websites about *Dark Shadows* have, in my opinion, enlarged *Dark Shadows* fandom" (e-mail).

Blog of Dark Shadows features Ed Gross's article "Spawn of *Dark Shadows: The Secret Circle*" and my reviews of the 35 Gold Key *Dark Shadows* comic books. *Collins Mausoleum* presents fiction by Joe Escobar and Geoffrey Hamell and the article "How Fans Kept the Torch Burning," Susan Ramskill's remembrance of the *Dark Shadows Mascots* fan club of the early 1970s. *Collinsport Historical Society* features *Dark Shadows* artwork by Bill Branch and a look back at Lambert Hillyer's *Dracula's Daughter* (1936). The U.K.-based *Dark Shadows Journal,* also known as *Collinwood-Dot-Net,* spotlights rare photographs and "News Bites" about the *Dark Shadows* stars' current appearances in plays (e.g., Jerry Lacy in Sonia Levitin's *Surviving Mama*), at fan conventions (e.g., Kathryn Leigh Scott at a memorabilia convention in Birmingham, England), and in movies (e.g., Lara Parker in Ansel Faraj's *Doctor Mabuse,* which also stars Lacy). In November 2012, the *Dark Shadows Journal* website joined Facebook as *Dark Shadows News Page. Dark Shadows Online,* managed by *Barnabas and Company* author Craig Hamrick until his death in 2006, still presents a definitive look at the plethora of *Dark Shadows* collectibles, as well as remarkable photographs of the 2006 Dark Shadows Festival in Brooklyn, New York. *Shadows of the Night* is the electronic reincarnation of Dan Silvio's long-running printed fanzine of the same name from the 1980s and 1990s. These diverse outlets have allowed fandom to grow by connecting more and more fans to each other through instantaneous online information and social media.

According to audiovisual technician and writer Nancy Kersey, "The establishment of online *Dark Shadows* message boards, group lists, websites, and e-mail allowed fans to have more intimate access to like-minded fans and easily share stories, poetry, artwork, and news about the actors and the series" (e-mail). Kersey, who in 2013 wrote a book about her friendship with *Dark Shadows* star Jonathan Frid, adds, "The immediacy of the Internet couldn't help but change the fandom from fans waiting for news and fanzines coming in the mail to having easy access to the same thing and even more online" (e-mail). Patrick Murphy concurs by noting, "With the Internet, information and communication can be obtained much more quickly and in greater volume than with the fanzines of the past. Fans who once enjoyed *Dark Shadows* as children are now enjoying it electronically with their children and even their grand-children, creating a dynasty of fandom" (Murphy e-mail 16 Aug.).

In the age of Facebook, many of the *Dark Shadows* actors and actresses have their own celebrity pages, and quite a few of them appear on personal Facebook pages where any and all fans can "friend" them. Lifelong *Dark Shadows* fans are delighted to have gone from writing fan letters to their favorite stars in the 1960s to meeting them at Dark Shadows Festivals in the 1980s to actually being Facebook friends with them and exchanging private messages with them in the 2010s. According to voice-over artist Sam Yates, "The single greatest aspect about *Dark Shadows* fandom is how wonderful the cast members are to their fans and how they go above and beyond in making themselves available and accommodating every fan request" (e-mail).

Indeed, on September 14, 2012, two *Dark Shadows* stars were the guests of honor at a devoted fan's birthday party when lifelong fan Scott Farris turned 50 in grand style at a party at Paris-on-Ponce in Atlanta, Georgia. The gala, complete with food, drink, costumes, music, dancing, and a red velvet cake in the shape of a coffin, was attended by 100 of Farris's friends — including Lara Parker (Angelique) and Kathryn Leigh Scott (Maggie). In my role as emcee, I warmed up the crowd as a coffin was wheeled onto the stage. Suddenly, Farris, dressed as Barnabas Collins, popped out of the coffin and welcomed everyone to his birthday bash. Next, Parker and Scott serenaded Farris with an *acapella* version of "Thanks for the Memories," with new lyrics all about

Farris and *Dark Shadows.* The night before (September 13), Parker and Scott had appeared at a book signing and Q&A at Barnes & Noble in Atlanta. Lara Parker, who now works as a college instructor, is the author of *Angelique's Descent* and *The Salem Branch* (both in new, expanded editions), and Kathryn Leigh Scott is the author of *My Scrapbook Memories of Dark Shadows* and *The Bunny Years* (both from Pomegranate Press, Scott's own publishing company), among other books. *Dark Shadows* fans enthusiastically support all of the stars' publications, from David Selby's novel *Lincoln's Better Angel* to Marie Wallace's memoir *On Stage & In Shadows* to Christopher Pennock's self-published *Fear and Loathing on Dark Shadows* #1–5, underground comic books of the early 2000s.

The aforementioned Scott Farris, who works in the health-care profession, runs *Dark Shadows Atlanta,* a 240-member-strong Facebook page devoted to his favorite TV series and its fans. Other highly participatory Facebook pages are *Dark Shadows Fan Site, An Evening at Collinwood, Jonathan Frid Fan Group, Jonathan Frid Material, Marie Wallace's Dark Shadows Fan Club, The Careys' Seaview Terrace Group* (Seaview Terrace is the mansion whose exterior is seen on the TV show), and *Remembering Jonathan Frid.* The *Dark Shadows Fan Site* specializes in pictures (3,000 of them), discussions of the TV show's storylines, funny captions, and fans' comments about the October 30, 2012, release of *House of Dark Shadows* and *Night of Dark Shadows* on DVD and Blu-Ray. *An Evening at Collinwood,* run in its initial months by *Dark Shadows* star Kathleen Cody (who played Hallie and Carrie), features fan fiction, memories of past Dark Shadows Festivals, and accounts of fans' real-life paranormal experiences. The *Frid Fan Group* page presents pictures of Jonathan Frid (who played Barnabas and Bramwell) at every point in his life and career, along with remembrances of Frid by his friend Nancy Kersey. *Jonathan Frid Material* features photographs of Frid along with fans' warm appreciations of the actor and the man. *Marie Wallace's Dark Shadows Fan Club* page showcases pictures of the *Dark Shadows* and *Somerset* star, plus Wallace's own comments about her roles, her photography, and her activities. In October–November 2012, the Marie Wallace page included up-to-the-minute news about Wallace's fall from the stage after a lighting black-out during her performance of *The Last Romance,* by Joe dePietro, at the Seven Angels Theatre in Waterbury, Connecticut, on October 20. Wallace herself provided many of the details of her hospitalization, surgery, and recuperation. *The Careys' Seaview Terrace Group* is devoted to the celebration, documentation, and preservation of the Newport, Rhode Island, mansion that served as Collinwood's exterior. The page features numerous vintage photographs of Seaview Terrace, as well as recent pictures of dozens of *Dark Shadows* fans' semi-annual sleepovers at "Collinwood." Seaview Terrace is owned by Denise Carey and her family and was featured on the September 7, 2011, episode of SyFy's *Ghost Hunters* (2004–present). The *Remembering Jonathan Frid* page offers in-depth discussions of every incarnation of *Dark Shadows*, fans' delighted reactions to mentions of *Dark Shadows* in two fifth-season (2012) episodes of AMC's *Mad Men* (2007–present)—the first name-checking "Burke Devlin" and "Collinsport" and the second calling *Dark Shadows* by name—and exuberant celebrations of the life of Jonathan Frid.

Indeed, the April 14, 2012, death of Frid was a major event in online *Dark Shadows* fandom as fans expressed their emotions on Facebook and established memorial pages. In the 2010s, almost every *Dark Shadows*-related event, from a star's new book or stage role to the release of *Fan Favorites* and *The Best of Barnabas* on MPI Home Video DVD to information about the new Dynamite Entertainment comic-book series, is publicized, discussed, and sometimes debated on Facebook and Twitter.

Coming one month after the death of Frid was the release of Tim Burton's *Dark Shadows* (2012) feature film, starring long-time fan Johnny Depp in Frid's Barnabas role. In the summer of 2011, Frid, as well as original stars Lara Parker (Angelique), Kathryn Leigh Scott (Maggie), and David Selby (Quentin), traveled to England to film cameo roles in a party scene in Burton's film. The Warner Bros. movie premiered in Los Angeles on May 7, in London on May 9, and across the United States on May 11, 2012. On May 10, the Vista Theatre in Los Angeles, in conjunction with the Dark Shadows Festival, presented a special double feature of *House of Dark Shadows* (1970) and *Dark Shadows* (2012), with stars of the original TV series in attendance. The stars signed autographs for the fans and then sat among them for the screenings.

Fans were delighted to see that Burton's film was dedicated to the memory of Dan Curtis. However, there was not enough time to add a similar nod to Frid. Yet again, Curtis's dream of the girl on the train was filmed as Burton's *Dark Shadows* opened on Victoria Winters' fateful Amtrak ride to the strains of "Nights in White Satin" by the Moody Blues. This time, Bella Heathcote played an unexpected amalgam of the Victoria Winters and Maggie Evans characters, as well as Barnabas's lost love Josette DuPres. Michelle Pfeiffer portrayed Elizabeth Collins Stoddard, and Jonny Lee Miller played her brother Roger Collins. The Victoria/Maggie twist took almost all fans by surprise, for that was not one of the facts that had been uncovered by any print or online sources prior to the film's release.

Ever since the first trailer for Burton's seriocomic film had appeared both on TV's *Ellen* (2003–present) and on the Internet on March 15, 2012, *Dark Shadows* fans had posted a firestorm of impassioned comments, both pro and con, on Facebook and Twitter. Both *Shadowgram* (in print and online) and *Dark Shadows Journal* (online) had released reliable, up-to-the-minute news

about Burton and Depp's film, so fans were better informed than they had
ever been in the history of *Dark Shadows* fandom. While many fans were over-
joyed that a feature-film version of *Dark Shadows* was on the horizon, many
other fans voiced their displeasure over the farcical quality of the trailers and
commercials for the film. The actual film proved not to be nearly as silly as
the trailers made it out to be. Although there are plenty of laughs, *Dark Shadows* also features many moments of drama, romance, and horror.

In April, May, and June of 2012, countless news outlets were covering
Dark Shadows— not only the new film but also the death of Jonathan Frid,
MPI's re-release of the 1225 TV episodes in a coffin-shaped boxed set, the re-
emergence of the original series through the Big Finish audio dramas and the
Dynamite Entertainment comic books, and the legacy of producer-director
Dan Curtis. Articles about the world of *Dark Shadows* appeared in *Vanity
Fair, TV Guide, Horror Hound, Entertainment Weekly, Down East,* and several
dozen other magazines and newspapers. Fans used social media to alert each
other to these publications and to write their own comments below online
articles at *Arts Forum, Daytime Confidential, Dispatch, Examiner, Zap2it,* and
many other websites.

Artist and library technician Sherry "Sherlock" Watson notes that much
of *Dark Shadows* fandom "is now online, I'd say. Earlier, it was through letters,
paper publications, and the occasional convention" (e-mail) and continues:

> Now, it is daily, non-stop, through social media, e-mail, e-groups, blogs, availability
> of the TV show in various formats [e.g., VHS, DVD, Netflix, streaming, etc.],
> availability of *Dark Shadows* offspring creations by artists, etc.
>
> I participate mostly through Facebook and Yahoo Groups at the moment; I did
> participate quite a bit on Jonathan Frid's website for some time, as well. The non-
> stop availability of all this now means anyone can easily explore *Dark Shadows* at
> any point, pick up ideas to turn into new creations, and keep the circle turning
> [Watson e-mail].

The *Dark Shadows* presence on YouTube consists mostly of fan-made
music videos, clips of stars' Q&As from past Dark Shadows Festivals, a few
of the Collinsport Players' skits (such as *Help Wanted, D.C.'s Behind-the-Scenes
Nightmare,* and *Curtains*) performed at Festivals, and various trailers and news
stories about Tim Burton's 2012 film. Dan Curtis Productions frowns on the
placing of the copyrighted 1966–1971 TV episodes online, so while there are
some brief clips online, full episodes that are put on YouTube are quickly
removed. The late Dan Curtis himself never interfered with fans' genuine
celebrations of *Dark Shadows, The Night Stalker,* and his other productions
through writing, drawing, costuming, acting, filksinging, and the like, but
he and the DCP lawyers have been very protective of the copying or selling
of the TV programs themselves.

Fans in the 21st century may not be able to agree on the merits of Dan Curtis's two and Tim Burton's first *Dark Shadows* movies, who the right woman for Barnabas Collins is, or whether the original show's 1795 storyline or 1897 storyline is better, but they are organized and mobilized through social media, websites, tweets, e-zines, and other hypermedia. According to college media professor Harry Benshoff, "One can see how drastically all media fan cultures have been reshaped due to the rise of the Internet and its ever-easier modes of web-based forums, complete with specialized chat rooms, list-servs, and ... on-line role-playing games" (107). Today's *Dark Shadows* fans are connected and bonded in their determination to express and perpetuate their love for a unique supernatural soap opera that began almost 50 years ago and continues to reincarnate itself. Sam Yates rates *Dark Shadows* fans "right up there with *Star Trek* fans as the most loyal of any television franchise," adding:

> And that loyalty not only saved the show from an early cancellation, but it also helped in creating a phenomenon which would lead to a giant hit soundtrack album [1969], three major motion pictures [1970, 1971, 2012], tons of merchandise, stars dominating the covers of teen magazines, a fan festival which is in its fourth decade, and the first television series of 1,200 episodes to be available in its entirety on VHS and DVD.... I believe the growing attraction and appreciation of *Dark Shadows* is because of its irresistible charm, mystique, and ability to draw more and more viewers into its romantic fantasy world. The horror element, to me, isn't nearly as important as the fact that it is *escapism* at its best. There's no better way to *escape* than *Dark Shadows!* [Yates e-mail].

Works Cited

Arsenault, Jeffrey. "Re: Dear *Dark Shadows* fan." Message to the author. 3 Aug. 2012. E-mail.

Benshoff, Harry. *Dark Shadows.* Detroit: Wayne State University Press, 2011. Print.

Booher, Mark. "Re: Dear *Dark Shadows* fan." Message to the author. 9 Aug. 2012. E-mail.

Jenkins, Henry. *Textual Poachers: Television Fans and Participatory Culture.* New York: Routledge, 1992. Print.

Kersey, Nancy. "Re: Dear *Dark Shadows* fan." Message to the author. 2 Aug. 2012. E-mail.

Murphy, Patrick. "Re: Dear *Dark Shadows* fan." Message to the author. 16 Aug. 2012. E-mail.

_____. "Re: Hello, Patrick!" Message to the author. 11 Nov. 2012. E-mail.

Myers, Phil. "Re: Dear *Dark Shadows* fan." Message to the author. 19 Aug. 2012. E-mail.

Samaras, Helen. "Re: Dear *Dark Shadows* fan." Message to the author. 7 Aug. 2012. E-mail.

Scott, Kathryn Leigh, and Jim Pierson, eds. *Dark Shadows Almanac.* Los Angeles: Pomegranate Press, 2000. Print.

Thompson, Jeff. *House of Dan Curtis: The Television Mysteries of the* Dark Shadows *Auteur.* Nashville: Westview, 2010. Print.

_____. *The Television Horrors of Dan Curtis:* Dark Shadows, The Night Stalker, *and Other Productions, 1966–2006.* Jefferson, NC: McFarland, 2009. Print.

Watson, Sherry. "Re: Dear *Dark Shadows* fan." Message to the author. 5 Aug. 2012. E-mail.

Yates, Sam. "Re: Dear *Dark Shadows* fan." Message to the author. 6 Aug. 2012. E-mail.

Spellbound

An Analysis of Adult-Oriented
Harry Potter Fanfiction

Don Tresca

On January 22, 2003, an attorney from the British law firm Theodore Goddard sent a letter to the webmasters of an Internet website known as *Shadow-Wrapped.net*. The purpose of the letter was to demand that the website discontinue publication of sexually explicit fanfiction and fan-art involving the characters from the Harry Potter series of books and films. The law firm, which represented both J.K. Rowling (the author of the books) and Warner Bros. (the film studio which produced and distributed the films), stated the reason for the cease and desist order was "to protect the integrity of [the] *Harry Potter* properties" (qtd. in Evans, "Why J.K. Rowling" 21). They made it clear that their complaint was about the sexually explicit material and that they had no complaint "about innocent fan fiction written by genuine *Harry Potter* fans" (ibid.) and that the concern of their clients was that there was

> a very real risk that impressionable children, who of course comprise the principal readership of the *Harry Potter* books, will be directed (e.g., by a search engine result) to your sexually explicit website, which you will appreciate most people would consider wholly inappropriate for minors [qtd. in Evans, "Why J.K. Rowling" 23].

Needless to say, this letter had a dramatic impact on the community of Harry Potter fanfiction writers. The number of Harry Potter fan stories on the web is phenomenal, nearing 750,000 works at last count, ranging from extremely short stories of one to two pages to massive novel-length works. Although the amount of adult Harry Potter fanfiction (stories containing graphically violent and sexual content) is a relatively small percentage of the overall amount of available fanfiction, it is not insignificant. There are numerous websites which specialize in presenting such fanfiction, including *The*

Daily Deviant (a play on *The Daily Prophet*, the wizarding newspaper in the Harry Potter series) and *Granger Enchanted*. Many of the webmasters of these websites balked at the suggestion by Rowling and Warner Bros. that they should remove their material from the Internet in the interest of protecting "impressionable children." They made claims of "fair use" and nonprofessional status as to the reasons why they should be allowed to continue to publish their works without fear of retribution by the author and the movie studio. But a central question remains in the minds of many when they read about the breadth of adult-oriented Harry Potter material available on the Internet: Why? Why has a literary (and filmic) work whose primary audience consists of children generated such an enormous amount of extreme fanfiction, works filled with graphic depictions of extreme and perverse elements including, but certainly not limited to, excessive gore, torture, rape, mutilation, pedophilia, necrophilia, incest, bestiality, and snuff (sexual murder)? Is it merely an aspect of the films (with their young and attractive casts), or is there something deeper at work, a dark psychological impulse among certain members of society that seek to corrupt the innocence of childhood icons in order to perversely destroy what others seek to celebrate? Or is it something else entirely?

One of the first things needed to begin is to provide some definitions of the works we are considering here. Like all other types of fiction, not all of the adult-oriented Harry Potter fanfiction is equal in its content or quality. Many of the writers of the more adult Harry Potter fanfiction are quick to differentiate between works they consider "erotica" and those they consider "smut" (Hansen 4). For these writers, "erotica" is writing dealing with characters in mature romantic relationships for whom sexuality is a natural extension of the love the characters share for one another. "Erotica" frequently contains some sexually-explicit content, but the main focus of the story is on the romance, not the graphic sexuality. "Smut," on the other hand, is pure pornography, a story which contains no artistic or literary merit and is designed completely to arouse the prurient interests of the reader (Chan 12). There are also numerous styles of adult fanfiction based on the content of the story and the relationship pairing discussed therein. In much of adult Harry Potter fanfiction (and a surprising majority of adult-oriented fanfiction in general), the primary style is "slash."

Slash fanfiction are stories in which the relationship at the center of the story is focused on a romantic coupling of two male characters. Both of the male characters are coded as heterosexual in the source text and engage in a homoerotic relationship within the fanfiction story based on a wide variety of factors that are contained within the secondary text. Slash began as a fanfiction subgenre in the 1960s with *Star Trek* (1966–1969) fanfiction based on the relationship between Kirk and Spock that appeared in various fan-produced magazines (known as fanzines). Since the designation for such stories was Kirk/Spock, the subgenre became known as slash because of the punctuation mark that appeared between the two characters' names. For the most part, slash is written by heterosexual women for an audience of heterosexual women. Researchers (such as Catherine Driscoll, Sonia K. Katyal, and Sharon Hayes and Matthew Ball) suggest that the subgenre, while frequently written with very explicit homosexual sex, is not about homosexuality at all, but is instead a female idealization of male-female relationships that are acted out on male bodies (Driscoll 83; Katyal 487; Hayes and Ball 223–224). The writer uses the men in the stories to ascribe emotions and behaviors that she craves from men in her own romantic life (Hansen 3). Slash stories frequently play with notions of gender roles, especially as they relate to sexuality, endowing one of the males in the slash relationship with typically feminine characteristics and the other with predominantly male characteristics (McCardle 11), thus allowing the writers to dismantle common stereotypes and assumptions regarding masculinity and femininity and reconstructing them in original and challenging ways (Hayes and Ball 225). Slash allows women to experience a fantasy of authentic love which can only exist between equals, people who are strong and share adventures as well as emotions (Cicioni 169). Because of the lack of strong female characterization and heterosexual romance narratives in early television science fiction texts such as *Star Trek* and *Doctor Who* (1963–present), the authentic love had to be expressed in a romantic relationship between two men. Female fans who wanted to engage with the programs in a more "feminized" manner were forced to use "male homosexuality to reconstruct men ... and change them into people with whom women can coexist more comfortably" (Bacon-Smith 248). While the Harry Potter stories do contain a strong feminine presence through characters as diverse as Hermione Granger, Ginny Weasley, Minerva McGonagall, and Luna Lovegood, they are sexually unavailable for a variety of reasons, such as age, authority, or lack of interest. Therefore, slash continues to be a popular subgenre amongst Harry Potter fans.

But, unlike the slash fiction of many other popular texts, Harry Potter slash has its dark side. Due to the age levels of the books' primary characters (the three main characters — Harry, Ron, and Hermione — begin at age eleven in the first book and end the series at age seventeen in the final book), many of the slash stories written by fans are written involving underage characters. One of the popular slash pairings in the Harry Potter fandom is Harry/Draco Malfoy. Draco is one of Harry's primary antagonists in the novels. Due to Draco's evil nature and the dislike the two characters exhibit towards one another throughout the books, many of the fanfiction stories contain elements such as torture (Sakai Michiba's "Sectumsempra Animi"), sadomasochism (dottyficons' "Severe Punishment"), and prostitution (elfflame's "Viridian 3: A Waiting Game"). Likewise, pedophilia raises its ugly head in a wide variety of slash stories involving Harry with a number of adult characters of dubious moral character including Severus Snape (hogwartshoney's "Snitches and Boxes and Brooms, Oh my!") and Voldemort (ships_harry's "Triad"). Such underage stories are frequently viewed as morally corrupt despite the arguments by those writers that their stories do not constitute child pornography because no child is actually used or harmed in the development of the story (Gooch 28). However, the mere presentation of children in a sexualized manner (even in a written fiction) is seen in a negative light. Many believe that because Harry Potter is viewed primarily as a children's text and that many children could gain access to the sexually-explicit material online, the purpose of the stories is to allow online predatory pedophiles to "groom" children in such a way as to corrupt them into believing that such sexual behaviors are acceptable and condoned by the general populace (Gooch 27). Some suggest that the stories contain the detailed fantasies of the writers for the actors who portray the characters in the Harry Potter films. As Dominick Evans observes, "what is sad about this is that more often than not, women see [Daniel Radcliffe, the actor who portrayed Harry Potter in the films] as Harry Potter, fantasizing about him as the character. This makes me wonder if they put Daniel's eleven-year-old face to the eleven-year-old Harry Potter porn that is written" ("Some Women" 8). Similarly, Emma Watson, the actress who portrays Hermione in the films, is one of the most popular actresses to appear in pornographic stories on websites such as *Celebrity Sex Stories Archives* (www.c-s-s-a.com) and *Television Sex Stories Archives* (www.t-s-s-a.com) and has been victimized by a stalker ("Emma Watson Confronted by Stalker" 3–4) and by a child pornographer who pasted her head atop the bodies of children in child porn images ("Emma Watson 'Distressed'" 1–3) to the point where she fears going out in public alone ("Emma Watson Afraid" 1–7). Such activities are of grave concern to researchers who investigate the psychosexual dynamics of celebrity stalking and attacking. While many claim that pursuit of a sexual relationship or a need for sexual dominance over a celebrity is rarely a primary motivating factor in celebrity stalking cases, "there are exceptions ... the investigation of psychodynamics in public figure cases would suggest that sexual dynamics are likely to be highly charged with aggression" (Hoffmann and Meloy 182–183). Fortunately, violence in such cases is very rare because "sexual activity toward the object of pursuit is likely to be limited to fantasy and masturbation, rather than an overt sexual attack" (Hoffmann and Meloy 183).

The darker elements of adult-oriented Harry Potter fanfiction occur outside the realm of slash and erotica. The far more pornographic aspects of "smut" within the fanfiction community allow writers to explore much murkier concepts such as incest, bestiality, and necrophilia. On the website *The Daily Deviant*, several stories feature content warnings that read like a catalog of the worst sexual perversities known to man. The story "A Little Wizard's Book of Slutty Goosings" by pre_raphaelite1 and thegildedmagpie contains warnings for "perversion of childhood memories, bad language, watersports, voyeurism, orgies, student/teacher, rectal exams/medical fetish, dubcon (dubious consent), various magical creature cameos which may or may not count as bestiality, references to public sex locations." Yet another story, "A Christmas Tale as Sung by Wormtail the Rat" by pre_raphaelite1 and snapelike, features the characters of Ginny Weasley, Arthur Weasley, "Mad Eye" Moody, Wormtail (a rat), Sirius Black, Regulus Black, Crookshanks (a cat), and Mrs. Norris (a cat) and contains content including "incest, chan [pedophilia], bestiality, cannibalism, snuff, cross-dressing, necrophilia, gang bang, non-con [rape], dubcon [dubious consent], scat, prostitution, and adultery, a bit of blasphemy, and generally yuckiness!" Such stories are generally considered the work of Harry Potter anti-fans, a group of individuals who actively dislike the books or the films (or both) and seek to degrade the characters in various and sundry ways (Hetcher 7). Such anti-fanfiction "shows a lack of respect for the author, their work, and the characters these individuals claim to love so much" (Evans, "Why J.K. Rowling" 2). Such major fads as the Harry Potter phenomenon cause tremendous consumer backlash, repelling as many individuals as it attracts. This backlash can lead to the rise of anti-fan movements that take to the web to voice their opposition in the strongest possible language, including giving rise to the anti-fan fiction movement (Brown and Patterson 159). Some of these anti-fans may even be former fans who have come to resent the control Rowling's fictionalized world has over their life. This leads inevitably to "revenge" writing in which these former fans subject the characters within the stories to compulsive or vengeful lust, sadomasochism, rape, or other even darker sexual impulses. In this manner, the fan seeks to regain control (Morrison 14). Still others use their "smut" fanfiction to turn the tables on those fans whom they perceive as perverting Rowling's original story by attempting to integrate too much of it into their own lives. A fanfiction writer named Kim P. turned to "smut" fanfiction when she realized that even the most devoted of fans were turning the Harry Potter franchise into an excuse for perverted debauchery:

> It's just gone Halloween, and the number of fake Harry Potters and Hermiones I saw on a night out was crazy. Big fat women trying to fool themselves that they look good dressed as Hermione when all they look like is a man in drag, bad drag at that! I don't know who they are trying to kid but the only guys that seemed to be attracted to them were Harry Potter wannabes. Where did all these people come from? All these people who think dressing up as school kids is a turn-on! Surely this is verging on perversion [qtd. in Brown and Patterson 157].

Fans frequently argue that pornographic fiction (and often slash fiction in general) centered around the Harry Potter universe is inappropriate because they consider the overly sexualized portrayal of various characters to be "character rape" (Jenkins, *Textual Poachers* 187), wildly "out-of-character" (Katyal 495), and out of touch with the original source material (Brandyback 4). Slash writers are often accused by fans of not so much making the books' gay subtext visible as inventing it outright (Pugh 97), introducing homosexuality into the stories in ways that make little to no "realistic" sense for the characters as they are portrayed and developed within the source text.

However, many Harry Potter fans who write slash and pornographic "smut" fanfiction claim they do so out of a deep love and respect for Rowling's original material and that they "regularly police each other for abuses of interpretative license, but they also see themselves as the legitimate guardians of these materials, which have too often been manhandled by the producers and their licensees for easy profits" (Coombe 388). For these fanfiction writers, the denial of sexuality for the teenage Harry Potter characters is unrealistic since "[s]exuality is one of teenagers' major concerns and interests" (Moore 17). Sexuality, for many young fanfiction writers, is a good way to connect to the characters on a much more personal level. One study found that many teenage writers created fanfiction in which Hermione became romantically and sexually involved with Harry because "Hermione is a role model for smart girls (and boys) who find themselves overshadowed by their flashier peers. There's a certain appeal to thinking that a young academic could couple with the hero of the wizarding world" (Chonin E1). Many psychologists even find that conjuring and writing sexual fantasies about fictional characters and celebrities might have a positive mental benefit. Such fantasies allow individuals who may be socially awkward and have difficulty forming pair bonding to create an emotional attachment (however artificial) with another human being (Hoffmann and Meloy 182; C. Lawrence 22). Unlike the "organ grinding" (Marcus 392) with "anonymous flesh" (Alexander 130) that represents the sexual couplings in most pornographic texts, the connections that writers and readers feel for the characters in a piece of erotic fanfiction based on a familiar text (like Harry Potter) can increase the metaphoric power and emotional exposition within the work to allow it to work in a much more positive way on their senses and emotions (Smith 25).

Many writers of adult-oriented fanfiction also point to Rowling herself for justification for the stories they choose to tell. Although publicly Rowling has stated her strong dislike for pornographic fanfiction based on her work (Evans, "Why J.K. Rowling" 20), several fans have pointed to instances within the books (or in subsequent materials, such as interviews) where Rowling has provided subtle clues to darker sexual intentions within the work. When

Rowling announced in 2007 during an interview at Carnegie Hall that Dumbledore was gay, her comment of "Oh, my God, the fanfiction!" shows that Rowling was fully aware and, in her own way, actively supporting the slash fanfiction involving Dumbledore and proves the contention of many writers that slash is not necessarily a perverse "resistance" to Rowling's books' presumed heteronormativity but rather "an actualization of latent textual elements" (Jones 82). Rowling's conviction that Dumbledore's homosexuality is "very clear in the book" (Ahearn 1) may be connected to her awareness of the slash fanfiction writers who are frequently accused of misreading and distorting the text but who, in the case of this text, actually function as "ideal readers" who were able to use their sensitivity to homoerotic undertones within the work to tease out the potential subtext of Dumbledore's sexuality from the text (Tosenberger 201–202). Dumbledore's status as Harry's teacher and mentor, however, does allow Rowling to distance herself from another element of slash: pedophiliac slash. She thoroughly rejects the notion that the relationship between Dumbledore and Harry was in any way sexual by using Rita Skeeter to make the point within the text. When Rita implies in her unauthorized biography of Dumbledore that his relationship with Harry was "unnatural" (Rowling, *Deathly Hallows* 27), the text clearly suggests that such an allegation is utterly ridiculous (Tosenberger 202–203).

Another primary example of dark sexuality pervading its way into Rowling's texts in such a way as to fuel the interests of adult-oriented fanfiction writers occurs in the fifth book of the Harry Potter series, *Harry Potter and the Order of the Phoenix.* In that book, Rowling introduces the readers to the unlikable Dolores Umbridge, who comes to Hogwarts School of Wizardry and Witchcraft to act as the Defense Against the Dark Arts instructor and to serve as a spy for the Ministry of Magic. She transforms the school into a living nightmare and makes life practically unbearable for Harry and his friends, subjecting them to all manner of tortures. When Umbridge threatens to perform an illegal curse on one of Harry's friends to get him to reveal information on Dumbledore's whereabouts, Hermione decides to formulate a plan to rid the students of Umbridge once and for all. She leads Umbridge into the forest and leaves her at the mercy of the centaurs who dwell there. According to legend, centaurs were notorious for their "violent lust" (E. Lawrence 63) and were considered especially dangerous because of their "exaggerated masculinity" due to their "human male element being combined with the sexual potency of stallions" (Ibid.). Clearly Hermione (and Rowling, well known for her detailed and knowledgeable research in all aspects of her work ["The Forgotten Rape" 6]) would know about the history of centaurs (she is the leading student in her class, after all). Therefore, one can assume that she led Umbridge into the forest knowing that she would suffer rape at the hands of the centaurs ("The Forgotten Rape" 5). When Umbridge arrives back at the school after her encounter with the centaurs, she is clearly suffering the after-effects of a terrible trauma: her "mousy hair was very untidy and there were bits of twig and leaf in it, but otherwise she seemed to be quite unscathed" (Rowling, *Order of the Phoenix* 849). Her reaction to the sound of Ron simulating horse hooves and her shock-like state throughout the scene are symptomatic of rape victims. The rape of Umbridge is perhaps the most primal example of sexual violence within the books ("The Forgotten Rape" 6). Clearly the fact that Rowling does not detail the rape (since the Harry Potter books are, as she explains [Evans, "Why J.K. Rowling" 20], for children) allows Umbridge's experiences in the forest to fall into the realm of a story "gap" which are then "filled in" by fanfiction writers who come along later (Haughtvedt 4), thus allowing Rowling to create a prime source of material for erotic fanfiction writers to work.

At the beginning of this essay, I asked one very distinct and simple question: "Why?" "Why do fanfiction writers use the characters in the children's book series Harry Potter as the subject of, in many cases, deeply disturbing and disgusting sexual fantasies?" As we have now seen, the answer to that question is not as simple as it would presumably appear. Many groups of individuals have had the kneejerk reaction in proclaiming all fanfiction writers who use these characters in this manner are simply "deviant" (Jenson 9), "perverted" (Goldman 6), or "a pedophile in disguise" (Evans, "Some Women" 13). But such a definition is an immense exaggeration. According to the author of the personal essay "Why Do I Write Fanfiction?," based on her experiences in interacting with fanfiction writers in various online forums, she claims the vast majority of adult-oriented fanfiction writers are well-adjusted individuals who would never actively condone the behavior they put down on paper if confronted with it in real life ("Why Do I Write Fanfiction?" 3). In fact, many scholars seem to conclude that adult-oriented fanfiction, even that with the darkest and most perverted content, has immense value in upholding a message of morality (Chan 3), showing people what not to do and showing the effects, positive and negative, of such activities by displacing them from an abstract character to a recognizable face. A story in which an unnamed and faceless teen girl is raped may trigger feelings of disgust and outrage, but transform the name and face of that girl to Hermione Granger (and Emma Watson, the actress who portrays her and thus becomes the facial image most fans see when they think of the character) and the impact of the story becomes stronger, more emotional, and more personal (C. Lawrence 22–23).

In a very real sense, the Theodore Goddard letter with which I opened this essay could have had a vastly chilling effect on not just writers of Harry Potter fanfiction but the writers of all fanfiction in general. Since so many

writers and artists guard their intellectual property so carefully, if it were not
for many of the Harry Potter fanfiction writers who refused to acquiesce to
the legal threats inherent in the letter, a chilling effect would have befallen
all fanfiction writers across the Internet. Their claims of "fair use" and nonprofessional status allowed them to fight for their ability to use their own
intellectual gifts and imaginations to develop "a helpful creative scaffolding"
(Jenkins 25) on which to build on the stories of their artistic heroes and create
new adventures for their beloved characters that fit more closely into the mold
of the world as the fanfiction writers understood it. Young adults, seeking to
intellectually explore the complex sexual desires they are beginning to feel, are
able to use the heroes of the fictional worlds that fascinate them (whether in
book, film, or television form) to comprehend those feelings, including desires
that may feel somewhat perverse or different. Fanfiction becomes a "safe" way
to explore those issues in a way that may be shocking to some but completely
understandable and relatable to others (Moore 17). Therefore, despite the
dark and somewhat deviant elements that permeate adult fanfiction (and
Harry Potter adult fanfiction specifically), it is vitally important to view the
stories within the context in which the fanfiction writers present their tales
in order to fully understand the value of them within the fan community.

Works Cited

Ahearn, Victoria. "Rowling Knew Early on Dumbledore Was Gay." *Toronto Star Online*. 23
    Oct. 2007. Web. 24 Oct. 2012. http://www.thestar.com/entertainment/ article/269527.
Alexander, Jenny. "Tortured Heroes: The Story of Ouch! Fan Fiction and Sadomasochism."
    Sex, Violence, and the Body: The Erotics of Wounding. Eds. Vivien Burr and Jeff Hearn.
    New York: Palgrave Macmillan, 2008. 119–136. Print.
Bacon-Smith, Camille. *Enterprising Women: Television Fandom and the Creation of Popular Myth*.
    Philadelphia: University of Pennsylvania Press, 1992. Print.
Brandyback, Celandine. "Slash Fanfiction: A Personal Essay." *Fanfic Symposium*. 2004. Web. 14
    Oct. 2012. http://www.trickster.org/symposium/symp158.html.
Brown, Stephen, and Anthony Patterson. "'You're a Wizard, Harry!' Consumer Response to the
    Harry Potter Phenomenon." *Advances in Consumer Research* 33 (2006): 155–160. Print.
Chan, Ivy. "The Morality of Writing: aka, Hazily Philosophical Rambling at Five A.M." *Live-
    journal.com*. Web. 24 Oct. 2012. http://ivy-chan.livejournal.com/ 87661.html.
Chonin, Neva. "If You're an Obsessed Harry Potter Fan, Voldemort Isn't the Problem, It's
    Hermione Versus Ginny." *San Francisco Chronicle* 3 Aug. 2005: E1. Print.
Cicioni, Mirna. "Male Pair-Bonds and Female Desire in Fan Slash Writing." *Theorizing Fandom:
    Fans, Subculture, and Identity*. Eds. Cheryl Harris and Alison Alexander. Cresskill, NJ:
    Hampton Press, 1998. 153–177. Print.
Coombe, Rosemary. "Author/izing the Celebrity: Publicity Rights, Postmodern Politics, and
    Unauthorized Genders." *Cardozo Arts & Entertainment Law Journal* 365.10 (1992): 371–
    402. Print.
Dottyficons. "Severe Punishment." *Livejournal.com*. 4 Jun. 2006. Web. 5 Nov. 2012. http://
    community.livejournal.com/_hpchallenge/41118.html.
Driscoll, Catherine. "One True Pairing: The Romance of Pornography and the Pornography

of Romance." *Fan Fiction and Fan Communities in the Age of the Internet: New Essays*. Eds. Karen Hellekson and Kristina Busse. Jefferson: McFarland, 2006. 79–96. Print.

Elfflame. "Viridian 3: A Waiting Game." *Can't Rain All the Time*. 13 Jan. 2012. Web. 5 Nov. 2012. http://elfflame.insanejournal.com/638065.html.

"Emma Watson Afraid to Go Out Alone." *Stuff Online*. 21 Aug. 2012. Web. 5 Nov. 2012. http://www.stuff.co.nz/entertainment/celebrities/7516472/Emma-Watson-afraid-to-go-out-alone.

"Emma Watson Confronted by Stalker." *FirstPost*. 13 Oct. 2012. Web. 5 Nov. 2012. http://www.firstpost.com/fwire/emma-watson-confronted-by-stalker-489594.html.

"Emma Watson 'Distressed' After Paedophile Pastes Her Head on Child Porn Images." *CelebrityFix*. 14 Oct. 2010. Web. 5 Nov. 2012. http://celebrities.ninemsn. com.au/blog.aspx?blogentryid=654062&showcomments=true.

Evans, Dominick. "Some Women (and Men) Who Obsess on an Underage Harry Potter Border on Pedophilia." *Li-Reviews.com*. 15 Aug. 2007. Web. 25 Oct. 2012. http://www.li-reviews.com/2007/08/15/harry-potter-obsession/.

_____. "Why J.K. Rowling Dislikes Harry Potter Adult Fan Fiction." *Li-Reviews.com*. 21 Aug. 2007. Web. 11 Oct. 2012. http://li-reviews.com/2007/08/21/jk-rowling-harry-potter-adult-fan-fiction/.

"The Forgotten Rape in Harry Potter." *Feminist Wetblanket*. Oct. 2007. Web. 27 Oct. 2012. http://www.dollymix.tv/2007/10/the_forgotten_rape_in_harry_po.html

Goldman, Daniel. "Perverse Fantasies More Common Than We Thought." *Healthy Place*. 10 Dec. 2008. Web. 25 Oct. 2012. http://www.healthyplace.com/sex/psychology-of-sex/perverse-fantasies-more-common-than-we-thought/.

Gooch, Betsy. *The Communication of Fan Culture: The Impact of New Media on Science Fiction and Fantasy Fandom*. Atlanta: Georgia Institute of Technology Press, 2010. Print.

Hansen, Brita. "The Dark Side of Slash Fanfiction on the Internet." *Inter-Disciplinary.net*. Feb. 2010. Web. 10 Oct. 2012. http://www.inter-disciplinary.net/wp-content/uploads/2010/02/bhansenpaper.pdf.

Hayes, Sharon, and Matthew Ball. "Queering Cyberspace: Fan Fiction Communities as Spaces for Expressing and Exploring Sexuality." *Queering Paradigms*. Ed. Burkhard Scherer. New York: Peter Lang, 2010. 219–239. Print.

Hetcher, Steven A. "Using Social Norms to Regulate Fan Fiction and Remix Culture." *University of Pennsylvania Law Review* 157 (2009): 1869–1935. Print.

Hoffmann, Jens, and J. Reid Meloy. "Contributions from Attachment Theory and Psychoanalysis to Advance Understanding of Public Figure Stalking and Attacking." *Stalking, Threatening, and Attacking Public Figures: A Psychological and Behavioral Analysis*. Eds. J. Reid Meloy, Lorraine Sheridan, and Jens Hoffmann. New York: Oxford University Press, 2008. 165–194. Print.

Hogwartshoney. "Snitches and Boxes and Brooms, Oh, My!" *The Daily Deviant*. 19 Dec. 2011. Web. 5 Nov. 2012. http://asylums.insanejournal.com/daily_deviant/ 458067.html.

Jenkins, Henry. *Textual Poachers: Television Fans & Participatory Culture*. New York: Routledge, 1992. Print.

Jenson, Joli. "Fandom as Pathology: The Consequences of Characterization." *The Adoring Audience: Fan Culture and Popular Media*. Ed. Lisa A. Lewis. New York: Routledge, 1992. 9–29. Print.

Jones, Sarah Gwenllian. "The Sex Lives of Cult Television Characters." *Screen* 43 (2002): 79–90. Print.

Katyal, Sonia K. "Performance, Property, and the Slashing of Gender in Fan Fiction." *Journal of Gender, Social Policy & the Law* 14.3 (2006): 461–518. Print.

Lawrence, Cooper. *The Cult of Celebrity*. Guilford, CT: Skirt!, 2009. Print.

Lawrence, Elizabeth A. "The Centaur: Its History and Meaning in Human Culture." *Journal of Popular Culture* 27.4 (1994): 57–68. Print.

Marcus, Stephen. "Pornotopia." *The Sexual Revolution*. Ed. Jeffrey Escoffier. New York: Thunder's Mouth, 2003. 380–398. Print.

McCardle, Meredith. "Fan Fiction, Fandom, and Fanfare: What's All the Fuss?" *Boston University Journal of Science and Technology Law* 9.2 (2003): 1–37. Print.

Michiba, Sakai. "Sectumsempra Animi." *Livejournal.com*. 20 Mar. 2007. Web. 5 Nov. 2012. http://sakaim.livejournal.com/23164.html.

Moore, Rebecca C. "All Shapes of Hunger: Teenagers and Fanfiction." *Voya* (Apr. 2005): 15–19. Print.

Pre_raphaelite and snapelike. "A Christmas Tale as Sung by Wormtail the Rat." *The Daily Deviant*. 10 Dec. 2007. Web. 5 Nov. 2012. http://asylums.Insanejournal.com/daily_deviant /92091.html#cutid1.

Pre_raphaelite and thegildedmagpie. "The Little Wizard's Book of Slutty Goosings." *The Daily Deviant*. 24 Mar. 2011. Web. 5 Nov. 2012. http://asylums.insanejournal.com/daily_deviant /394107.html#cutid1.

Pugh, Sheenagh. *The Democratic Genre: Fan Fiction in a Literary Context*. Bridgend, Wales: Seren, 2005. Print.

Rowling, J.K. *Harry Potter and the Deathly Hallows*. New York: Scholastic, 2007. Print.

_____. *Harry Potter and the Order of the Phoenix*. New York: Scholastic, 2003. Print.

_____. *Harry Potter and the Sorcerer's Stone*. New York: Scholastic, 1997. Print.

Ships_harry. "Triad." *The Daily Deviant*. 28 Nov. 2007. Web. 5 Nov. 2012. http://asylums.insane journal.com/daily_deviant/90035.html?thread=847027.

Smith, Clarissa. "Pleasing Intensities: Masochism and Affective Pleasures in Porn Short Fictions." *Mainstreaming Sex: The Sexualization of Western Culture*. Ed. Feona Attwood. LONDON: I.B. Tauris, 2009. 19–35. Print.

Tosenberger, Catherine. "'Oh My God, the Fanfiction!' Dumbledore's Outing and the Online Harry Potter Fandom." *Children's Literature Association Quarterly* 33.2 (2008): 200–206. Print.

"Why Do I Write Fanfiction, Especially That Fanfiction Which Is of an Erotic Nature?" *Livejournal.com*. 17 May 2008. Web. 24 Oct. 2012. http://spacefic.livejournal.com/.

Recut Film Trailers, Nostalgia and the Teen Film

Kathleen Williams

Recut film trailers have been a popular form of video on YouTube since 2006. They typically involve the splicing together of footage from one or more sources to adhere to the form of commercially released film trailers (trailers that appear in theaters before films). While they take the structure of an advertisement, recut trailers most commonly advertise a film — or a version of a film — that will not exist. The popularity of recut trailers on YouTube (many have millions of views) suggests not only a willingness in audiences to watch a trailer by choice, but also to engage with a past film from a different perspective. Rather than reading the trailer only as an advertising text, recut trailers allow audiences to see an old film in a mode of anticipation — as though they were seeing it for the very first time.

This essay discusses recut trailers in relation to nostalgia and how they are created and played with. This will be achieved through the use of a case study of recut trailers for popular teen films where new trailers are created either through re-editing original material from the film or through "mash-up" trailers that promote non-existent films derived from two or more pre-existing films. By focusing on the creation of nostalgia in the production and consumption of recut trailers on YouTube, this essay will address nostalgia in relation to fan practices. Digital spaces and technologies such as YouTube both encourage nostalgic interaction with past films and provide easier ways to augment and play with a past text.

Some of the recut film trailers that involve rereading a past teen film, such as *Ferris Bueller's Day Off* (1986), are created to uncover a storyline that was latent in the film's narrative. By comparison, some recut trailers incorporate films outside the teen genre, such as *The Ten Commandments* (1956), to give them the aesthetic and narrative world of a teen film. These trailers allow audiences, through their close reading of a film, to augment their memories by alternating storylines or displacing the original genre of the film.

Defining Recut Trailers

Recut trailers have become a recognizable and popular form of video on YouTube. The trailers involve "cutting" or mashing up footage from one or more source texts in order to create a trailer for a film, or a version of a film that will never exist. These trailers, in turn, seem to strip the trailer of its advertising function and instead signal how commercially released trailers have come to inform and reflect cinematic desires. Lisa Kernan, in the first comprehensive study of commercially released trailers, highlights how film trailers signal an act of faith between film-goers and the feature film. They attempt to appeal to an audience through a focus on stars, genre, or narrative. This can be seen in numerous ways in the structure of commercially released trailers today: the trailer works to situate the upcoming feature film in relation to a broad genre (claiming that this new horror film is as scary as a past horror film), the trailer can announce the presence of an actor whose past body of work comes to signal how that actor will draw audiences to a film based on their expectations, and the trailer can present a version of the film's narrative in a way that will appeal to as many potential audiences as possible. As such, film trailers have become both an entry point into a film and a way for studios to build a future film-going audience, providing links and a meta-narrative to where a potential film will be situated in relation to past films.

This leads to, as Victor Burgin (12) argues, audiences being familiar with a film prior to having seen it. However, film trailers are unstable links to a feature film; they omit or amplify parts of a film in order to draw an audience to the cinema and rental services such as Netflix, or to purchase a DVD. This amplification and omission is common practice (Kernan), and as such does not go unnoticed by film audiences. These recut trailers play with conventions of the theatrically released trailer that provide a version of a film that might differ from the actual feature. By amplifying and omitting to an even greater extent than commercially released trailers to uncover and share a new version of a film or a dormant storyline, recut trailers subvert studio attempts to create an audience for a feature film by denying the end product of a film that can be consumed.

The recut trailer comes in many different forms. Some groups of trailers will focus on a specific film. For instance, a number of trailers were uploaded from 2006 that recut footage from films featuring two male leads, such as

Back to the Future (1985) or *Dumb and Dumber* (1994), to mimic or copy the narrative and aesthetic world of the *Brokeback Mountain* (2005) trailer (Williams). Other recut trailers do not revolve around a particular film; popular examples include *The Shining* (1980) recut as a family comedy, *Mary Poppins* (1964) recut as a horror film, or *Must Love Jaws*— the misunderstood love story between a man and a shark. Often, recut trailers attempt to draw out a storyline that was latent in the original footage for the feature film. This in part mimics the role of the commercially released trailer, which picks and chooses aspects of a feature film to "sell" to an audience (Tryon 161).

Many recut trailers are nostalgic in that they playfully evoke a past text and bring it into the form of a trailer so that it can be revisited and desired as if it were a new film. Recut trailers that deliver a new storyline for an existing feature can be seen as an act of rereading. This rereading also demonstrates nostalgia for a past film as it seeks to draw older texts into the present. The recut trailers that change the storyline of an existing feature also demonstrate the joy of revisiting and altering existing memories of a film. This relates to the culture of YouTube as a "portal of cultural memory" (Hilderbrand, *YouTube* 54) where clips are consistently uploaded of forgotten films, television shows, and music videos as a form of nostalgia.

Situating Nostalgia

Nostalgia has been studied in relation to many different texts and media and in numerous academic disciplines and fields. The following discussion of nostalgia is not intended as a comprehensive overview of the available literature but instead focuses upon creating an impression of how nostalgia may function in spaces such as YouTube and in objects such as recut trailers. As mentioned before, the theoretical work on nostalgia is varied, particularly in terms of media production. In relation to media consumption, numerous works exist that discuss, for example, the presence of nostalgia for technological media of the past through the lens of fan-like adoration, or the collecting of outmoded technologies such as vinyl collections (Plasketes), VHS tapes (Hilderbrand, *Inherent Vice*), or retrogaming (Suominen). Often this involves being nostalgic for a time that an individual did not personally experience. Nostalgia can exist beyond individual experiences as something that has been *lived*, and can, as Boym notes, often become collective nostalgia for bygone eras or items that were not directly experienced.

In basic terms, nostalgia can be seen as the romanticization of a representation of the past through a text or object. In relation to popular media consumption and production, there are tropes and signifiers of the past that are readily employed in music, films, magazines, posters, and so on to evoke nostalgia in media consumers. The use of sepia-tone in newly shot footage, music from artists or genres associated with a specific generation or period of time, or costumes of a bygone era all have the potential to evoke nostalgia in audiences or even to make the audience feel as though they should be nostalgic for the past.

Johannes Hofer, a Swiss doctor, coined the term "nostalgia" in 1688 as a scientific and medical term (Natali). Its popular usage since then has come to connote an affective method of engaging with the past. The literal meaning of nostalgia comes from Hofer's combination of the Greek words *nostos* (homecoming) and *algos* (pain or ache) "to describe the pain resulting from the desire to return to one's home" (Natali). However, nostalgia takes on a meaning outside of the longing and inherent pain (regardless of its severity) that is implied by its original meaning. Fred Davis discusses the "nostalgia boom" (90) of the 1970s, seen through such TV shows such as *Happy Days* (1974–1984) and movies that romanticized past eras such as *Grease* (1978) and *American Graffiti* (1973), each of which was set in the 1950s. He claims that nostalgia is a "distinctive aesthetic modality" (Davis 30) that rises in times when culture is in "transition and in response to the yearning for continuity" (Grainge 27), suggesting that instead of yearning for a home, it is the yearning for continuity that creates nostalgia.

This culture of transition can be seen in the attempts to shift cinematic culture and texts into digital spaces and temporalities. The search for continuity rather than a yearning for the past can be seen in the way that the life of a narrative or cultural style is extended into the present. Considering this search for continuity as a cultural mode involves evoking a collective understanding of the past through cultural symbols (for instance, through the use of clothing to signify a particular era such as the 1950s), which in turn symbolizes stability, nuclear families, and rock 'n' roll. This can be seen as negotiating symbols of the past into current culture.

Importantly, Grainge notes that the production of nostalgia might not necessarily have to do with longing or mourning, but instead suggests that "modes of (media) nostalgia have developed in a culture that is neither reeling from longing nor forgetting, but that is able to transmit, store, receive, reconfigure, and invoke the past in new and specific ways" (28). Grainge's conception of nostalgia is the basis for the understanding of nostalgia in reference to recut trailers. Instead of discussing nostalgia purely in terms of longing or yearning, we should instead look for and attempt to understand "nostalgia as a cultural style" (Davis) that is born out of a culture that can "transmit, store, receive, reconfigure" objects from the past (Grainge 28).

Nostalgia is often considered in terms of what has been lost; however, it is important to consider how nostalgia itself has been produced. Nostalgia for a time and place is produced and created by acknowledging an absence, but this does not necessarily mean that it is a loss, or that it is melancholic. As many of these trailers demonstrate, nostalgia can also be seen as a celebration or reworking of our understanding of history and memory. Scanlan argues that "nostalgia may be a style or design or narrative that serves to comment on how memory works" (4). If this popularized form of entertainment on YouTube repeatedly evokes nostalgia, it is important to consider how nostalgia is figured in our cinematic mediation and the importance of nostalgia in our understanding of how we interact with media.

Cameron's Day Off: Nostalgia, Faux-Nostalgia and the Teen Film

In analyzing how these trailers augment and question teen advertising and appeals made to teen markets, it is important to look at how the recut trailer seeks to interact with notions of nostalgia. Some of the trailers discussed appeal to teens through parody, playfully revisiting and altering the storyline of canonical teen films, or placing a film that was not created to appeal to teens in the realm of a teen film by using the same methods used in commercially released trailers.

Teen films are popular source material for recut trailers. Popular teen films of the past few decades have at times been nostalgic; examples include the 1970s films *Grease* and *American Graffiti* (both of which are set in the 1950s), and *Dazed and Confused* (1993), filmed in the 1990s and set in the 1970s. This is also a popular trope in television series aimed at teens such as the cult show *Freaks and Geeks* (1999–2000) filmed at the end of the millennium but which was set in the late 1970s, and *That '70s Show* (1998–2006). Each of these films and television shows could be categorized as a "coming of age" story that depicts the supposedly universal characteristics of teenagers coming to terms with and finding one's identity while attempting to integrate into society.

These teen films depict times that their target audience was not alive to experience. In the above examples, the setting of the films is closer to the era of their parents' coming of age than their own. Lesley Speed identifies this tension as a broader comment on generational difference:

> Teen films are fundamentally concerned with reversing age-defined privileges. The nostalgic teen film is distinctive in the genre because it augments the ostensible themes of rebellion and anti-authoritarianism with an adult perspective. Whereas most teen films emphasize an adolescent point of view, the nostalgic teen movie

reveals tensions between youth and adulthood at the level of narration, which can be seen as the site of a quest to contain adolescence [24].

While Speed notes that there are exceptions to this tension (*Dazed and Confused* being a notable example), there is an expectation in nostalgic teen films that the trials and tribulations of teenage life are something that has been experienced before. This is highlighted by the popular use of an aged narrator such as in the film *Stand By Me* (1986) in which the narrator looks back on his teen experiences and explicitly considers how those events shaped his adult life. More broadly, the nostalgic treatment of teen years shows the universal problems that teens encounter as a rite of passage that must be endured by all. The nostalgic teen film also commonly presents the teen experience through the retrospective wisdom of adults, who marvel at what they did as teenagers. With nostalgia being such an integral part of teen films, it is likely that this mode of nostalgia should also appear in recut trailers that augment teen films.

The trailer *10 Things I Hate About Commandments* satirizes the teen film genre through the reworking of a well-known biblical story and appropriates footage from the film *The Ten Commandments*, which documents the story of Moses. By using editing, voiceover, text, and music, *The Ten Commandments* is placed in the realm of a twentieth-century teen romance comedy (while directly referencing 1990s teen film *10 Things I Hate About You* [1999]). While the characters in the imagined film are not youthful and are placed within the religious and historical settings, the use of voiceover and other editing techniques places the action within the trailer as belonging to the supposed universal narratives of the teen film. This, in part, highlights the inauthenticity of historical film — the recut trailer is no more authentic than the historical film made thousands of years after the time Moses supposedly parted the Red Sea.

The story of Moses is likened to schoolyard trivialities over popularity and image: Will Moses make it from "zero to hero" and "get the girl"? Thus, the original meaning attributed to the story of Moses in the original film is bypassed and historical representation is brought into question. More notable, however, is the disdain towards the predictable nature of the teen film genre and the way that teen films are marketed to appeal to youthful audiences. The trailer also upends star appeal, in both anachronistic references as well as in playfully coopting star appeal used in other trailers. For instance, Sinead O'Connor plays a bald man, and Samuel L. Jackson is inserted as "Principal Firebush" — the burning bush that appears to Moses. This also places the tradition of the Bible within the realm of popular culture, in the context of popular knowledge, and as a collective cultural artifact.

10 Things I Hate About Commandments parodies the techniques used in trailers to appeal to teen audiences. By taking what could be one of the furthest points in history — well before teenagers were considered a different category of age — and placing it in the advertising mode of what should appeal to young audiences, the trailer signals that youth are easily identified as commodities. Part of that commodification can be seen in the way that the teen genre is communicated, but also in the focus on a particular type of star appeal. *10 Things I Hate About Commandments* uses Sinead O'Connor and Samuel L. Jackson as appeals to a youth audience (arguably, Sinead O'Connor would not appeal to a youth audience in 2012, suggesting how film studios often get this appeal wrong). Samuel L. Jackson appears as his character Jules Winnfield from *Pulp Fiction* (1994), playing on the use of biblical passages his character famously recited in the film. Jackson thus becomes a character in and of himself, who traverses time and space to appear as the same character through different historical eras and genres. This goes beyond merely being intertextual. *10 Things I Hate About Commandments* hints at a timelessness to media consumption and textuality.

The recut trailer *Back to the Future—Trailer Recut* takes the time traveling premise of the film *Back to the Future* (1985) and plays the nostalgic references to excess. In this trailer, Marty McFly is depicted as a teenager who brings part of the future back to the 1950s. While this is part of the storyline of the original feature film, the trailer presents the footage in black and white, with nods to the B-movie science fiction trailers of the 1950s. The temporality of the original film (shot in the 1980s with footage depicting both the 1980s and the 1950s) is displaced by making the film appear as though it was made in the 1950s with a depiction of the future, instead of the past.

The trailer constantly asserts that a "teenager from the future" will come to the 1950s and bring music from the 1980s as a futuristic omen of what is to come. Rather than the past appearing as a novelty — as it did in the original feature — this trailer places the futuristic teenager as the historical curiosity. This trailer demonstrates the expected aesthetics of creating nostalgia with the use of black and white, the altering of clean footage to make it as appear as though it was created with antiquated technology, and the understanding that trailer and film viewers have about science fiction films of the 1950s. The trailer also reflects the notion that teenagers appear as outsiders and attempt to place new ideas and tastes on older people with more conservative sensibilities. The message is that teenagers *always* appear to be from the future. Speed argues:

> The nostalgic teen film reveals a tension between semantic excess and syntactic containment, mapped across the themes of generational differences and historical distance. Here, the syntactic dimension is designed to contain and dominate the semantic details of the narrative. Perceiving adolescence from a distance, the nostalgia text is less concerned with historical detail than with *attaching significance to the past*. Here, youths' concerns tend to be restricted to the semantic and contained within a syntax that privileges nostalgia and fetishizes historical distance. The rites-of-passage film is inclined to disavow the immediacy and, at times, the vulgarity of youth culture [26, my emphasis].

Nostalgia thus functions as a way of placing what seems new — teen culture — in a long-running narrative that is inter-generational. While nostalgia may seem, in the typical teen film, as a longing for the past, these trailers show that this can also function as a way of revisiting and reordering the past and, in the process, reordering and revisiting the present. The privileging of historical distance that is apparent in many teen films is augmented and challenged through the recut trailers by either provoking the ways that teens are depicted in films or by reworking the past to appear as new.

In his discussion of nostalgia in postmodernism and pastiche, Fredric Jameson presents *Star Wars* (1977) as a nostalgia film (8). In his case for moving beyond describing historical fiction or films as such, but instead looking to pastiche and nostalgia as a way of explaining why these texts exist, he points out that *Star Wars* is "not a historical film about our own intergalactic past" (8), but rather it evokes the history of 1930s to 1950s afternoon serials set in space such as *Buck Rogers* (1950–1951). Jameson claims that "*Star Wars* reinvents this experience in the form of pastiche: that is, there is no longer any point to a parody of such serials since they are long extinct" (8). By "reinventing the feel" (8) of the earlier serials, *Star Wars* appeals in two ways: as a vehicle for longing that older viewers will experience, but also as a straight narrative to younger viewers who did not view the texts that *Star Wars* draws upon. Thus, nostalgia can also appear aesthetically and affectively, not just in the clear representation of the past.

Teen films are designed to appeal to a teen audience that will later mature and look back fondly on them. They act as an aesthetic time capsule for the era teens grow up in. But there is a grander narrative to the presence of nostalgia in teen films — one that moves beyond merely revisiting the world of one's youth. Nostalgia plays a role in the construction of many teen films that look back to the experiences of generations before them and place that future within the present. Rather than attempting to present an accurate depiction of the past, nostalgic teen films seek to create the feeling of pastness, which is played within the recut trailers discussed here.

Rather than merely recutting an older film to readjust it, recut trailers also seek to revisit and alter the history of a film. One such example of this is *Ferris Club*, which shows edited footage from *Ferris Bueller's Day Off* to reveal an alternate storyline: Ferris Bueller is a figment of his long-suffering friend Cameron's imagination, following the plot from *Fight Club* (1999). *Ferris Club*, as of February 2012, has received over 600,000 hits on YouTube and has been discussed on numerous blogs and sites as an example of a clever reworking of what was potentially always in the film.

By taking the form of a trailer rather than a short clip to suggest the presence of this plot, *Ferris Club* also advertises this alternate narrative and seeks to persuade the audience of its legitimacy. It appeals to the literacy of consumers who have seen *Ferris Bueller's Day Off* and *Fight Club* and allows not only for a communal act of consumption, but also a communal production of a new memory of what *Ferris Bueller's Day Off* is about. Rather than nostalgia being figured only as a way of looking back and a longing for the past, *Ferris Club* suggests that there is also a longing for a teen film to be altered through the literacy and knowledge of its audience who can revisit their past and alter it based on their consumption of texts.

Nostalgia and Fandom

In his work *Digital Fandom,* Paul Booth discusses how a "philosophy of playfulness" is a useful lens for analysis in digital mediated fan creations and interactions:

> One key characteristic we can witness in Digital Fandom is how fans' use of technologies brings a sense of playfulness to the work of active reading. The work that fans put into creating fan fiction, fan videos, fan wikis of other fan works can all be boiled down to the fact that they are fun to share. What these examples illustrate is an approaching trend in contemporary media to ludicize texts, or for audiences to create a philosophy of playfulness in their writing to each other [12].

As Booth acknowledges, this playfulness does not seek to portray fandom as lacking in seriousness or drive. What can be taken from this idea of a philosophy of playfulness, when applied to recut trailers, is the enjoyment that comes from augmenting and playing with films and their legacies. As Booth suggests, fan creations are fun to *share*: to participate in a culture that facilitates and promotes sharing and creation is a type of playfulness within media systems. Fandom, in a sense, is about striving for the continuity that nostalgia provides; by pulling objects from the past consistently into the present and augmenting and shifting them, fan practices seek to both disrupt and extend time. This occurs while ensuring the continuity of the object and its audience.

While, arguably, fans do not create all of the recut trailers on YouTube, Booth's concept of the philosophy of playfulness is still relevant. As he notes, "fans make explicit what we all do implicitly: That is, we actively read and engage with media texts on a daily basis" (12). While fandom is not the only lens of analysis that can be employed in order to understand why these trailers are created and shared, fandom studies do provide insight into and acknowledgment of, the ways that very active audiences have engaged with texts and formed networks that augment, play with, and disrupt the usual lifespan of a text.

The relationship between fandom and nostalgia for past texts and their reworking can now be seen in a variety of mediated forms such as the recut trailer and the popularity of sharing older media forms on YouTube. Fan creations leave traces and articulations of how nostalgia has operated in fandom for some time. While nostalgia is arguably part of how we interact with media, the ways that fandom has documented nostalgia show how a complex relationship with the past is central to fandom.

Nathan Hunt discusses nostalgia in fan film cultures through their reiteration of popular film and film histories. Hunt looks at how popular film magazines and other vehicles for film criticism draw upon Stringer's notion of the "memory narrative" which involves "fondly" evokes the past (81). Using popular film magazines *Empire* and *Total Film* as examples, Hunt demonstrates how film journalism "circulate[s] these 'memory narratives' in relation to film fan culture" (97), through a constant remediation and evocation of the past by making reference to the production of a film or the context in which it was originally viewed, or by providing trivia. Hunt suggests that there needs to be a shift away from considering film as being a filmic text to "move beyond the text itself and its direct relationship with the viewer and explore the way that nostalgia is employed in the discursive spaces that surround film consumption" (98). According to Hunt, these discursive spaces form an integral part of fan cultures as they become vehicles for fans to learn film histories and serve as an "exchange between fan culture and cultural texts and intertexts" (98).

Hunt's analysis of nostalgia and the significance of the relationship between spaces and consumers is useful to apply here. Hunt identifies knowledge as "vital currency in fans' sense of place" (98). In particular, nostalgia "constantly calls upon imagined histories, both cultural and institutional, evoking notions of particular historical periods of production and reception as contexts for popular film" (98). These imagined histories are concerned with both the remembered aspects of fans' individual consumption of films, and also of the shared knowledge between fans and institutions of the production of films.

Not all admirers of a film can be considered fans or have the same attitude toward a film (Hunt 98–99). For example, some viewers who choose to create their own media such as a trailer may be appreciating a film ironically in the realm of kitsch. Others may have a general "fan-like" attitude towards a film, leading the film to be categorized as a cult film. Part of this cult status — which could be achieved through an ironic appreciation of a past text, such as Hunt's example of *Top Gun* (1986), or films that have been appreciated increasingly retrospectively after their release date — is nostalgia in the appreciation and yearning for a return to a time and place. This can be seen at play in the recut trailers: arguably, in order to create *10 Things I Hate About Commandments* a viewer need not be a fan of either *The Ten Commandments* or *10 Things I Hate About You*. However, it is fairly clear that the trailer creator was appreciating both films ironically. To that end, Hunt argues for nostalgia to be considered:

> as a *way* of reading as much as it is a film language; that nostalgia is not just a product of the moment of textual reading, but a mode of interpretation that has become central to the way that film is read within popular film fandom. The primacy of the present in reading the past is visible in the constant packaging of the history of cinema in terms of its value to the contemporary moment. As such, the memory narratives circulated in fandom are nostalgic in that they seek to fix or reiterate histories of production as essential contexts for the contemporary reading of film [98].

This "constant packaging of the history of cinema" (98) and its relation to reading a film in the present can be seen in popular contemporary uses of the trailer. The inclusion of trailers as a special feature on DVDs, for instance, allows the viewer to engage in the history of the film through its promotion and to acquire insider knowledge of the production and reception of the film, building a seemingly more authentic sense of nostalgia. Further, YouTube's architecture allows for the past to be evoked through linking to related videos and thus linking to a plethora of source footage from numerous eras. Memory operates and circulates in the consumption of film trailers on YouTube, and YouTube provides avenues for a viewer to engage with their memories of popular culture. Hunt's "memory narratives" can be seen at play here, in the literal evocation of supplementary footage that aims to provide fan-like insider knowledge alongside the text, as well as providing links between texts. In terms of recut trailers specifically, the memory narratives that seek to draw upon histories of production can be seen through the links provided to the source footage used by the trailer's creator. Increasingly, these memory narratives that Hunt mentions have become "essential contexts for the contemporary reading of film," (98) supplemented by YouTube's architecture, which have long existed through the popularity of film magazines, websites, the packaging of DVDs, and other cultural objects that contribute to the popular and shared histories of film.

While the teen trailers discussed here may not necessarily be made by fans, they do draw upon common fan practices: that is, reworking a past text. Some recut trailers clearly demonstrate fandom, such as trailers for *Twilight* (2008) made before the release of the feature film (Williams). However, what the recut trailers demonstrate is the way that users collectively augment and engage with film culture in online spaces. While being a fan is not a prerequisite to create a recut trailer, an understanding of individual narratives, film culture, and marketing is necessary. The teen recut trailers demonstrate, as a subset of a larger body of videos, that YouTube users and audiences are not only willing to nostalgically evoke media, they are also willing to augment it, shift it, and play with their own memories.

Conclusion

Recut trailers are apt examples of remix and mash-up culture online. However, as I have discussed, they demonstrate broader engagement with media and the communal production of cultural and filmic knowledge. They demonstrate that media users are not only literate when it comes to the narrative of feature films but also literate to the ways that films are marketed and sold to ensure future audiences.

While many recut trailers may not be created by fans per se, the willingness in producers and consumers of the recut trailer to nostalgically rework and play with media memory speaks to current modes of engagement with media. Teen films, in particular, are useful vehicles through which to discuss the potential of nostalgia as a lens of analysis; teen films act as time capsules for a generation. The recut trailer, however, seeks to upend and subvert the role of the teen film as a time capsule. They rework the narrative of a feature film and in the process rework our memories of media we've consumed. They ask their audience to draw upon their memories of a feature film and to accept the latent storyline that was lying between individual shots.

As I have discussed, trailers released in theaters have traditionally amplified or omitted parts of a feature film in order to appeal to an audiences, and as Kernan argues, they rely on stars and genre to generate interest in the films. The teen recut film trailers that have been analyzed show that the identifiable trademarks of a teen film in terms of genre, narrative and stardom can be easily drawn upon and parodied. Any actor can be recut as a teenager as long as he or she is accompanied by particular music, narrative, and editing effects that signal to an audience that they are watching a teen film.

Recut trailers are a useful vehicle through which to discuss the relationship audiences have to cinema and media. Due to the ease of dissemination on YouTube, those who have traditionally been considered consumers of media are not regulated to private practices of engagement with texts and media. Recut trailers are traces of the way that audiences participate in filmic culture. Nostalgia, in turn, allows us to broaden the reasons why people create their own media and draw upon their memories of films — from recut trailers it can be seen that nostalgia can be playful, clever, and subversive.

Works Cited

American Graffiti. Dir. George Lucas. Universal, 1973. DVD.

Back to the Future. Dir. Robert Zemeckis. Universal, 1985. DVD.

Booth, Paul. *Digital Fandom: New Media Studies*. New York: Peter Lang, 2010. Print.

Boym, Svetlana. *The Future of Nostalgia*. New York: Basic, 2001. Print.

Burgin, Victor. *The Remembered Film*. London: Reaktion, 2004. Print.

Classyhands. "Ferris Club **Original Version**." *YouTube*. 11 Jul. 2010. Web. 12 Jan. 2013. http://www.youtube.com/watch?v=eiMuj85ngEo.

Davis, Fred. *Yearning for Yesterday: A Sociology of Nostalgia*. New York: Free Press, 1979. Print.

Dazed and Confused. Dir. Richard Linklater. Gramercy, 1993. DVD.

Dumb and Dumber. Dir. Peter Farrelly. New Line, 1994. DVD.

Ferris Bueller's Day Off. Dir. John Hughes. Paramount, 1986. DVD.

Fight Club. Dir. David Fincher. 20th Century–Fox, 1999. DVD.

Grainge, Paul. "Nostalgia and Style in Retro America: Moods, Modes and Media Recycling." *Journal of American and Comparative Culture* 23.1 (2000): 27–35. Print.

Grease. Dir. Randal Kleiser. Paramount, 1978. DVD.

Hilderbrand, Lucas. *Inherent Vice: Bootleg Histories of Videotape and Copyright*. Durham: Duke University Press, 2009. Print.

_____. "YouTube: Where Cultural Memory and Copyright Converge." *Film Quarterly* 61.1 (2007): 48–57. Print.

Hunt, Nathan. "Nostalgic [Re]membering: Film Fan Cultures and the Affective Reiteration of Popular Film Histories." *Image and Narrative* 12.2 (2011): 96–117. Print.

Jameson, Fredric. "Postmodernism and Consumer Society." *The Cultural Turn: Selected Writings on the Postmodern 1983–1998* London: Verso, 1998. 1–21. Print.

JohnnySwitchblade. "Back to the Future — Trailer Recut." *YouTube*. 19 Aug. 2009. Web. 12 Jan. 2013. http://www.youtube.com/watch?v=CdhALpGqA5U.

Kernan, Lisa. *Coming Attractions: Reading American Movie Trailers*. Austin: University of Texas Press, 2004. Print.

Mary Poppins. Dir. Robert Stevenson. Buena Vista, 1964. DVD.

Moviemker. "THE ORIGINAL Scary 'Mary Poppins' Recut Trailer." *YouTube*. 8 Oct. 2006. Web. 12 Jan. 2013. http://www.youtube.com/watch?v=2T5_0AGdFic.

Natali, Marcus Piason. "History and Politics of Nostalgia." *Iowa Journal of Cultural Studies* 5 (2004): 10–25. Print.

Neochosen. "The Shining Recut." *YouTube*. 7 Feb. 2006. Web. 12 Jan. 2013. http://www.youtube.com/watch?v=KmkVWuP_s00.

Plasketes, George. "Romancing the Record: The Vinyl De-Evolution and Subcultural Evolution." *The Journal of Popular Culture* 26.1 (1992): 109–122. Print.

Pretty in Pink. Dir. Howard Deutch. Paramount, 1986. DVD.

Scanlan, Sean. "Introduction: Nostalgia." *Iowa Journal of Cultural Studies* 5 (2004): 3–9. Print.

Shary, Timothy. *Generation Multiplex: The Image of Youth in Contemporary American Cinema*. Austin: University of Texas Press, 2002. Print.

The Shining. Dir. Stanley Kubrick. Warner Bros., 1980. DVD.

Speed, Lesley. "Tuesday's Gone: The Nostalgic Teen Film." *Journal of Popular Film and Television* 26.1 (1998): 24–32. Print.

Stand By Me. Dir. Rob Reiner. Columbia, 1986. DVD.

Star Wars. Dir. George Lucas. 20th Century–Fox, 1977. DVD.

Stringer, Julian. "Raiding the Archive: Film Festivals and the Revival of Classic Hollywood." *Memory and Popular Film*. Ed. Paul Grainge. Manchester: Manchester UP, 2003. 81–96. Print.

Suominen, Jaakko. "The Past as Future? Nostalgia and Retrogaming in Digital Culture." *Proceedings of the 7th International Digital Arts and Cultures Conference: The Future of Digital Media Culture*. Ed. Andrew Hutchison. 15–18 Sep. 2007. PDF file.

The Ten Commandments. Dir. Cecil B. DeMille. Paramount, 1956. DVD.

Ten Things I Hate About You. Dir. Gil Junger. Touchstone, 1999. DVD.

Top Gun. Dir. Tony Scott. Paramount, 1986. DVD.

Tryon, Chuck. *Reinventing Cinema: Movies in the Age of Media Convergence.* New Brunswick: Rutgers University Press, 2009. Print.

Vayabobo. "Must Love Jaws." *YouTube.* 14 Mar. 2006. Web. 12 Jan. 2013. http://www.youtube .com/watch?v=92yHyxeju1U&list=PL7F8FFA8F1CD02068&index=.

_____. "10 Things I Hate About Commandments." *YouTube.* 14 May 2006. Web. 12 Jan. 2013. http://www.youtube.com/watch?v=u1kqqMXWEFs.

Williams, Kathleen. "Fake and Fan Film Trailers as Incarnations of Audience Anticipation and Desire." *Transformative Works and Cultures* 9 (2012). Print.

Bringing Piety Back

Tim Tebow, Sports and American Culture

SUSAN ORENSTEIN

Faith and football aren't contradictions; our popular culture reinforces that viewpoint. *Friday Night Lights* (2006–2011), a long-running television show, features members of a high school football team who play as well as pray together. The movie, *The Blind Side* (2009), narrates the heartwarming story of a Christian family that decides to take in a homeless football player and give him a better life. Religion has always factored heavily into every facet of America's lay experience. America's first social critic, Alexis De Tocqueville, hypothesized that our secular democracy depended upon its Christian roots to provide a moral framework for its citizens (Douthat 2). In recent times, though, that dependency has been changing. Cultural revisionists such as Ross Douthat, David Campbell and Robert Putnam have commented upon this movement away from structured forms of worship. According to the 2012 Pew Report on Religion, over a quarter of all adults have left the faith they were raised in for another religion or for no faith at all, and a whopping 16.1 percent of all young Americans are unaffiliated with any religion whatsoever. More importantly, religion, once a social bulwark, is complicating individual responses towards hot button issues like same sex marriage, stem cell research and abortion. When people choose to vote according to their religious values, can a game of football, infused with a rousing religious message, encourage social harmony and widespread understanding?

Tim Tebow seems to think so. Using America's favorite sport (Harris) as a launching pad for his religious agenda, Tebow, an evangelical from Florida, has become to football what Lady Gaga is to modern music: a trend setter. Over his brief career, he has achieved tremendous name recognition. It is this iconic popularity, coupled with his pleasant personality, that separates him from the more sanctimonious evangelicals of yesteryear. And yet, in spite of tremendous faith-based credentials—a larger than life back-story and a commitment to numerous humanitarian deeds — he has merely moved fans to believe in an urban legend and to practice a popular meme which is devoid of religious content. It was highly probable that Tebow would fare well with fans who were religious, but how he would be perceived by fans who were merely engaged in following football religiously could not be predicted. In fact, how he will relate to fans who were religiously disaffected is still slowly emerging. What has become evident, though, is the extreme way in which fans have misconstrued religious meanings contained within his modeled behavior. Giving his actions a secular, sacrilegious or superstitious spin, his most loyal fans prove that determinations made by *Time* in 1966 are even truer for contemporary times: God and religion are passé ("Is God Dead?"). Although Tebow is earnestly planting seeds of faith on the football field, in America's arid religious environment, those seeds cannot take root.

D. Michael Lindsay defines the evangelical movement as "Christians who hold a particular regard for the Bible, embrace a personal relationship with God through a conversion to Jesus Christ, and seek to lead others on a similar spiritual journey" (4). In most press conferences or interchanges, Tebow discusses the importance of religion in his life, stating and restating that God takes precedence over not just football, but also family. He tells reporters and fans that he believes in spreading the word of God and in helping others to achieve the same personal relationship that he has with his Savior. In a discussion with Jake Plummer, Tebow declares that he will use any opportunity to shout God's name out to the listening public: "It is the most important thing in my life, so anytime I get an opportunity to tell Him that I love Him or give Him an opportunity to shout Him out on national TV, I'm gonna take that opportunity" (qtd. in Gagnon). Growing up in a family that has always been involved in missionary work and outreach, Tebow has naturally come to believe in spreading the Gospel and in using his position as a sports figure to reach both young and old in the football community. Indeed, George Barna, an evangelical pollster and a Tebow advisor, has counseled all evangelicals to grab young people and bring them to God during their tender years: "If people don't embrace Jesus Christ as their Savior before they reach their teenage years, the chance of their doing so at all is slim" (qtd. in Lindsay 10–11). Not surprisingly, believing that he has the charisma to convince young people to return to the faith, Tebow's media team are bent on marketing Tebow as that youthful face on Barna's brand.

A quick litany of facts proves that Tebow has earned more attention than most statesmen as well as the adoration of his enthusiastic fans. He has authored the best-selling sports book of 2011 (Rovell). He inspires many by his example; in 2012, some 30,000 people came to Georgetown, Texas, just to hear Tebow's Easter sermon (Alper). He has over 1.3 million friends on

Facebook and more than 800,000 people follow him on Twitter. In addition to Tebow's Jets jersey selling out in just hours, MacFarlane Toys released not just one, but rather three different Tim Tebow action figures in 2012 (McGuire). Even his name has become iconic, creating new popular culture terminology. Fans who adore his come-from-behind response have affectionately christened the second half of the game "Tebow time" since this is when Tebow makes his unique, game-changing moves (Dodd). Tebowing is a term for bowing down in prayer. His diverse array of fans maintain that they are part of "Tebow Nation," the term used to categorize his loyal enthusiasts. Fan loyalty can be glimpsed in games like the Broncos-Patriots matchup (January 14, 2012), which scored 19.5 million overnight views, the best regular season game in four years (McKay). His supporters have a variety of reasons for being devotees. Among the nearly 225,000 fans listed on his official fan webpage are people who find positive motivation in Tebow's wholesome personal demeanor, his unbridled philanthropy, his consistent embrace of a Christian lifestyle and his persistent ability to stimulate controversy and drama in the game (Dyer). Since his trade to the Jets, ardent fans, anxious to catch a glimpse of this cultural phenomenon, have boosted the hotel bookings and shop sales in the region near the Jets' upstate training camp (Braconier). This loyalty is highlighted by Deborah Braconnier, who analyzes the effect of Tebowmania on the upstate New York economy: "Bernard's Custom Logo and Trophy Source are offering various shirts featuring Tebow and Tebowmania... The store has already received calls from churches requesting large orders of these shirts." In addition, area newspapers can't get enough of him because he sells papers. *The Daily News* has featured articles about Tebow on an ongoing basis. When Tebow stripped off his shirt during a morning run in the rain, *Star Ledger* photographers quickly took some 99 *Baywatch*-esque shots in just under a minute for publication on their website (Vrentas).

Nonetheless, Tebow enthusiasts are counterbalanced by equally vocal detractors. Noting that it is duplicitous to promote Tebow as an underdog since he has won a Heisman Trophy, Andrew Sharp, one of Tebow's detractors, asks the media to stop painting Tebow as a David who made it to the big leagues in spite of prevailing viewpoints from a host of Goliaths. In doing so, Sharp raises a pertinent issue, since it is Tebow's skill packet that disturbs so many hardcore tradition-oriented football fanatics. Those who count themselves as Tebow critics generally dislike his unorthodox playing style. In fact, one Internet critic has remarked that some 22 percent of America's football fans are actually rooting for him to fail (Lourie) because of his playing style. Angrier commentaries have surfaced during game time on Twitter (Bishop) when debate rages among those angered by Tebow's uneven abilities. Chuck

Klosterman, a well-known sports commentator, observes that ambivalence about Tebow's talents has contributed to fan discomfort and discord. That dichotomy in Tebow's playing skills — his weaknesses as an intermediate passer and the limits in his throwing range — places him "at the fulcrum of the see-saw debates on college success and professional potential of athletic quarter-backs versus pocket passers" (Klosterman). Indeed, this splintered skill set has been largely responsible for the negative undercurrent that emerged during Tebow's short tenure in Denver. Noting that there was relief from this divisiveness when Tebow left Denver for New York, Julie Hayes, a writer for Yahoo! Sports, indicates that although Tebow's final drives were three minutes of pure excitement, the other "10, 077 minutes of the week were frustrating for Broncos fans not sold on the Tebow phenomenon." His terrible play the first 57 minutes of the vast majority of his games was too disconcerting for purists who railed openly against his often indelicate playing technique.

This fractured response to Tebow's performance on the field has been heightened by the controversy raised by Tebow's religious agenda. Although many in the NFL line-up have championed their faith, athletes like Colt McCoy, Sam Bradford and Devin Hester have remained more low-key about their relationship with Christianity. Tebow, on the other hand, has never been silent about affirming his faith. Eliciting strong reactions from his fans because of these interjections, he has subdivided football devotees into two warring camps. One set of fans views criticism of Tebow as an indictment of religion itself while the other faction, which finds "delight in every wayward pass" (Bishop), has been labeled as religiously detached and disinterested. Fan division fostered along religious lines is unfortunately reminiscent of America's larger social-political divide; sociologist have noted that over the last decade, a pattern of red and blue states has emerged during election years as Americans declare party loyalty based on religious leanings (Nivola and Brady). Just as religion increases tension in the nation, talk about religion in football has increased hostility between Tebow's proponents and critics. Anger bubbled over on November 2, 2011, when resentment with Tebow's evangelical stand spilled onto a discussion thread on ESPN's site. Comments on "X>Tebow" turned so negative that some of the threads had to be moderated or hidden by ESPN staffers. Within hours, patently offensive statements which were anti–Christian in nature spread to other comment sections (Petchesky), forcing ESPN officials to abandon the threads on November 3. As a result of ESPN's capitulation, a number of anti–Christian comments were left exposed and open to public scrutiny (Petchesky). Incidents like this have prompted *The New York Times*, *The Atlantic*, *The Christian Post* and *The Huffington Post* to use the words "polarizing" and "divisive" when discussing Tebow's effect upon football enthusiasts.

Such perceptions are shockingly different from previous gauges of Tebow's popularity among fans, which were made in 2010, the year in which he left college. Nielsen ratings of his popularity and likeability qualities from 2010 are some nine points higher than ratings made in 2012 (Bishop). His negative appeal to football admirers was so negligible that Nielsen rated him as extremely marketable. After making repeated protestations about his faith during the 2012 season, Tebow's appeal plummeted among the football public, with several responders dismissing him as a "religious nut job" (Bishop). As admirers and detractors went to war on the Internet over Tebow's behavior, the magnitude of the fan fracture could have irreparably upset the Broncos' upper management. According to one insider, Denver Broncos beat writer Dan Karpiel, fan division may have had an negative effect upon the trajectory of Tebow's career: "Elway and his staff were no longer willing to deal with those headaches and those distractions." A similar outlook is echoed in a Yahoo! Sports survey which intimates that talks about trading Tebow might have grown out of his fans turning the game into a "circus" (Crum).

Was all this commotion over religion really an unexpected repercussion? In contemporary America, religion is frequently associated with right-wing social and political movements that are held to be not particularly attractive (Campbell and Putnam). That is why Tebow's affiliation with some extreme movements has been so unsettling to football enthusiasts. Footballers turn to the game as an escape from national, social and personal woes. It is meant to relax them and not to offend them. Although some defenders can argue that players paid homage to God long before Tebow came on the scene by pointing to post-game huddles in the 1990s (Moring), Tebow has categorically moved God out of the clubhouse and onto the field. For example, his support for airing Focus on the Family's pro-life film clip during the 2010 Super Bowl generated debate among many football fans. During that controversy's most heated moments, Tebow assumed an evangelical's pose, hunkering down and staying the course, hoping that perhaps he could reshape partisan visions over time (Layman 207). Many fans were offended by this since they felt that leaving football out of the debate was the appropriate move. In his autobiography, Tebow glosses over the negative aspects of the incident, choosing to focus upon Barna's post-game statistics. His excitement over the some five and a half million people who had cause to rethink their position on abortion because of the short video (Tebow 246) defines his direction as a pro-life believer. And even though he may not have caused a tectonic shift in the battle lines over abortion, there are football fans who fear that his repeated articulation of his birth story might have an effect upon his young admirers. Studies by Putnam and Campbell confirm that Barna's assumptions about the upcoming generation's possibilities as a political game-changer may be spot-on. More than any other generation, this "Juno generation" is primed to embrace pro-life without rancor due to their familiarity with birth control and their vision of abortion as an unsettling procedure (Putnam and Campbell 412). Not surprisingly, any indication of Tebow's ability to persuade youth on this topic is sure to heighten tension that already exist in the social-political arena.

In contrast, not all of Tebow's fans want him to remove God from the football field. Amazingly, most fans find him to be a wildly attractive figure because of his religious commitment and in spite of his ties to right-wing thinking. Part of the reason why these fans are mesmerized by Tebow grows out their limited knowledge of religion. Amazed at his religious enthusiasm, they can only view him through their limited and often solipsistic lens that is rooted in America's religious transformation. During the sixties, Americans became fascinated with finding spiritual values and embraced a variety of religions, including Buddhism, Scientology and the occult. In recent times, though, religions with any structure to them have been replaced by what Douthat calls a "do it yourself" religion (214), a religious outlook that demands little of the convert in the way of knowledge. This type of religious adherence focuses on feelings and on the self, not on rituals, dogma or scholarship. Elizabeth Gilbert's *Eat, Pray, Love*, a memoir about an unstructured search for God's spirit, was a national best seller because audiences empathized with her spiritual quest; many bloggers have incorporated quotes from the book about religion into their forums. That God lies within the inner core of every being is a theme that is advanced by many a contemporary philosopher, such as Karen Armstrong, a former Catholic nun (118). Deepak Chopra, Eckhart Tolle and James Redfield, other contemporary religious philosophers, express similar beliefs, speculating that God can be sensed within one's self because of a heightened state of consciousness. Young people have also assimilated some of this feel-good religion, Kendra Creasy Dean confirms. Ill-educated contemporary Christian youth, she postulates, are seeing Him as either a "cosmic therapist" or the "divine butler" (qtd. in Mooney). Unlike Tebow, who views God as standing outside him as an accountability partner (qtd. in Associated Press), urging him to make all necessary sacrifices (qtd. in Legan), fans who are the graduates from the "feel good" school of thinking have a more frivolous way of viewing religion; they tend to focus on the happiness quotient in any religious response. That Tebow and his followers are on divergent paths when it comes to knowledge of God is crystallized in this accounting of their interactions: "While Tebow often tweets references to Bible verses to his 1 million-plus followers, just 7 percent of the social media conversation about Tebow deals with religion" (Klemko). Because they have a flawed sense of organized religion, fans who have created Tebowing prove that the scope of America's religious acculturation makes them unable to connect to Tebow's deeply spiritual stance. There is nothing about what Tebow is personally espousing that is "feel good" in nature. His well-forged relationship to God, which he hopes his fans will embrace, has been misconstrued by many of his devotees.

For those who are either informed or devout, the purpose behind true prayer is to establish a connection between the supplicant and the Heavenly Spirit. John Wesley, the Methodist reformer, paid prayer the ultimate compliment: "God does nothing but by prayer, and everything with it" ("Quotes on Prayer"). When he chooses to bow down on one knee on the football field, Tebow is engaging in a gesture that is filled with reflective commentary. Real prayer involves men in a communication process with their Maker. The fans who created Tebowing have, however, chosen to ignore how their imitation undercuts Tebow's real spiritual purposes. Eviscerating the religious connection from this delivery system, Tebowing merely celebrates the form itself while ignoring the more important object — the content of that interchange. Fans who engage in Tebowing must complete a sequence of actions which emphasize a connection to Tebow, rather than a connection to God. First the participant must get down on bended knee. Next the participant needs to immortalize the event in a photo shoot that is, in the last step, posted on the Web. This three part action synthesizes various aspects of Tebow's interaction with the media, but not his interaction with God. When Tebowing, the fan's camera takes the place of the television monitor. It is the imitative nature of this process that converts Tebowing into a style or a fashion statement rather than a religious event. More of a meme than a fad, Tebowing has "overtaken planking, owling and batting in popularity" (MJD) because it can be spread through e-mails, blogs, social networks, instant messaging and video streaming site like YouTube. In addition, a meme, unlike a fad, must always be spread by an electronic medium; its electronic identity is the source of its power. A meme's triumph of a form over function is effected through millions of postings on the Web. In the case of Tebowing, any of these iterations can take place in a setting that is antithetical to the religious content that was the original stimulus for the form. A quick glance at the 500 fans in Lodos' Bar and Grill, poised on bended knee (davidtheincredible303), clarifies how far afield this picture is from the pose Tebow affects. Without its links to prayer, Tebow's model is significantly less recognizable than a shoddy knock-off of a designer's logo. Because he is interacting with deeply secular fans who lack the foundation needed for achieving spiritual understanding, Tebow's religious message has been jettisoned. In contrast, Lady Gaga, another fashion-forward icon, has shaped opinion on sexual identity and same sex marriage because copying her style statements cannot affect the substantive content.

It isn't just adults who lack the necessary knowledge to seize upon Tebow's message; unfortunately, Tebowing has made it clear that young people are spiritually blocked. Barna, who has urged evangelists to get young people thinking about the faith, has miscalculated the extent in which an increasingly secularized society might misconstrue Tebow's evangelical mission. Indeed, this lack of understanding about where Tebow stands on many religious issues factors into Tebow's relationship with teens, where clouded judgments and flawed assumptions have also proliferated. For example, the three young men from Riverhead High School who decided to engage in Tebowing in their school's crowded hallway in December 2011 clearly misunderstood Tebow's intentions when they used Tebow's religious stance to express their defiance against authority. Viewing Tebow's on-the-field expression of faith as a breaking away from the herd and thus a counterculture position, they defined Tebow as an anti-establishment figure. This is not who Tebow is. Learning about their suspension, Tebow re-affirmed the necessity for all young people to follow established rules of conduct: "You have to respect the position of authority and people that God's put as authority over you" (Associated Press). Although he pushes the envelope on where and when and how far he should advance his agenda, Tebow is far from a revolutionary. When fans like these young people admit that they were Tebowing in order to pay homage to Tebow (the man) and to be part of Tebowmania, they transfer the attention contained in the process of prayer to the individual. Prayer is about God and man and about their close relationship; it is not about an individual man's power. All five types of prayer — prayers of praise and thanksgiving, which are devotional in nature; prayers of confession, supplication and intercession, which ask for God's intervention or help with a problem — focus on God's goodness and greatness (Shewmake). When the Riverhead Three admitted that it was Tebow's greatness that they are honoring with their actions, they reduced his galvanizing religious model to dust. Turning Tebow into a false god or a godlike figure will not help Tebow achieve his real goal, which is stimulating the disinterested to connect with the Holy Spirit: "It was basically just a tribute to Tim Tebow," confesses Carroll Connor, a seventeen-year old, who had planned the prank with his brother and friends as tribute to Tebow and Tebow alone (Algar and Greene).

The fans who have created Tebowing and who have carried it into the popular culture are no less confused than the fans who, in embracing an urban legend that is associated with John 3:16, have mistakenly substituted superstition in the place of logic and theology. One can't totally blame fans for this. Their shaky foundation in religion coupled with the media's slick human interest story about Tebow's conception and birth prepared them to be seduced by coincidences and mythic events. Knowing that hardcore fans spend some thirty five percent of their free time watching sporting events (Queenan 167), television and print outlets are prone to create feature stories that turn an athlete's life into a "powerful nexus of symbols" (Amidon 200), embellishing and polishing real facts until the story seems to have been "purposely designed for the big screen" (Amidon 206). Hindsight clarifies the extent to which ESPN's film about a seventeen-year old Tebow has shaped Tebow's relationship with his fans. Merging human interest with powerful innuendos, ESPN's video essay on Tebow, *The Chosen One*, uses the power of suggestion to condition viewer response. Imbuing Tebow's life story with layers of symbolism that are suggested by the emblematic title, the film's producers psychologically manipulate viewers to believe that Tebow is meant to lead. The creators of this video present the public with a variety of the reasons why Tebow is amazing and thus chosen. These human interest tidbits include his conception because of his father's dream about his future, his mother's unflagging faith in God which leads her to defy her doctor's urging to abort her fetus as well as the some sixty schools that are clamoring to recruit him. In a few short clips, the writers depict Tebow, the player, as surrounded by supernatural happenings. The cumulative effect of these suggestions turn Tebow into a larger-than-life mythic figure who, they infer, God saw fit to choose. In fact, these suggestions about his relationship with God can always be accessed, courtesy of YouTube, so that the myth of supernatural intervention can always be powered "right into the core of the spectator's brain" (Amidon 205). Not surprisingly, such associations with larger than life events prepared brainwashed fans to accept the Broncos-Steelers January 8, 2012, game as more proof of Tebow's amazing and mythic powers. After all, hadn't God intervened on his behalf before?

Since the media believes that athletes "are now supposed to inspire us with more than just their play" (Amidon 206), television and print outlets have chosen to detail Tebow's outside interests to his fans. It was the media that first presented the Bible verse John 3:16 to football fans as one Tebow's favorite verses (Jonsson), and it was television cameras that got the now famous and iconic close-up of the signage during the 2009 BCS Championship game. Commentators played up on the fact that Tebow, unlike Reggie Bush, was not using his eye black messages to advertise his area code, but rather to present the Bible verses that had special meaning for him. On January 8, 2009, the John 3:16 message stimulated some 94 million people to Google that citation during a twenty-four hour period (Tebow 209). As remarkable as that event was, what is equally remarkable about the Broncos-Steelers game is how many fans recalled this signage some three years later on January 8, 2012. When Tebow achieved an astonishing 316 yards in ten passes fans did the math and researched the verse again. Once again, some 94 million people Googled the Bible citation. Needless to say, fan excitement was immediately amplified by media outlets recording the game results and evaluating fan reactions; these outlets took part in the fact-checking and moved the emerging 3:16 numbers game into overdrive. The media quickly noted that the Steelers' time of possession was 31 minutes and 6 seconds. Then, when the CBS network share during the peak hours of the game reached 3.16 (Callery), many believed that the rash of coincidences had finally ended. But then, in yet another curious turn of events, Mark Neuman-Lee, an attendee at the game, photographed a "Mile High Halo" over the playing field ("Mile High Halo Forms"). Primed to believe in Tebow's supernatural powers, it didn't take long for fans to express their belief that a special covenant existed between Tebow and God. A survey taken just days after the game proved that some 43 percent of all football fans strongly believe that God is somehow involved in Tebow's football victories (Poll Position).

Meanwhile, within the same time frame, many print outlets began to address the God-Tebow conspiracy theory, which spread through the social media like wildfire. Newspapers like *The Wall Street Journal* and online news outlets like *The Huffington Post* and *The Bleacher Report* chose to meet the rumor mill head-on, hoping to blunt the theory that God was a part of the football betting pool. In a heartbeat, the numbers 3 and 16 took on a new and intense significance as football devotees ran with them. The signage became part of an urban legend which played up on the fans' subconscious tendency to believe in Tebow's supernatural powers, a concept disseminated to them by media services. An urban legend is folklore that can be circulated among a specific community. Legends of this sort usually lead to simplistic and fallacious conclusions because they lack verification (Brunvand 2). They can be seen as a "culture's version of Grimm's fairy tales" (Zacher) with one added twist. Offering the hope of a miraculous event, they are seductive because they provide society an escape from the fears and anxieties of daily life. Jan Harold Brunvand, an expert on this subject, reaffirms that urban legends are embraced earnestly because they prove to believers that "our prosaic contemporary scene is still capable of producing shocking or amazing occurrences" (12). It is not surprising then that Americans, living through tense social, political and economic events, would embrace a miracle wrapped in a legendary and spell-binding football game. While there were reporters who refuted God's connection to this phenomenon, there were reporters galore who used words like "miracle" and "illogical" and "not understandable" in reviews after the game. Mark Kiszla of *The Denver Post* evinces an overt belief in Tebow's divine covenant: "The magic of Tim Tebow is bigger than football and grows larger with each late-game miracle by the Broncos. Logic fails to explain this no-way-in-heaven, overtime victory against Chicago, unless you consider: Denver played as if victory were preordained." In his earlier evaluation of Tebow's wins, Yahoo! Sports columnist Les Carpenter had set the groundwork for the urban legend, noting that "there is no scientific explanation" for what occurred when Tebow was at the Broncos: "There is no other plausible way to make sense of these games and the amazing, miraculous way with which they win week after week. ... It just happened." When legitimate sources affirmed their belief in the urban legend, the media reinforced their readers' faith in a myth which magnifies Tebow's standing as the chosen one and God as the helper.

What does all this mean for fans and football? That he has done more to reshape relationships between his fans and football than between fans and God is confirmed by one Christian scholar, Anthony Bradley of King's College, who urges Tebow to abandon the verses on his face, the bended knee and the public actions that have alienated so many: all he has accomplished thus far is to increase "the faith of the mothers — they want their sons to be him and their daughters to marry him" (qtd. in Bettis). To this harsh judgment, one might add that imitation is not always the sincerest form of flattery. Tebowing, like all fads, has added a "disconcerting sameness" to our popular culture (Hoffer 33). It has obliterated any hope that fans will find in Tebow's actions an uplifting message about spiritual interchange and for some fans, that might make a difference. The emergence of an urban myth about John 3:16 is equally unsettling since a belief in God intervening in a football game doesn't elevate God. It merely elevates Tebow's importance in the universe. To his credit, Tebow isn't responsible for any of his fans' reaction. He is just doing what he believes in wholeheartedly. However, he should see by now that something is missing in the translation of his ideas.

As for his effect on football, that is another story. Because he incites so much debate about things that America needs to confront and work through, Tebow has had a strong influence on football that is both positive as well as negative. Football has always been a spectator sport which cuts cross the audience's economic lines, with subdivisions occurring because of team loyalty. It has promoted unity and camaraderie over a beer and a sub sandwich. One's regard for certain players and teams was heretofore done without rancor. It is not that way now. Without a doubt, because of his religious stance, Tebow has left his mark on the game and on the fans who watch it. Because of Tebow, religious content has been allowed in the Super Bowl, with yet another advertisement from Focus on the Family appearing during the 2011 AFC playoffs. People now choose to discuss serious topics like faith after the game ends. This is not to say that making people react to an important subject is a bad thing. Getting a group of individuals to feel strongly about anything is a rare skill in our "feel good" society. However, making people find productive solutions to their differences is a rarer one. If Tebow really wants to reshape football and the religious lives of his fans, he needs to get his fans to reach some form of an understanding and reconciliation. Matthew 5:9 notes, "Blessed are the peacemakers for they will be called sons of God." Our national divide is great, but there are many among us who believe that bridges to understanding can be forged if the debate turns to an earnest and productive discussion (Putnam and Campbell 494). Since he has made football a place where that divide is clearly visible, Tebow should turn to teachings in The Gospel of Matthew for advice on how to move his followers forward to a higher ground. Matthew 5:47 suggests that cultivating compassion and understanding will provide mankind with the tools needed for conflict resolution: In the end, if one is kind only to one's friends and to those who think like he does, how is he different from other false messengers?

Works Cited

Algar, Selim, and Leonard Greene. "Long Island High School Students Suspended for Tebowing." *New York Post.* 16 Dec. 2011. Web. 21 Aug. 2012. http://www.nypost.com/p/news/local/li_tebow_taunters_02qRP4jvTksWW1XIyleMqI#ixzz249T5bzOH.

Alper, Josh. "Tim Tebow's Easter Sermon Draws a Big Crowd." *NBC Sports.* 8 Apr. 2012. Web. 25 Jul. 2012. http://profootballtalk.nbcsports.com/2012/04/08/tim-tebows-easter-sermon-draws-a-big-crowd/.

Amidon, Stephen. *Something Like the Gods: A Cultural History of the Athlete from Achilles to LeBron.* New York: Rodale, 2012. Print.

Armstrong, Ari. "Guest Commentary: Tebowmania Isn't Just for Christians." *Denver Post.* 19 Dec. 2011. Web. 25 Jul. 2012. http://www.denverpost.com/opinion/ci_19565147.

Armstrong, Karen. *The Case for God.* New York: Knopf, 2009. Print.

Associated Press. "Tim Tebow Leans on 'Accountability Partner.'" *USA Today.* 13 Aug. 2012. Web. 15 Aug. 2012. http://www.usatoday.com/sports/football/nfl/jets/story/2012-08-15/Tim-Tebow-accountability-partner-faith/57067664/1.

Bell, Justin. "Tim Tebow Motivates, Challenges Catholics." *NCR Register.* 30 Dec. 2011. Web. 25 Jul. 2012. http://www.ncregister.com/daily-news/tim-tebow-motivates-challenges-catholics/#ixzz21d8R6hRD.

Berger, Peter. "The Religiously Unaffiliated in America." *The American Interest.* 21 Mar. 2012. Web. 21 Aug. 2012. http://blogs.the-american-interest.com/berger/2012/03/21/the-religiously-unaffiliated-in-america/.

Bettis, Kara. "How Has Tim Tebow's Faith Affected Young Christians." *Religion Today.* 21 Jan. 2012. Web. 23 Jul. 2012. http://www.religiontoday.com/news/did-tim-tebow-s-faith-affect-young-christians.html.

Bishop, Greg. "A Quarterback Controversy Involving God." *New York Times.* 7 Nov. 2011. Web. 25 Jul. 2012. http://www.nytimes.com/2011/11/08/sports/football/in-tebow-debate-a-clash-of-faith-and-football.html?pagewanted=all.

Braconnier, Deborah. "New York Jets' Training Camp Attracts Church Groups: Fan Perspective." *Yahoo! Sports.* 16 Jul. 2012. Web. 25 Aug. 2012. http://sports.yahoo.com/news/york-jets-training-camp-attracts-church-groups-fan-160900635-nfl.html.

Branch, John and Mary Pilon. "Tebow, a Careful Evangelical." *New York Times.* 27 Mar. 2012. Web. 25 Jul. 2012. http://www.nytimes.com/2012/03/28/sports/football/tebow-professes-his-evangelical-faith-carefully.html?pagewanted=all.

Brunvand, Jan Harold. *The Vanishing Hitchhiker: American Urban Legends and Their Meanings.* New York: Norton, 1981. Print.

Callery, Sherri. "Tim Tebow's Message, John: 316, Gets Communicated Without the Use of Eye Black." *Examiner.com*. 10 Jan. 2012. Web. 8 Jul. 2012. http://www.examiner.com/article /tim-tebow-s-message-john-3-16-gets-communicated-without-the-use-of-eye-black.

Campbell, David and Robert Putnam. "God and Caesar in America: Why Mixing Religion and Politics Is Bad for Both." *Council on Foreign Relations*. Mar./Apr. 2012. Web. 19 August 2012. http://www.cfr.org/religion-and-politics/god-caesar-america/p27468.

Carpenter, Les. "Run by Tebow, Broncos Gets Harder to Explain." *Yahoo! Sports*. 12 Dec. 2011. Web. 27 Aug. 2012. http://sports.yahoo.com/nfl/news?slug=lc-carpenter_tim_tebow_ broncos_comeback_bears_121111.

Crum, Amanda. "Tebow Being Traded Because of His Fans? Speculations Begins on Reasons For Trade Rumors." *WebProNews*. 12 Mar. 2012. Web. 5 Aug. 2012. http://www.web pronews.com/tebow-being-traded-because-of-his-fans-2012-03.

Davidtheincredible303. "500 People Tebow at Lodos." *YouTube.com*. 9 Jan. 2012. Web. 5 Aug. 2012. http://www.youtube.com/watch?v=3xouPToV-to.

Dodd, Patton. "Tim Tebow: God's Quarterback." *Wall Street Journal*. 10 Dec. 2011. Web. 5 Aug. 2012. http://online.wsj.com/article/SB100014240529702034133045770847709731 5282.html.

Douthat, Ross. *Bad Religion: How We Became a Nation of Heretics*. New York: Free Press, 2012. Print.

Dyer, Kristian. "Tebow Fans Aren't Jets Fans." *Yahoo! Sports*. 19 Aug. 2012. Web. 21 Aug. 2012. http://sports.yahoo.com/blogs/nfl-shutdown-corner/tebow-fans-aren-t-jets-fans-181221282-nfl.html.

Eckman, Jim. "Tim Tebow and Evangelicalism: Issues in Perspective." Grace University. 21 Jan. 2012. Web. 20 Aug. 2012. http://graceuniversity.edu/iip/2012/01/12-01-21-2/.

Gagnon, Brad. "On Tebow's Public Relationship with God." *TheScore.com*. 22 Nov. 2011. Web. 21 Jul. 2012. http://blogs.thescore.com/nfl/2011/11/22/on-tim-tebows-public-relationship-with-god/.

Gibbs, Charles. "Football: America's National Religion." *Washington Post*. 3 Sep. 2010. Web. 6 Jul. 2012. http://onfaith.washingtonpost.com/onfaith/guestvoices/2010/09/football_ americas_national_religion.html.

Harris Interactive. "Football Is America's Favorite Sport as Lead Over Baseball Continues to Grow." *Harris Interactive*. 25 Feb. 2012. Web. 5 Jul. 2012. http://www.harrisinteractive.com /NewsRoom/HarrisPolls/tabid/447/ctl/ReadCustom%20Default/mid/1508/ArticleId/950/ Default.aspx.

Hayes, Julie. "Tebow Circus Finally Pulls Out of Denver, Heads to Big Apple: Fan's Take." *Yahoo! Sports*. 22 May 2012. Web. 4 Aug. 2012. http://sports.yahoo.com/nfl/news?slug=ycn-11141512.

Hoffer, Eric. *The Passionate State of Mind*. New York: Harper and Row, 1955. Print.

"Is God Dead?" *Time Magazine* 8 April 1966: cover. 6 July 2012. Print.

Jonsson, Patrik. "Top Five Tim Tebow Biblical Verses." *Christian Science Monitor*. 3 Feb. 2010. Web. 3 Jul. 2012. http://www.csmonitor.com/USA/Society/2010/0203/Top-5-Tim-Tebow-eye-black-biblical-verses.

Judge, Clark. "Tebow in Wildcat Will Be Potent Weapon for Jets, Teammate Scott Says." *CBS Sports*. 29 Jul. 2012. Web. 5 Aug. 2012. http://www.cbssports.com/nfl/story/19682210 /tebow-in-wildcat-will-be-potent-weapon-for-jets-teammate-scott-says.

Karpiel, Dan. Quoted by Noel Sheppard in "ESPN Leads with 'Polarizing Quarterback Tim Tebow.'" *Newsbusters.org*. 21 Mar. 2012. Web. 5 Aug. 2012. http://newsbusters.org/blogs /noel-sheppard/2012/03/21/espn-leads-polarizing-quarterback-tim-tebow#ixzz221g0qs2V.

Kiszla, Mark. "Tim Tebow Has the Broncos Believing They Can't Lose." *The Denver Post*. 12 Dec. 2011. Web. 24 Aug. 2012. http://www.denverpost.com/sports/ci_19527521#ixzz24zntGA8j.

Klemko, Robert. "With Loss, Tebowmania Takes Breather." *USA Today*. 16 Jan. 2012. Web. 23 Aug. 2012. http:www.usatoday.com/sports/football/nfl/broncos/story/201-01-15/after-loss-tim-tebow-mania-cools/52585224/1.

Klosterman, Chuck. "The People Who Hate Tim Tebow." *Grantland.com*. 6 Dec. 2011. Web. 4 Aug. 2012. http://www.grantland.com/story/_/id/7319858/the-people-hate-tim-tebow.

Layman, Geoffrey. *The Great Divide: Religious and Cultural Conflict in American Party Politics.* New York: Columbia University Press, 2001. Print.

Legan, Kenny. "Tim Tebow Urges Sacrifice at Father's Day Event." *NFL.com.* 26 Jul. 2012. Web. 20 Aug. 2012. http://www.nfl.com/news/story/09000d5d829e992f/article/tim-tebow-urges-sacrifice-at-fathers-day-event.

Lindsay, D. Michael. *Faith in the Halls of Power.* Oxford: Oxford University Press, 2007. Print.

Lourie, Steven. "Hate Tim Tebow." *The Football Fan Spot.* 12 May 2012. Web. 4 Aug. 2012. http://footballfanspot.com/hate-tim-tebow.

Martin, James. "Is God Answering Tim Tebow's Prayers?" *Wall Street Journal.* 9 Jan. 2012. Web. 3 Jul. 2012. http://blogs.wsj.com/speakeasy/2012/01/09/did-praying-to-john-316-really-help-tim-tebow-win/.

McClure, Vaughn. "Religious Devotion Prevalent in the NFL." *Chicago Tribune.* 10 Dec. 2011. Web. 3 Jul. 2012. http://articles.chicagotribune.com/2011-12-10/sports/ct-spt-1211-bears-chicago — 20111211_1_tim-tebow-devin-hester-christian-athletes.

McGuire, Kevin. "Tim Tebow, Peyton Manning, Cam Newton Highlight Latest Line from McFarlane Toys." *Examiner.com.* 15 Jun. 2012. Web. 3 Jul. 2012. http:www.examiner.com/article/tim-tebow-peton-manning-cam-newton-highlight-latest-line-from-mcfarlane-toys.

McKay, Tom. "Don't Worry: Tim Tebow Evangelicalism Not Swaying Many Minds." *Policymic.com.* 2012. Web. 5 Aug. 2012. http://www.policymic.com/articles/2974/don-t-worry-tim-tebow-evangelicalism-not-swaying-many-minds.

Meacham, Tom. "Tebow's Testimony." *Time.* 16 Jan. 2012. Web. 20 Aug. 2012. http://www.time.com/time/magazine/article/0,9171,2103742-3,00.html.

"'Mile High Halo' Forms Over Tim Tebow and Mile High Stadium During Broncos Steelers Game." *Huffington Post.* 9 Jan. 2012. Web. 27 Jul. 2012. http://www.huffingtonpost.com/2012/01/09/mile-high-halo-over-broncos_n_1194204.html.

MJD. "Introducing Tebowing: It's Like Planking, but Dumber." *Yahoo! Sports.* 27 Oct. 2011. Web. 23 Jul. 2012. http://sports.yahoo.com/nfl/blog/shutdown_corner/post/introducing-tebowing-its-like-planking-but-dumber?urn=nfl,wp10549.

Mooney, Deborah Arca. "Almost Christian: An Interview with Kenda Creasy Dean." *Patheos.com.* 22 Jun. 2010. Web. 27 Aug. 2012. http://www.patheos.com/Resources/Additional-Resources/Almost-Christian-Kendra-Creasy-Dean.html.

Moring, Mark. "Fumbling Religion?" *Christianity Today.* 11 Sep. 2007. Web. 5 Jul. 2012. http://www.christianitytoday.com/ct/2007/september/21.32.html?start=1.

Nivola, Pietro, and David W. Brady. *Red and Blue Nation: Consequences and Correction of America's Polarized Politics.* Baltimore: Brookings, 2008. Print.

Petchesky, Barry. "How Contempt for Tim Tebow Caused an ESPN.com Commenter Revolution." *Deadspin.com.* 2 Nov. 2011. Web. 18 Aug. 2012. http://deadspin.com/5855575/how-contempt-for-tim-tebow-caused-an-espncom-commenter-revolution.

The Pew Forum on Religion and Public Life. "Religious Affiliation." 7 May 2012. Web. 10 May 2012. http://religions.pewforum.org/reports.

Poll Position. "Do You Believe That Any of Tim Tebow's Success Can Be Attributed to Divine Intervention?" *PollPosition.com.* 10 Jan. 2012. Web. 5 Aug. 2012. http://media.pollposition.com.s3.amazonaws.com/wp-content/uploads/Poll-Position-crosstabs-divine-intervention.pdf.

Press, Bill. "Tim Tebow Trivializes Religion." *BillPressShow.com.* 16 Dec. 2011. Web. 6 Aug. 2012. http://www.billpressshow.com/2011/12/16/tim-tebow-trivializes-religion/.

Putnam, Robert, and David Campbell. *American Grace: How Religion Divides and Unites Us.* New York: Simon & Schuster, 2010. Print.

Queenan, Joe. *True Believers: The Tragic Inner Life of Sports Fans.* New York: Holt, 2003. Print.

"Quotes on Prayer." *Smithworks.org.* Web. 10 Jan. 2013. http://www.smithworks.org/quotes/prayerquotes.html.

Rovell, Darren. "Tim Tebow's Autobiography 'Through My Eyes': The Best Selling Sports Book of 2011." *CNBC.com.* 9 Jan. 2012. Web. 26 Jul. 2012. http://www.cnbc.com/id/45931888

/Tim_Tebow_s_Autobiography_Through_My_Eyes_The_Best_Selling_Sports_Book_Of_
2011.
Sharp, Andrew. "It's Okay to Hate Tim Tebow." *SBNation.com*. 12 Jan. 2012. Web. 4 Aug. 2012.
http://www.sbnation.com/nfl/2012/1/13/2702190/tim-tebow-nfl-playoffs-2012-denver-
broncos-haters-gonna-hate.
Shewmake, John and Carol Shewmake. "Types of Prayer." Web. 9 Aug. 2012. http://www.prayer
partners.com/HowTo/PrayerTypes.htm.
Tebow, Tim, and Nathan Whitaker. *Through My Eyes*. New York: HarperCollins, 2011. Print.
Vrentas, Jenny. "Tim Tebow Laughs Off Attention from Shirtless Run Through the Rain."
NJ.com. 30 Jul. 2012. Web. 4 Aug. 2012. http://www.nj.com/jets/index.ssf/2012/07/tim_
tebow_laughs_off_attention.html.
Zacher, Elissa Michele. "Urban Legends: Modern Morality Tales." *The Epoch Times*. 20 Jul.
2010. Web. 15 Aug. 2012. http://www.theepochtimes.com/n2/life/interpreting-the-message
-in-urban-legends-39382.html.

Fan-Made Time

The Lord of the Rings and *The Hobbit*

OWAIN GWYNNE

Once, a group embarked on a journey.

The road was long, seemingly unending, and fraught with hardships and obstacles so that the goal was ever in doubt. Nevertheless, they persevered, remaining loyal and true to their cause, ever hopeful of reaching their journey's end.

If what I've just described sounds like a summary taken straight from Tolkien, think again. I've just described the long wait that fans eager for the release of the first film in Peter Jackson's three part adaptation of Tolkien's *The Hobbit* have endured for the last nine years. For the purposes of this essay, I refer to *The Hobbit* as the collection of films that comprise the trilogy, including *The Hobbit: An Unexpected Journey* (2012), *The Hobbit: The Desolation of Smaug* (2013), and *The Hobbit: There and Back Again* (2014).

The Wait Is Killing Me

When it was announced in December 2007 that Peter Jackson would be too busy to direct the new *Hobbit* production, a discussion arose on the message boards of the popular Tolkien fan-site *TheOneRing.net* about whether members would be content to wait longer until Jackson was available to direct or whether they preferred his role be sacrificed to allow the movies to be made and released earlier. The outcome was mixed, with many loyal supporters observing the necessity to grant Jackson the opportunity to return to the directing chair, while others arguing that delaying the films for Jackson's return would simply be too long a wait; as one fan put it: "No! I don't want to wait. I've been waiting since Extended ROTK [*Return of the King*] came out."

On the one hand, the fans who rejected any delay as a result of coaxing Peter Jackson back to the project perceived the act of waiting as something painful, torturous, and unbearable: "But we are really talking about waiting till 2015 which is the year I saw quoted somewhere? That's enormously too long a wait." On the other hand, fans who were prepared to wait demonstrate the realization that their waiting, though un-pleasurable, would be required for the benefits the results would yield: "*The Lord of the Rings* movies are what they are because of Peter Jackson! I for one am willing to wait for his schedule to allow him to direct *The Hobbit* and its sequel... The wait is MORE than worth it."

However, neither of these points of view indicate any enjoyment in waiting. Those holding to the latter, while recognizing the necessity of a delay, view it as something to be endured for the greater good. It is something to be tolerated, rather than embraced with any real enthusiasm. In his reading of Henri Bergson's philosophy of time, Harold Schweizer outlines several important points regarding the *experience* of waiting. In reference to an experiment conducted by Bergson where a lump of sugar was allowed to dissolve in a glass of water, Schweizer contends that the act of waiting forces the waiter to confront the absoluteness of time:

> The hour is intensive not extensive, felt not thought, embodied not applied. The waiter is the embodiment of the hour; it has taken possession of him. Like the lump of sugar, the waiter has become time's unfolding, its manifestation. He *must* wait. Rather than seizing it — as when he would seize that hour to eat lunch — time has seized him [17].

In waiting, Schweizer states, the individual's desire to obtain mastery over time is thwarted by his realization that he is powerless in its grasp. This defeat manifests itself in acts of impatience that may include glancing at one's watch or restless pacing (22). Waiting for the first film in *The Hobbit* series also entails the knowledge that one cannot take control of time in order to make the films come out any faster. Distasteful quotes plagued a discussion thread lamenting the delay of a major announcement regarding *The Hobbit*:

> "This waiting is going on forever, the anticipation is unbearable!"
> "I was so hoping for news by now. Unfortunately, we still have a long way to go for the movie."
> "I try to be patient but it's hard! I can wait for news as long as I have to, but it won't be easy."

Here, the wait for news is depicted as anything but pleasurable: "unbearable," "unfortunate," "hard"— words that connote dissatisfaction. Waiting is an inconvenience, a hurdle, murky and intangible (so much that it cannot be grasped, cannot be changed) on the road towards solid, exciting information. Elsewhere, phrases such as "chewing my fingernails down to the nub" and "but I'm patient * taps fingers on desk" demonstrate a sense of restlessness comparable to Bergson's pacing as he waits for the sugar lump to dissolve. Could the act of posting be construed as a form of virtual pacing? Were the posts of fans the product of restless impatience during the wait for *The Hobbit*? If this is the case, the boards merely fill a void, serving as a distraction for fans as they await the finished films.

We're Not Just Going to Wait Around

But are fans really waiting? As the opposite of action, of doing, waiting implies a lack of activity, such as sitting in a chair waiting for an appointment at the doctor's office. Fans have not spent the last few years of their lives sitting down in one place, putting all other activities on hold, merely waiting until the films are released. Many of these fans have jobs, are at school or college, have families, and have busy social schedules, all of which likely preoccupy their time. Giovanni Gasparini distinguishes between different kinds of waiting: Firstly, there is "interstitial time," where the wait period can be viewed as an interruption to one's actions (waiting for a train), or as a more meaningful experience (where the wait is substituted with more meaningful activities such as reading or listening to music). Secondly, Gasparini considers waiting as "sacred time," where waiting serves as an important part of the Christian faith (37).

To what extent can we consider fans' waiting as meaningful? This will require more significant unpacking of Gasparini's arguments than space in this essay allows. For now, it is enough that we can still describe the fans on *TheOneRing.net* as waiting, yet it is a wait filled with meaningful activities. It is active, rather than passive waiting. In participating regularly on the forums, fans are actively and periodically engaging with the object of their waiting. The message boards offer fans more than the means to simply tolerate the wait; they become a way of taking back control of, and actively defying, the waiting period.

It is not my intention to provide an overview of fan studies in this essay. However, a dominant theme in the earlier stages of the discipline has been concerned with the idea of fan resistance. Henry Jenkins' influential *Textual Poachers* draws upon Michel De Certeau's model of "poaching" to posit the fan as resisting the dominant meaning of a text. Fans, according to Jenkins, seize (or "poach") content from a particular media text and rework it in their own image. Matt Hills has suggested that fans can take this resistive stance even prior to the broadcasting of a media text: "Unlike 'poachers' of the early 1990s, they are instead contesting producers' control over pre-transmission information. These fans are "pre-textual poachers." Their struggles with fan-producers necessarily pre-date rather than follow the text's transmission" (*Triumph* 72).

What differentiates "pre-textual poachers," Hills suggests, is that their struggle with producers does not involve acting on a text once it has materialized. Rather, their defiance is in searching for information about an unreleased text before the information is made public by the producers. Struggles for control of the text that take place between fans and media producers have often led to legal struggles over issues of copyright, especially in the closely guarded pre-release as a period.

Simone Murray, for example, in comparing the different pre-release strategies adopted by New Line for The Lord of the Rings films and Warner Bros. for the Harry Potter films concludes that the marketing strategy adopted by the studios of each film incorporated notably different relationships with their fan bases. Warner Bros. set off on the wrong foot, imposing strict restrictions on the ability of fans to create and promote their own sites, whereas New Line sought to embrace its fan base from day one. Ways in which New Line achieved this included unveiling its official website a full five months before the start of production and closely monitoring discussion boards and chat rooms (18–19). Through the use of social media sites such as Facebook and fan communities such as *TheOneRing.net*, *The Hobbit* continues this tradition, adopting a similar "collaborationist" strategy (Jenkins, *Convergence* 134) in the build-up to the films' release.

Fan-Made Time

This research began as a desire to explore the importance of waiting in fan engagement with a text that had yet to be released. The ways in which fans engage with a pre-release period has been examined before by Will Brooker, who provided a fascinating analysis of the activities of fans prior to the release of the second film in George Lucas' Star Wars prequels, *Star Wars: Episode II — Attack of the Clones* (2002), and by Chin and Gray, who did the same with fans awaiting *The Lord of the Rings: The Return of the King* (2003). However, my intention with *The Hobbit* is to delve deeper into the waiting period itself, in order to consider what kind of *experience* fans gain by waiting. To make sense of this, I propose that what fans engage in is "fan-made time." Fan-made time can be defined in relation to eight characteristics.

1. It is a block of time that is created by fans. It is, after all, fans that have chosen to wait for the release of *The Hobbit*. Forums dedicated to discussion of the films were created with that very purpose in mind; *TheOne Ring.net* declares itself to be "forged by and for fans of J.R.R. Tolkien." While discussion is sometimes driven by announcements or incidents directly related to the event at the heart of fan-made time (announcements by the studio, for example), it remains the case that discussion may occur even in the absence of external forces. Furthermore, it is the fans that turn this waiting period into something significant. They transform a process that generally passes without much interest for the average viewer into part of a much larger experience with the text.

2. Fan-made time, in addition to being a period time that fans create, is one that fans can shape as they see fit. The wait period can be extended, with discussion having begun years prior to the release of a film and undoubtedly set to continue long after. This time can also be contracted, with fans responding as quickly as possible to breaking news events (for example, the forums on *TheOneRing.net* were inaccessible for some time after the news emerged that Guillermo del Toro was stepping down as director of *The Hobit* films). Fan-made time, then, is flexible. This is in contrast to the more rigorously defined production time.

3. Fan-made time is also time that fans can take possession of and hold some sort of claim over. With most details pertaining to the films kept under heavy guard by studios and producers, fans take satisfaction from the knowledge that the period before the films' release is a period of speculation, fantasizing, and imagining. During this time, the films can be anything and everything the fans want them to be. Although producers disapprove of information being leaked online, they have no power over the way the films are being imagined by fans on the forums. This can also be thought of as a form of pre-textual poaching.

In addition to these three key points, there are a number of characteristics that fan discussion should adhere to in order for it to be described as fan-made time as I define it.

4. Fan-made time is a period of intense engagement with a text. That is to say, any discussion taking place around a particular object must recur regularly and frequently for it to be considered fan-made time. Of course, fan discussion may continue to revolve around a television show that is no longer on the air (*Lost* [2004–2010], for example). However, if the discussion is not taking place several times a day, on a daily basis, then it becomes an instance of general fan discussion as opposed to fan-made time.

5. Fan-made time must revolve around an event that is taking place around

the object of fandom. For discussion to occur frequently and regularly, it needs to take place in the aftermath of, or prior to, some sort of happening — most likely the moment of physical engagement with, or consummation of, a particular text. Examples of such events could include a recently aired episode of a given television show, an upcoming release in a series of books or films, or some kind of celebrity appearance or organized convention. The event forms an integral part of fan-made time, serving as both a driving factor of communication as well as a way of extending or prolonging a particular event.

6. In order for fan-made time to feature regular discussion, it must take place within a shared community. It also must take place within a group of considerable size in order for the conversation to be constantly changing and growing. Fan-made time is a collective and collaborative process, drawing together a number of different thoughts, ideas and opinions from a range of individuals, each possessing different backgrounds and different levels of commitment towards the particular object of fandom.

7. Another characteristic of fan-made time is that it can be measured. Fan-made time can be measured quantitatively and qualitatively. Discussions are often archived on particular forums, where fan engagement is transformed into a physical, tangible presence that can be observed, referred back to and, indeed, measured (convenient indeed for the researcher interested in analyzing online fan communication).

8. Finally, in order to meet these other requirements, fan-made time should always take place online. This is not to say that fans do not, and cannot, use periods surrounding the exhibition or consummation of texts in other ways that do not take place on the Internet. Indeed, fans may physically gather together at regular intervals to talk about upcoming or recent textual engagements. However, the online space provides an instant link to a wider population of fans and allows for the kind of rapid interaction through forums, chat rooms and other forms of social interaction necessary for the constitution of fan-made time. As a result, fan-made time is a product of its technology. Different forms of online communication may affect the flow or structure of fan-made time, yet they are linked by the immediacy they provide the individual.

To summarize, fan-made time is a period of intense discussion revolving around an event tied to the object of fandom. It is a period that is made, shaped, and owned by fans. Because it takes place online, within a shared community, it can be stored, revisited and measured. Having set the parameters for my discussion of fan-made time, I turn now to the example of *The Hobbit* and a brief introduction to the troubled process of making those films a reality.

The Unexpected Journey of The Hobbit *Film Production*

The tragic story of *The Hobbit's* production began in September 2006, when MGM Studios teamed up with Peter Jackson and New Line Cinema to produce a film version of J.R.R. Tolkien's successful novel. But the production was in doubt from the very beginning. In March 2005, Peter Jackson filed a lawsuit against New Line Cinema, the studio that had produced his critically and financially successful The Lord of the Rings trilogy. This lawsuit resulted in New Line co-founder Robert Shaye severing ties with Jackson and kick-starting a series of events that would have disastrous implications for production of *The Hobbit* (Johnson).

On December 16, 2007, it was announced that Jackson would serve as executive producer of the two-part *Hobbit* adaptation, which was now to be co-financed by New Line and MGM Studios. Release dates for the two films were announced following New Line's merger with Warner Bros. Studios for the Decembers of 2011 and 2012. The mantle of director was given to Oscar-nominated filmmaker Guillermo del Toro. At this point, the first film was set out to be a stand-alone film, a unique interpretation of Tolkien's Middle Earth, with the second serving as a "bridge film," linking del Toro's vision with Peter Jackson's (Wee and Fixmer).

The next major hurdle arrived in the form of MGM Studios, whose developing financial problems led to the studio filing for bankruptcy on November 3, 2010, placing a number of its forthcoming films, including *The Hobbit*, in jeopardy. The studio emerged from bankruptcy on December 10, 2010. However, the damage had been done. On May 28, 2010, del Toro announced that he was withdrawing from the project, citing repeated delays caused by MGM's financial situation as the reason for his departure. On October 15, 2010, it was announced that the films would still be moving forward and would be directed by Peter Jackson. The films would now be a simple two-part adaptation of Tolkien's novel and would be shot in 3D (Sibley 19).

Still this was not the end of the saga. On September 24, 2010, the International Federation of Actors took industrial action over a supposed breach of union-negotiated agreements. The impact of this action was felt on *The Hobbit*, with several actors siding with the union. The resulting decision to move production of the film outside New Zealand was met with anger and concern for the effect this would have on tourism, leading to mass protests and involvement from the government (Sibley 19). Finally, on August 27, 2010, it was announced by Warner Bros. that production of the films would remain in New Zealand. The two films became a trilogy and, at the time of writing, revised release dates stand as December 2012, December 2013, and December 2014.

Methodology

A content analysis of the message boards on *TheOneRing.net* allowed for an in-depth analysis of "fan-made time" in relation to *The Hobbit*. The purpose was to see how fans shape and make use of this prolonged waiting period.

A sample size of 400 threads (a collection of messages under various topics) was investigated over a period of six months in the first half of 2010. The sample size and date range were selected due to the limits of space. Due to the limited date range selected for this essay, it may not be possible to obtain a comprehensive view of fan-made time. Nevertheless, the threads offer a suitable representation of how fan-made time occurs on the boards. The year 2010 was chosen as a result of the key events that occurred during this period that heavily influenced discussion on the forums, while the first six months specifically provided an opportunity to examine the effects of production delays and the departure of director Guillermo del Toro on fan discussion.

The methodology consisted of coding keywords throughout the forums, thereby exposing trends and identifying recurring themes and ideas. The aspects that were chosen for scrutiny included Topic of Thread, Length of Thread, Number of Views, and Overall Tone. In terms of Topic, a total of twelve categories were identified, with the most common including:

- Cast Speculation (any discussion revolving around issues of casting)
- Production (discussion involving any aspect of production, including directing, writing, set design and music)
- Adaptation (discussions pertaining to aspects of the films' translation of its source material. This includes how certain scenes from the book would be adapted for the big screen)
- Faithfulness (those discussion relating to issues of faithfulness regarding the adaptation of Tolkien's world versus that of Peter Jackson established in his Lord of the Rings trilogy)
- Technology (discussions around any aspect of the films' technological aspects — special effects, use of 3D, etc.)

Length of Thread refers to the number of posts (messages) that compose a single thread, while Number of Views refers to the number of people who read or contributed to a particular thread. Overall Tone was measured in terms of four categories: optimistic, pessimistic, mixed, or neutral. Threads that were overwhelmingly optimistic were those where the majority of posts anticipated the upcoming films in a positive way. Optimistic threads displayed hope and confidence that the films would come into being, any and all problems would be resolved, and that the movies would be everything that fans wished them to be. Negative threads, on the other hand, feared or anticipated a less favorable outcome. Such threads often bemoaned the lack of information and the repeated delays to production. Mixed threads contained posts that were considered both positive and negative, while threads labelled neutral contained no specific tone. Upon coding the threads, a statistical analysis program, SPSS, was used to interpret the data.

Results

The first half of 2010 was a period of intense uncertainty, worry, and frustration on the message boards. A period marred by MGM's continuing financial turmoil, the absence of news, together with the repeated signs of further delays, threatened to put the very future of *The Hobbit* in doubt. Fans were still very much in the dark as to who would be playing Bilbo, how the two films would be structured, and when the films would receive the elusive "green-light," allowing them to finally enter production. It is unsurprising, then, that the two most discussed topics throughout the first six months related to Casting and Production.

The number of threads composed on these topics stood out in overwhelming majority to others. Production received slightly below forty percent (39.89 percent), while Casting received just under twenty-five percent (23.36 percent) of the total proportion of topics. This was followed by issues of Adaptation (7.98 percent), Other (5.70 percent) and Plot Speculation (4.27 percent).

Discussions around casting set the year off on a fairly positive note, with suggestions and rumors surrounding which actors would be best suited for certain roles. The casting of the films' main protagonist, Bilbo Baggins, remained a key point of speculation, with several fans already anticipating Martin Freeman for the role (which would not be officially announced until November 2010). As the months progressed, discussion shifted elsewhere. Playful speculation regarding casting made way for less enthusiastic musing over the state of the films' production.

With regards to Production, fans largely lamented over the lack of information, the recurring delays and the uncertainty that went with it, whilst remaining quietly optimistic that the situation with MGM would be resolved and the films could begin shooting. Threads pertaining to production issues were most prominent during the months of March and June. These spikes in activity occurred as the early months dragged on with no sign of any progress being made, and fans began to question the state of the upcoming films. The hardest blow came in June when Guillermo del Toro announced via *TheOne Ring.net* that he was stepping down as director. Discussion on the boards immediately became dominated by expressions of disappointment over losing a director many had come to respect as greatly as Peter Jackson, as well as feelings of anger directed mainly towards the studios for costing the project its commander-in-chief. It truly seemed like the beginning of the end for *Hobbit* fans.

Reflecting these sentiments, overall Tone for the threads shifted steadily from overwhelmingly neutral during the first few months, to mixed and pessimistic by the end of July. The dominance of neutral threads early on in the year is tied to the prominence of casting-related discussions during this period. By their nature, such discussions (revolving primarily around speculation, rumors and guesswork) display no strong opinions that could be considered in either a positive or negative tone. This is in contrast to discussions around matters of production, which involve fans responding to news stories and actual happenings. As Production topics became more dominant, the tone of the threads became increasingly more opinionated, and due to the nature of the news the fans were responding to, this tone was overwhelmingly either mixed or entirely pessimistic.

With regards to Length of Threads and Number of Views, it was found that the longest threads and those that attracted the most views during this period occurred during June. Again, this comes as little surprise, considering the unfolding saga of del Toro's resignation that was taking place during this month and fans' need to keep up to date with a particularly fluid situation.

Overall, threads throughout the six month period tended to consist mostly of between 6 and 10 posts, and this formed 21.37 percent of the total sample. Threads consisting of 11 to 15 posts came in second (15.95 percent). The total number of views per post during this period tended to lie within 500–999 views (28.21 percent).

What Are We Waiting For?

One thing that becomes apparent from studying fan-made time on *TheOneRing.net* is that fans are not just waiting for a film, they are waiting to receive a special filmic *experience*. To make better sense of this idea, I turn first to the work of philosopher and theologian Paul Tillich who, in his book *Theology of Culture*, defines man's relationship with God as one of absolute waiting. It is a condition of religion, specifically within the Christian faith, in that waiting for that which man does not possess is paramount. And in that act of absolute waiting, Tillich argues, man already possess the essence of that which he is waiting for:

> Waiting anticipates that which is not yet real.... He who waits passionately is already an active power himself, the greatest power of transformation in personal and historical life. We are stronger when we wait than when we possess. When we possess God, we reduce Him to that small thing we knew and grasped of Him; and we make it an idol. Only in idol worship can one believe in the possession of God.

We can draw upon certain aspects of Tillich's argument in trying to make sense of fans' relationship with *The Hobbit*. Though it is neither feasible nor necessary to compare fans' few years of waiting for the upcoming films with man's lifelong wait for affinity with a higher power, there are nevertheless important parallels that we can draw in terms of waiting and possession.

Fans who waited for the 2012 release of the first *Hobbit* movie can certainly be said to have been waiting passionately. According to Tillich, this implies an "active power," which applies to fandom more generally. As we have seen, the time leading up to *The Hobbit*'s release has been a period of intense and focused activity. Fan-made time is a product of this active power — an online message board chronicling years of speculation, debate, and discussion.

Despite this, however, fans are not waiting in an *absolute* sense. According to Tillich's philosophical outlook, those who possess something reduce that thing to a mere idol. It becomes clear through the actions of fans on *TheOne Ring.net*, that they are in the process of trying to "possess" *The Hobbit*. This can be seen through their attempts to gather as much information about the films as they can and to embrace *The Hobbit* experience as much as possible. Furthermore, they are already in possession of *The Hobbit*, in the sense that they have likely read the book and seen Peter Jackson's Lord of the Rings trilogy. *The Hobbit*'s transformation into an idol is reminiscent of Emilé Durkheim's notion of the totem; fans develop an attachment to *The Hobbit* as a sacred object on a level comparable to the worship of religious icons. But does this attempt at possession reduce the power of fan-made time? Not when we return to consider fans' waiting in terms of resistance. We have already seen how fan-made time functions as a period where fans retain a degree of power over their *Hobbit* experience. In the months leading up to each film's release, fans remained in a position to create the idea of the perfect film. This becomes an example of the active power obtained through their waiting. As soon as the films are released, this power is diminished; fans now see the films in their complete and unchangeable states. Thus, in this instance, fan-made time can be seen as bridging the gap between waiting and possessing.

In order to relate Tillich's ideas back to fans' experience of waiting for *The Hobbit*, we can turn to the work of Francesco Casetti, who addressed the shifting cinema experience. Casetti argues that despite the rise in popularity in new technologies allowing the screening of movies outside of the traditional space of the movie theater, the cinema experience remains intact. For example, with regard to watching films on DVD, Casetti suggests that we are in possession of "fragments" of a larger whole: "What I possess is only a remnant; but it is a remnant that had been part of the large body of the cinema" ("Cinema"). These fragments, or "relics," may not give us the same authentic feel of actually visiting the movie theater, yet they are still able to offer a cinema experience: "They are fragments belonging to an entity that has now been dispersed, but nevertheless they are able to make cinema present — they are able to convey its sanctity" (Casetti "Cinema").

Fans expected their experience of watching *The Hobbit* to be something special. Fan-made time has played a vital role in making this the case through providing them with fragments of that experience. That is to say, it is in waiting for *The Hobbit* that *The Hobbit* becomes something worth waiting for. This cyclical approach demonstrates that fan-made time forms an integral part of fans' *Hobbit* experience. In Tillich's words, "they already possess that which they are waiting for."

Playing the Waiting Game

One of the ways in which fans enact and negotiate their experience on the forums is through play. There are a number of ways in which fans' participation on the boards constitutes a playful experience. For instance, the process of collecting and organizing information about the films is comparable to the assembling of a jigsaw puzzle; fans gradually obtain the pieces and strive to put them together in the pursuit of assembling the complete picture. One could also examine the way fans engage with the message boards as a form of emergent game system, drawing upon recent video game scholarship, as well as Nancy Baym's work on virtual communities, to demonstrate how a limited rules structure affords fans the relative freedom to explore the game system. This, in turn, bestows fan-made time with a considerable amount of unpredictability in terms of its goals and outcomes. Alternatively, we might examine the ways in which fans adopt a level of role-play into their engagements with the forums through the use of on-screen avatars (Booth).

Fans negotiate the fragile boundaries between the real world and their online experience with *The Hobbit* through what is known as a "magic circle." Introduced by Johan Huizinga in his 1938 dissertation exploring the role of play in culture (Salen and Zimmerman 24), the term refers to the idea that games construct a magic circle, separating the game from the outside world. Within this circle, Huizinga contends, players abide by a system of rules which has no bearing on the outside world. Though contested by many for its degree of usefulness, the term has been adapted for use by video game scholars

(Castronova) as well as being used by theorists of social media. The boards on *TheOneRing.net* become suggestive of such a magic circle, a space where various games unfold between fans and producers (pre-textual poaching), between fans and other fans (in terms of competing levels of commitment), and between fans and the waiting period more generally. This space, too, is defined by its own set of rules and rituals, albeit one that exists on the very cusp of the real world (it can be accessed anytime and anywhere the individual has access to a computer or mobile device).

We can draw comparisons between Huizinga's magic circle and Durkheim's notion of sacred time. According to Durkheim, the profane and the sacred cannot occupy the same time: "In consequence religious life must have specified days or periods assigned to it from which all profane occupations are withdrawn" (313). Participation on the forums of *TheOneRing.net* by fans share some similarities with the rituals of which sacred time consists, an instance of what Hills terms "neo-religion" (*Fan Cultures* 118–119). The act of returning regularly to the boards, posting a comment, or checking the latest topics, constitutes a ritual that makes up the fan's everyday life. Moments are taken out of their day to engage with the boards, time that abandons the profane world to engage in, what Durkheim terms, a collective "effervescence" (Hills, "Virtually" 148).

Hills is keen to point out that Durkheim's concept of rituality is not appropriate for thinking about online forums ("Virtually" 148–149). He argues that the close proximity to the everyday, made possible through the accessibility and timeliness of new media, conflicts with Durkheim's notion of the ritual as a physical gathering of individuals at a designated time in a designated place. This is a fair reservation: activity on *TheOneRing.net* does not take place at one specific time — it is accessible at any hour of the day and it does not require its members to participate at the exact same time. Unlike a chat room, members do not have to be online together at any given time. However, I propose a counter argument, returning to Casetti's discussion of the filmic experience where rituality is identified as one of several defining characteristics:

> It is as a result of these rites — linked to the fact that spectators respond in a uniform way to the solicitations emanating from the screen, like the faithful at a religious or lay ceremony — that the crowd gathered in the theater is transformed into a collective, into a public. In the theater a spectator joins or rejoins a social group and becomes a member of a community thanks to a rite ["The Filmic Experience" 9].

In both accounts, it is the "collective," then, that becomes important to the ritual. On the boards, fans respond collectively to new information and developments. An example of this can be seen when del Toro announced his departure from the project in 2010. The boards were inaccessible for a time due to the sheer amount of traffic to the site. This demonstrates that the boards become a sacred space for fans to go to when and as they desire. While this reinforces Hills' position to some extent — the idea that online space constitutes a kind of "rituality on demand" ("Virtually" 148) it also becomes a case of "just-in-time fandom" (Hills, *Fan Cultures* 178) — where fan capital is reinforced by members responding as quickly as possible to major developments. In this case, it would appear that fans not only have a specific "affective" space (Hills, "Virtually" 148) to go to, but also a specific time (as close to the timing of the event as possible) to engage with other members over that particular event. In conclusion, it becomes possible to consider fan-made time as sacred time; there remains an element of "ritual on demand," but it is shaped, to a certain degree, by the need to respond instantly and collectively to breaking news events. As Hills claims, the sacred/profane separation is eroded ("Virtually" 148), though some aspect of rituality remains. Certain rites must be enacted: the fans must turn on their computer or Smartphone, they must conform to a certain structure, and they must abide by a certain set of rules (Casetti, "The Filmic Experience" 16).

Fans are keenly aware of the thin line that exists between the real world and the fictional, "sacred" space in which they play. Indeed, a crucial factor of fans' engagement on the forums lies in the close proximity it shares with "real life." It is through the playful enacting of rituals on the forums that fans explore and develop their experience with *The Hobbit*, hopping back and forth between two worlds, much like the One Ring's capability to transport its bearer to and from the "wraith world" in Jackson's first film trilogy.

Conclusion

There are many other ways in which we might address the phenomenon of fan-made time. For example, we might consider the extent to which fans are being used by the studios, their ideas and creative input being harnessed by producers to create a product that will ensure the maximum success at the box office (Andrejevic 29). Whether or not this is the case, for the most part fans remain largely oblivious, or at least uncaring, as to how their efforts are serving the purposes of a money-driven enterprise. This lack of awareness, conscious or unconscious, bears similarities to the relationship Bilbo keeps with the magic ring he found in Gollum's cave in Tolkien's novel.

Slipping the ring on his finger, Bilbo can disappear at will. He uses it to escape from danger and outwit his foes. For years following his adventure, he keeps hold of what later turns out to be the One Ring, forged by none other than the Dark Lord, Sauron, in his ambitions to conquer all of Middle Earth. Blissfully unaware of its greater, darker significance, Bilbo uses it mainly to hide from his neighbors. One might indeed draw parallels between Bilbo's relaxed use of the One Ring and fans' sometimes tenuous grip over fan-made time...

But, just as was the case for a certain hobbit, this is best left for another story.

Works Cited

Andrejevic, Mark. "Watching Television Without Pity: The Productivity of Online Fans." *Television and New Media* 9.1 (2008): 24–46. Print.

Baym, Nancy. *Personal Connections in the Digital Age: Digital Media and Society Series.* Cambridge, UK: Polity, 2010. Print.

Booth, Paul. *Digital Fandom.* New York: Peter Lang, 2010. Print.

Brooker, Will. *Using the Force.* New York: Continuum, 2002. Print.

Casetti, Francesco. "Cinema Lost and Found: Trajectories of Relocation." *Screening the Past* 32 (2011). Web. 17 Jan. 2012. http://www.screeningthepast.com/2011/11/cinema-lost-and-found-trajectories-of-relocation/.

_____. "The Filmic Experience: An Introduction." *Cinema in the Post-Medium Age.* Mar. 2007. Web. 16 Jan. 2012. http://francescocasetti.files.wordpress.com/2011/03/filmicexperience1.pdf.

Castronova, Edward. *Exodus to the Virtual World: How Online Fun Is Changing Reality.* New York: Palgrave Macmillan, 2007. Print.

Chin, Bertha, and Jonathan Gray. "One Ring to Rule Them All: Pre-viewers and Pre-texts of the Lord of the Rings Films." *Intensities: The Journal of Cult Media* (2001). Web. 5 Feb. 2011. http://intensities.org/Essays/Chin_Gray.pdf.

Durkheim, Emilé. *The Elementary Forms of Religious Life.* 1912. New York: Free Press, 1995. Print.

Gasparini, Giovanni. "On Waiting." *Time & Society* 4.1 (1995): 29–45.

Hills, Matt. *Fan Cultures.* New York: Routledge, 2002. Print.

_____. *Triumph of a Time Lord: Regenerating Doctor Who in the Twenty-first Century.* London: I.B. Tauris, 2010. Print.

_____. "Virtually Out There: Strategies, Tactics and Affective Spaces in Online Fandom." *Technospaces: Inside the New Media.* Ed. S.R. Munt. London: Continuum, 2001. Print.

Jenkins, Henry. *Convergence Culture: Where Old and New Media Collide.* New York: New York University Press, 2006. Print.

_____. *Textual Poachers: Television Fans and Participatory Culture.* New York: Routledge, 1992. Print.

Johnson, Ross. "The Lawsuit of the Rings." *New York Times.* 27 Jun. 2005. Web. 14 Oct. 2012. http://www.nytimes.com/2005/06/27/business/media/27movie.html?pagewanted=print&_r=0.

Jones, Steven E. *The Meaning of Video Games: Gaming and Textual Strategies.* New York: Routledge, 2008. Print.

Juul, Jesper. *Half-Real: Video Games Between Real Rules and Fictional Worlds.* Cambridge: MIT Press, 2005. Print.

Murray, Simone. "Celebrating the Story the Way It Is: Cultural Studies, Corporate Studies, Corporate Media and the Contested Utility of Fandom." *Journal of Media and Cultural Studies* 18.1 (2004): 14–17. Print.

Salen, Katie, and Eric Zimmerman. *Rules of Play.* Cambridge: MIT Press, 2003. Print.

Schweizer, Harold. *On Waiting.* London: Routledge, 2008. Print.

Sibley, Brian. *The Hobbit: An Unexpected Journey. Official Movie Guide.* London: HarperCollins, 2012. Print.

Tillich, Paul. *The Shaking of the Foundations.* New York: Wipf & Stock, 1955. Print.

Thornton, Sarah. *Club Cultures: Music, Media and Subcultural Capital.* Oxford: Polity Press, 1995. Print.

Wee, Gillian, and Andy Fixmer. "New Line Settles Dispute, Plans Two 'Hobbit' Films." *Bloomberg.* 18 Dec. 2007. Web. 14 Oct. 2012. http://www.bloomberg.com/apps/news?pid=newsarchive&sid=a4r00glLX3jM.

The Fandom Is Out There

Social Media and
The X-Files Online

BETHAN JONES

On September 10, 1993, the pilot episode of *The X-Files* (1993–2002), featuring FBI Special Agents Fox Mulder and Dana Scully, aired on the Fox network. On December 1, 1993, the Usenet group alt.tv.x-files, one of the first *X-Files* online fan sites, was created. Fan cultures and fan communities, particularly those such as the David Duchovny Estrogen Brigade, which were formed by women, have received much attention in scholarly circles over the last thirty or so years. In *Reading the Romance,* Janice Radway explored women's subversive reading of romance novels, while Camille Bacon-Smith's *Enterprising Women* and Henry Jenkins' *Textual Poachers* both explored how fans create new discourses out of their fascination with a specific series. Much academic work has also been done on *The X-Files* fandom. David Lavery, Angela Hague and Marla Cartwright's *Deny All Knowledge: Reading The X-Files* features essays discussing the series' function in the development of cult TV and the role of the Internet in *X-Files* fan communities, while Christine Scodari and Jenna L. Felder investigate the online community of *X-Files* fans known as "shippers" (fans who desire a relationship between Mulder and Scully) in "Creating a pocket universe." Both Rhiannon Bury (*Cyberspaces of Their Own*) and Sarah R. Wakefield ("Your Sister in St. Scully") have undertaken analyses of female online fan communities, examining the David Duchovny Estrogen Brigade and the Order of the Blessed Saint Scully the Enigmatic, respectively.

The X-Files ended in 2002, but fans' adoption of social media sites such as Facebook and Twitter has led to a resurgence of online activity. Academic analysis of these new social media sites and their use within *The X-Files* fandom is understudied, however. My intention in this essay is then to analyze *The X-Files* fans' use of new social media and assess whether the participatory aspect of these sites plays a role in the development of closer collaborations with content producers. I begin this essay by examining the history of *The X-Files* fandom online, from the Usenet groups of the early 90s to the LiveJournal blogs and fanfiction archives of the early 21st century. I then turn my attention to the new forms of social networks that appeared in the mid–2000s, analyzing Facebook and Twitter in particular. I suggest that these new forms of social media have blurred the boundaries between fans and producers and turn to the *X-Files* fansite *XFilesNews.com* (XFN) to analyze this further. My case study involves examining three XFN campaigns. I first examine the site's Twitter campaign, *X-Files* [XF]: Tweet-a-thon campaign. I then turn my attention to its relationship with the show's producers by analyzing its Frankenbear the Bear charity fundraising. Finally, I assess its position in fandom through examining the XFN Productions documentary *Fandom: The Film*. I argue that there is a case to be made for examining how post-series fandoms adopt and use social media and suggest that XFN provides us with a unique way of looking at the changes taking place in fans' and producers' adoption these technologies. However, I also demonstrate that social media repositions some fans and situates them as gatekeepers, thus extending existing (and at times negative) fan practices, communities and spaces.

It is worth noting, at this point, my involvement in fandom and how this has affected my approach to this study. Just as Henry Jenkins positions himself as an "acafan" in his 1992 work on *Star Trek* fandom, I consider myself an acafan in my study of *The X-Files* fandom. I am a member of various *X-Files* fan communities, have developed close relationships with many fans — including those running XFN — and am a fanfiction writer as well as an academic. In writing this essay, therefore, I have been very much aware of my dual identities as fan and scholar, and I have attempted to achieve a balance between these positions.

The X-Files *Fandom Online*

Fans of *The X-Files*, or X-Philes, as they refer to themselves, are often considered as "among the first to use cyberspace to create their own virtual fan culture and specialized interest groups" (McLean 3). Brian Lowry suggests that "fan reaction to the series has become as much a part of *The X-Files* story as the show itself, from the conventions that have sprung up around the country to the hours of chat about the series whipping around each week on the Internet" (239), while Jimmie L. Reeves, Mark C. Rodgers, and Michael Epstein note that fans of the show maintained a "high profile on the express lane of the information superhighway" (22). At the height of the show's popularity, fans were congregating on newsgroups, email lists and chat rooms to compile detailed episode guides, share information on the actors' other roles and appearances, and analyze and interpret the show's multilayered text as well as reading, writing and sharing fanfiction.

One of the first *X-Files* online fan sites was alt.tv.x-files. Among the posts made to the group on its first day were messages discussing Mulder's mysterious informant (known as Deep Throat), nitpicking over Scully's medical diploma, and analyzing the show's standing in the Nielsen ratings. Its initial purpose was to allow fans to discuss the stories aired each week, as evidenced in the first few months' posts. But as the series developed cult status, topics covered in the group included analysis of feminism in the series, other shows such as *Fringe* (2008–2013) and *Lost* (2004–2010), and discussions of the cast and crew's other commitments. Official and unofficial websites also began to appear online shortly after *The X-Files* aired. Bambi Haggins notes that, in addition to The Official Fan Club, *The X-Files* fan pages arguably set the standard for impressive sites of fandom (12). Despite the well-publicized attempts by Fox to limit fans' access to and sharing of images and sounds from the series, the number of websites for the virtual community of X-Philes has grown, and the advent of new social networking sites, such as Tumblr, has continued this trend. Haggins writes that in 1996, a search for websites would yield just over 100 hits and in 1999, there were over 700; at the time of my writing, a search on Google yielded over 672,000 results.

In the early nineties, online chats with series creator Chris Carter and *The X-Files* team were held on The Official *X-Files* website, and rumors persisted that the writers and producers lurked in newsgroups and chat rooms to gauge fan reactions to story developments. Frank Spotnitz, former *X-Files* producer and writer, remembers going online during the early days of the show's second season:

> A lot of writers were reluctant to see what the fans were writing, but I was always curious to see how the show was being received... I only browsed and never contributed to the forums, but it was extremely useful to see how the episodes were playing — what fans liked, what they didn't like, and where they thought the show was going [Email].

Haggins suggests that the producers' interest in what fans thought of the show seemed to hearken a new age of interactivity between the two sides of the screen, and the ongoing story arc was indeed influenced by fans, as Spotnitz notes:

> I remember one specific instance where I was actually inspired to write an episode because of something I read on a message board. It was during the third season, and I was flying back from a fan convention in Minnesota when I read one comment noting that we hadn't followed up on the death of Scully's sister earlier in the year. I realized that this was not only true, but an enormous oversight. I thought about

it all the way to the airport, and by the time my plane landed in Los Angeles, I'd outlined most of the episode that became "Piper Maru" [Email].

By frequenting fan forums and allowing fan opinion to shape the storylines, *The X-Files'* creators openly embraced their fans, and indeed that recognition of fans became a part of the show through the use of fans' names in the opening sequences of season nine. Each opening sequence for the duration of the show's final season highlighted the online monikers of different fans and, as Chin suggests, was intended to be a public thank you note from the producers to the fans. The appearance of Special Agent Leyla Harrison in the season eight episode "Alone" (8:19) also demonstrates the ways in which fans were recognized: the character was named in honor of an *X-Files* fanfiction writer who had died in 2001 after a two-year battle with cancer (Lo).

Despite their willingness to draw references to both fans and fandom, however, Susan Clerc argues the increased contact between fans and producers did not change the essence of fan activities (51). It wasn't until the advent of new social media sites that this began to change.

Social Media

The emergence of social networking sites such as Facebook and Twitter provides fans with news ways of communicating with both other fans and media producers and has led to a resurgence of fan activity, with fans adopting these new media technologies as easily as their predecessors adopted Usenet and AOL. In *The X-Files* fandom, for example, the release of the 2008 feature film *The X-Files: I Want to Believe* was followed by the "XF3 Army" fan campaign for a third film, and fan groups such as Aussie X-Files Fans @ Facebook [sic] use their presence on social media to raise money for charity (Jones). Web 2.0 has changed the proximity fans have to media producers as studios also begin make use of social networks and blogs to communicate with fans, either directly or via an assistant who writes the blogs or tweets on their behalf. David Duchovny, star of *The X-Files*, briefly blogged about his experiences of filming *I Want to Believe* in a blog set up by 20th Century–Fox and Frank Spotnitz maintains a blog through his production company, Big Light Productions. Spotnitz invites fans to write in and pose questions, which he in turn attempts to answer, and considers the blog "less a blog than a conversation" (Welcome). Chin notes that reading the blogs of media producers and/or celebrities heightens the possibility that the celebrity may respond directly to the fan's questions or comments, subsequently elevating the fan's social status within fandom, even if that elevation may just be momentary (202–203).

Spotnitz's blog also plays host to a social network for fans, however.

Discussing the decision to host such a network, he writes, "I didn't really know where this would lead — I just thought it was a unique opportunity to connect with fans and see what they were thinking. Since that time, my relationship with the fans has grown much closer. We have an ongoing dialogue and I know many of them by name" (Interview). Through the blog, Spotnitz arranged for fans to be able to attend the *I Want to Believe* premieres in Los Angeles and London and continued to give fans information on schedules for promotional events. He also began to get a sense for the people communicating with him through the blog:

> A group of frequent correspondents ... emerged so I started to get a sense of who the people were who were most frequently on the social network ... then you started to get a sense of their personalities and their sense of humor and it's all over the world, from Australia to Europe to the Middle East to Russia ... I can tell you about *X-Files* fans now on every continent [Interview].

Among the fans who corresponded with Spotnitz were those on X-Files News.com.

XFilesNews.com: The CNN of Fandom

XFilesNews.com (XFN) is an *X-Files* fansite created in October 2007 by Holly Simon. Currently staffed by a team of up to 40 volunteers who are responsible for maintenance, reporting, organization, research and clerical duties, XFN's original purpose was to promote *The X-Files: I Want to Believe*, and it tracked the film's progress from casting announcements through the film's release. XFN's reporting included obtaining video of David Duchovny and Amanda Peet dancing between takes, a leaked cast sheet and breaking the very first pictures from WonderCon, where the first teaser trailer for the film was shown. In July 2008, Simon was contacted by representatives from 20th Century–Fox who offered to officialize the site for the release of the second film. XFN thus, as Tiffany Devol, Content Director and Public Relations Director, notes, "became the only authorized fan site in conjunction with *IWTB* [and] a link to XFN was placed on Fox's official *X-Files* site" (qtd. in Chin 250). XFN was also the only fansite on the red carpet for the Los Angeles premiere of *IWTB*, and the only fansite whose staff were granted press access to interview cast and crew.

In the autumn of 2008, XFN started to promote the forthcoming DVD and Blu-ray releases of *I Want to Believe* and was also able to interview Frank Spotnitz, William B. Davis, Robert Patrick, and Annabeth Gish. In the spring of 2009, XFN attended a book signing by *X-Files* creator Chris Carter and asked him what fans could do to convince Fox to greenlight a third feature film. Carter suggested that fans should write letters to Fox, stating that this approach had worked for the second movie. XFN staff therefore opted to keep the site running and launched the XF3 Army Campaign: Believe in the Future. The campaign consisted of a multitude of phases, including collecting fan-made postcards showing images from the series, the creation of fan videos which were uploaded to XFN's YouTube channel, and designing a uniform for the "XF3 Army." In January 2011, XFN launched "phase four" of the XF3 campaign, calling on fans to create posters and trailers for a third film. This was followed by its "10,013 photos for a green-light" campaign in April 2011, and a 10/13 Greenlight Baby video project, which asks Philes to contribute videos of themselves singing XFN's Greenlight Baby (to the tune of "Call Me Maybe"), in September 2012. The number 1013 is of significance to Philes as it is both Chris Carter's birth date (October 13) and the name of his production company. XFN campaigns thus often feature the number in some way.

Chin refers to fans such as those running XFN as "fan journalists" (241) and suggests that they retain a semi-professional status in volunteering their time to maintain their fan sites while also balancing a relationship with both the producers and the fans. Perla Perez, one of the site's editors, reinforces this notion of XFN as a journalism site, saying, "We are a news site, not a fan board... And that makes us different ... from the hundreds of sites out there, we are primarily news. We schedule interviews, send our correspondents to events, initiate worldwide campaigns" (qtd. in Chin 276). This focus on raising awareness about the show and the fandom make these kinds of fans perhaps the most influential in disrupting the traditional relationship between fans and producers, and both *X-Files* producers and Fox are aware of XFN through their various social networking sites. I would also suggest, however, that XFN has disrupted the traditional relationship between fans. While the concept of the "Big Name Fan" is well known in fandom, the (sometimes pejorative) term is more usually applied to fans in possession of cultural capital or information, and often encompasses fanfic writers or fan artists who have a large following (Zubernis and Larsen 30). The accrual of cultural capital and information about the series by XFN has, however, both situates the organization in the realm of Big Name Fandom and forces it to act as an intermediary, policing requests for access to the cast and crew of *The X-Files*:

> Even for ourselves contact with XF alumni is controlled... [To] maintain a healthy relationship with these sources, you need to be very diplomatic, delicate and smart. There are times that we help out depending on the case to create links between these fans and the producers or cast, but it really depends on the case. We have helped very specific cases after we evaluate them and determine if it would influence our relationship with them in anyway, good or bad [Quijada qtd. in Chin 266].

In this way, XFN acts as gatekeeper of access to the producers and is thus placed in a position of power over other fans, consolidating its relationship with the cast and crew through its use of social media.

XF: Tweet-a-Thon

One of the main ways in which XFN has utilized social media in garnering attention for *The X-Files* is through its various Twitter campaigns. The first of these began on September 10, 2011, after a fan approached XFN and asked if they would consider doing a tweet campaign to celebrate 18 years since *The X-Files* first premiered. Tiffany Devol, in an interview with Patrick Munn, suggests that this has been one of XFN's proudest moments: almost 17,000 tweets containing the hashtag "#XF3" were sent to 20th Century–Fox, and actors Annabeth Gish and BD Wong also threw their support behind the campaign. The second Twitter campaign took place on October 13, 2011, to celebrate the birthday of *X-Files* creator Chris Carter. By the end of the second campaign, over 32,000 tweets had been sent and #XF3 ranked at number 15 on Twitter's top 500 hashtags (Munn). More recently, XFN has coordinated Twitter campaigns designed to get *X-Files* related hashtags trending, as well as demonstrating to Fox fan desire for a third film. The tweet-a-thon on March 10, 2012, ran from the moment the first time zone (New Zealand) hit midnight on March 10th until the last time zone (Hawaii) hit midnight on March 11. In order to have the best possible chance to trend, XFN also changed hashtags through the course of the event and held three separate trending windows, using different hashtags for each one. Due to the way Twitter works, hashtags frequently trend if they are new and haven't yet been used on the site. By utilizing the hashtags #txf3, #xfiles3movie, and #thexfiles3, XFN was thus able to influence the site's algorithms and #txf3 trended fifth worldwide (Quijada, "Trending").

Axel Bruns, Stephen Harrington, and Tim Highfield suggest that Twitter is used as a technology of fandom during such major media events as the MTV Music Awards and the UEFA Champions League final, arguing that it serves as a backchannel, enabling users to offer their own running commentary on the universally shared media text. This "communion" of fans around the shared text is facilitated by the use of Twitter hashtags, though XFN's Twitter campaigns demonstrate that the shared media text need not be live (nor, indeed, even in production) for fans to commune around it. Nancy Baym contends that "More than any other commercial sector, the popular culture industry relies on online communities to publicize and provide testimonials for their products," and XFN's use of Twitter certainly aims to publicize and provide testimony for *The X-Files'* popularity. In an interesting twist, however, it is the fansite which aims to publicize the show to the studios, demonstrating that the fandom still exists and that a desire for a third film is still there. Indeed, XFN's approach does seem to be working, to some extent: Munn notes that XFN's campaign has received some attention from Fox, with one source at the studio describing the site as being "surprisingly consistent and well organized" although no feature is forthcoming at the time of this writing.

The What Would Frankenbear Do? Worldwide Tour

If XFN's tweet-a-thons are evidence of the traditional notion of fan activism, its Frankenbear campaign is more closely aligned with the idea of fan charity (Jones). The campaign was created by XFN in association with the Skype Files and IBG, Inc., two other fan-created organizations. The premise of the campaign was that a stuffed teddy bear called Frankenbear (named after Frank Spotnitz) would travel the world while raising money for the UCLA–Santa Monica Rape Treatment Center. X-Philes from around the globe took turns "hosting" Frankenbear, taking him on sightseeing tours of their cities and uploading pictures with him to XFN and a range of social networking sites before sending him on to his next "family." Souvenirs were sent on in the packages, including badges and items of clothing, and a scrapbook of messages was also collated and presented to Spotnitz, along with Frankenbear, in November 2009.

While Twitter has been regarded as the primary tool through which celebrity and/or fan activism has taken place, with celebrities such as Lady Gaga and Misha Collins using the site to activate their fanbase (Bennett), the Frankenbear project drew on a range of social networking sites to encourage participation amongst Philes. The project was announced on XFN and the Big Light blog, and shortly afterwards, Twitter, Facebook, and Big Light accounts were set up for the bear. A blog was also updated for the duration of the campaign, detailing the bear's exploits with various Philes. Although the goal of the campaign was to raise funds for the UCLA–Santa Monica Rape Treatment Center, and indeed almost $1,500 was sent to the organization, I would argue that the larger impact was on the fandom itself. Discussing the campaign, Avi Quijada wrote:

> Inspired by the kindness of his namesake, after a trip 9 months long, and visiting over 20 different countries and hundreds of *X-Files* Fans, Frankenbear managed to create a community experience that allowed philes [sic] from over the world share a sentiment that conquered distances. As a final perk of this feat, Frankenbear also raised awareness and gathered donations for the UCLA-Santa Monica Rape Treatment Center ["Frankenbear"].

Frankenbear traveled to 25 countries and stayed with dozens of fan communities. As part of the group of Philes who hosted the bear in London, I was able to experience the community-making effect the campaign had firsthand. I spent a week in London with a group of friends I had met through *The X-Files* fandom, including Philes from the U.S. and Australia who had traveled to the UK for Gillian Anderson's play *A Doll's House.* During the course of the week, we took possession of Frankenbear and took him with us to attractions such as the Tower of London, Buckingham Palace and the London Eye. We also journeyed down the Thames by boat before sending him off to his next hosts. Photographs that we took during Frankenbear's stay were uploaded to our personal Facebook pages, as well as being sent to XFN and appearing on Frankenbear's Big Light profile page. Writing about my own experiences of fandom in an academic essay may seem counterintuitive, but Jenkins stresses the need for it from a standpoint of immersion rather than distance, writing:

> These aspects of popular culture are difficult to understand from a stance of contemplative distance. To understand how popular culture works on our emotions, we have to pull it close, get intimate with it, let it work its magic on us, and then write about our own engagement [*Convergence* 10].

Immersing myself in the Frankenbear world tour thus enabled me to feel a closer engagement with *The X-Files* fandom. Furthermore, it allowed me to contribute to a worthwhile charitable cause. I would also argue, though, that the elements of participation required by the project extend past the duration of the project itself. Re-reading Frankenbear's blog post about his London trip, for example, reinforces the sense of community I personally felt while in London:

> The next day, Sandy arrived from Australia! The Inner Circle was complete, at last! These guys kill me! They even have matching jerseys! That night they went out and I stayed behind while they went to the Pub... The following days were filled with more food and sightseeing: we went to Trafalgar Square and couldn't pass taking at picture with the lions, as this is the safest and closest I'll ever get to one of these fellows, and even met Caileigh, that came from California all the way over here for some of the European summer experience.

In *Textual Poachers,* Jenkins describes participatory culture as activities that involve people enjoying, discussing, and reimagining a specific text. In their 2009 report, Jenkins et al. expand upon this earlier definition to consider participatory culture as "a culture with relatively low barriers to artistic expression and civic engagement, strong support for creating and sharing creations, and some type of informal mentorship" (*Confronting* xi). In these terms, the What Would Frankenbear Do? World Tour would perhaps not fall under the definition of participatory culture, but without the participation of Philes the project would not have taken off. The Frankenbear project suggests, then, that in an age of social media, what happens offline is as important to the notion of participation as what happens online.

Fandom: The Film

The final XFN project I wish to examine in this essay better fits Jenkins et al.'s definition of participatory culture. *Fandom: The Film* is a documentary being made by XFN Productions, the production arm of XFN. The project was presented to Neil Canton (producer of the *Back to the Future* films), David Streit, and Bob Kaplan of the AFI Production Faculty on October 13, 2011. Avi Quijada, director and producer, detailed the importance of the project, not only to fans but also because of its value to TV history enthusiasts, and approval was granted for its production. A call for participants for the film, which aims to "show the unknown characteristics and misconceptions of this world of Fandom, seen through the eyes of X-Philes, the hardcore fans of The X-Files, all over the world," was circulated on Facebook on May 7, 2012. Interested fans were sent a series of questions on their involvement in fandom, which included questions on what drew them to liking the show they were fans of and whether they had made friends through the fandom. Questions also covered relationships with non-fans, asking whether fans had felt rejected or judged because of their fandom, and whether they had applied their fandom to their "real life." The initial questionnaires were followed by more detailed questions, also sent via email. At the time of this writing, these questionnaires are still being sent out and will continue to be until XFN is ready to interview interested fans in person or remotely. XFN also undertook interview at the San Diego Comic-Con in 2012.

Work on *Fandom: The Film* is still underway at the time of writing, but what interests me most about this project is its reception by other fans. As well as updating fans on the status of *Fandom: The Film*, the Facebook page also shared information about a documentary being produced by French Philes, called *X-Philes: Ils voulaient croire / they wanted to believe* [sic]. Relations between the two groups appeared to be frosty, however, with the producers of *X-Philes: Ils voulaient croire / they wanted to believe* insinuating that XFN is "crowding other fans out [and] hogging attention" (Zubernis and Larsen 30). Zubernis and Larsen note that "wank" (used in a metaphorical sense to describe fans who have gotten carried away) is an integral part of fandom: "the popularity of online sites such as Fandom Wank ... the existence of 'hate memes,' and the subtle and not-so-subtle relational bullying attest to fandom's passionate disagreements" (13). Quijada notes that the relationship between XFN and fandom has changed since the website became officialized by Fox:

It's not that we wanted to put distance between us and the fans, because that's not what we wanted to do. We still wanted to seem normal, we still wanted ... people to understand that we were part of the fandom as much as they were ... but part of having the status now ... falsely put us in another level where people looked up to us or people looked down on us because ... people get jealous about them not getting that attention or they create ideas in their head about how we're better than other people but we're not and that's something I wanted to stress ... but that didn't really come through at all [Interview].

As Derek Johnson points out, it is important that "we must not uncritically accept this shift [in the relationship between audiences, texts, and institutions of production] as evidence of growing audience power" (73). The proximity between producers and consumers, encouraged by social media, often results in conflicts, not just between fans and producers but also between different groups or factions of fans. I would suggest that XFN, particularly in its production of *Fandom: The Film* reinforces some of these conflicts. MacDonald observes that hierarchies exist in fandom along multiple dimensions, including knowledge, level of fandom, and access to "inside" information. Through both its officialization by Fox and its contact with Frank Spotnitz, XFN has developed a closer connection to *The X-Files* media producers than most other fans. Hills contends that fandom should be viewed as a "social hierarchy where fans share a common interest while also competing over fan knowledge, access to the object of fandom, and status" (46) and, as Chin suggests, the fan-producer relationship or collaboration prioritizes certain factions of fans, which ultimately alters the relationship fans have with other fans, particularly if the collaboration is an ongoing one (253). Thus, although XFN does allows for more participation between and amongst fans, in many areas the sites' creators are in possession of more (or at least a different kind) of knowledge than those using the site, and are also given access to media producers, which other fans aren't, reinforcing the us/them divide.

Conclusion

Through the course of this essay, I have examined the ways in which *The X-Files* fandom has existed and adapted since the series first aired. I have also suggested that the participatory aspect of social media plays a large role in the development of closer collaborations with content producers in *The X-Files* fandom, making the fan-producer boundary more blurred than previously considered. Chin suggests that "the existence of a site like XFN displays a change in the relationship between media producers and fans, in particular for a media text that had debuted at a time when fans were starting to make use of the Internet for fannish activities" (245). Devol concurs:

The goal has always been to bring the fans, the creators, and the studio together and let everyone know that this campaign is fighting for what is mutually beneficial for all of us. The fans want closure to the mythology that helped make the show phenomenal; the creators want another chance to explore that world and to tell a compelling story, the studio wants to make a successful film because at the end of the day, success is what pays the bills. Our decision was to bring all of these sides together because we felt that while any fan campaign could demand a film, we wanted to be the campaign that convinced the studio why it would be good for them, and not just good for us [qtd in Munn].

I have also, however, noted that we must not blindly accept the idea that social media encourages participation amongst fans. In some areas, for example XFN's *Fandom: The Film*, tensions arise when other fans undertake similar projects.

A final way in which XFN's use of social media has changed the relationship between fans and fandom is in the way it has changed the fans behind the site. Quijada says "We are no longer fans ... being totally free to say whatever we want or do whatever we want because of the seriousness we want to bring to XFN. It's kinda hard.... Sometimes it's not fun anymore" (Interview). Without social media, however, Quijada states that XFN would not exist: without Facebook, the Frankenbear campaign would not have happened, and without Twitter, and Big Light, XFN would not have been able to relate to other fan communities (Interview). Through social media, XFN has been able to develop relationships with other fan sites such as Back to Frank Black, thus promoting *The X-Files* to fans who may not otherwise have been as aware of the show and drawing support from similar fan endeavors.

The way in which social media use by fansites is perceived by corporations such as Fox, however, should not be overstated. Spotnitz suggests that "perception of fans ... has changed and the Internet is why.... There's so much two-way communication now through websites, through Facebook, through Twitter, that people are much more aware these are not crazy people, they're passionate people" (Interview). He does concede, however, that studios recognize the people who go online are a small percentage of the fandom and are thus not seen as representative of the wider audience. While fan campaigns such as the XF Tweet-a-thons do make it harder for the studios to forget about a show, no matter how devoted or passionate the fanbase is, the studio will still question whether the online activism alone justifies making another movie. Spotnitz does believe that social media allow for a closer relationship between fans and producers, not just the illusion of such a relationship. The use of social media by *X-Files* fans generally, and by XFN more specifically, thus helps develop this relationship, and it does so while reworking and extending existing fan practices, communities and space.

Acknowledgments

I am indebted to Frank Spotnitz and Avi Quijada who gave up their time to answer my questions. I am also grateful to Bertha Chin and Lucy Bennett for their invaluable feedback on the first drafts of this essay.

Works Cited

Baym, Nancy. "The New Shape of Online Community: The Example of Swedish Independent Music Fandom." *First Monday* 12.8 (2007). 14 Oct. 2012. Print.
Bennett, Lucy. "Fan Activism for Social Mobilization: A Critical Review of the Literature." *Transformative Works and Cultures* 10 (2012). 15 Jun. 2012. Print.
Bruns, Axel, Stephen Harrington, and Tim Highfield. "#Oscars, #Eurovision: Twitter as a Technology of Fandom." Paper presented at the Internet Research 13 Conference, Salford, October 2012.
Bury, Rhiannon. *Cyberspaces of Their Own.* New York: Peter Lang, 2005. Print.
Chin, Bertha. "From Textual Poachers to Textual Gifters: Exploring Fan Community and Celebrity in the Field of Fan Cultural Production." Diss. Cardiff University, 2010. Print.
Clerc, Susan J. "DDEB, GATB, MPPB, and Ratboy: *The X-Files'* Media Fandom, Online and Off." *Deny All Knowledge: Reading* The X-Files. Eds. David Lavery, Angela Hague and Marla Cartwright. London: Faber & Faber, 1996. 36–51. Print.
Haggins, Bambi L. "Apocrypha Meets the Pentagon Papers: The Appeals of *The X-Files* to the X-Phile." *Journal of Film and Video* 53.4 (2002): 8–28. Print.
Hills, Matt. *Fan Cultures.* New York: Routledge, 2002. Print.
Jenkins, Henry. *Convergence Culture: Where Old and New Media Collide.* New York: New York University Press, 2006. Print.
_____. *Textual Poachers: Television, Fans and Participatory Culture.* New York: Routledge, 1992. Print.
Jenkins, Henry, Ravi Purushotma, Margaret Weigel, Katie Clinton, and Alice J. Robison. *Confronting the Challenges of Participatory Culture: Media Education for the 21st Century.* Cambridge: MIT Press, 2009. Print.
Johnson, Derek. "Fan-tagonism: Factions, Institutions, and Constitutive Hegemonies of Fandom." *Fandom: Identities and Communities in a Mediated World.* Eds. Jonathan Gray, Cornel Sandvoss and C. Lee Harrington. New York: New York University Press, 2007. 285–300. Print.
Jones, Bethan. "Being of Service: *X-Files* Fans and Social Engagement." *Transformative Works and Cultures* 10 (2012). 15 Jun. 2012. Print.
Lo, Malinda. "Fanfiction Comes Out of the Closet." *AfterEllen.* 4 Jan. 2006. Web. 3 Oct. 2012. http://www.afterellen.com/archive/ellen/Print/2006/1/fanfiction4.html.
Lowry, Brian. *The Truth Is Out There: The Official Guide to* The X-Files. New York: HarperCollins, 1995. Print.
MacDonald, Andre. "Uncertain Utopia: Science Fiction Media Fandom and Computer Mediated Communication." *Theorizing Fandom: Fans, Subculture and Identity* Eds. C. Harris and A. Alexander eds, Creskill, NJ: Hampton Press, 1998. 131–152. Print.
McLean, Adrienne L. "Media Effects: Marshall McLuhan, Television Culture, and 'The X-Files.'" *Film Quarterly* 51.4 (1998): 2–11. Print.
Munn, Patrick. "Tiffany Devol Talks About XF3 Campaign: 'We Were Blown Away.' *Suite 101.* 30 Oct. 2011. Web. 11 Jan. 2013. http://suite101.com/article/tiffany-devol-talks-about-xf3-campaign-we-were-blown-away-a394973.
Quijada, Avi. "Frankenbear's Rare Footage." *X-Files News.com.* 5 Mar. 2012. Web. 5 Mar. 2012.

http://xfilesnews.com/index.php/xfiles-news/featured-stories/37-frankenbear-s-rare-footage.

Quijada, Avi. Personal interview. 30 Sep. 2012.

_____. "Trending #XF3." *X-Files News.com.* 10 Mar. 2012. Web. 12 Mar. 2012. http://xfilesnews .com/index.php/xfiles-news/latest-news/48-trending-txf3.

Reeves, Jimmie L., Mark C. Rodgers, and Michael Epstein. "Rewriting Popularity: The Cult Files." *Deny All Knowledge: Reading* The X-Files. Eds. David Lavery, Angela Hague and Marla Cartwright. London: Faber & Faber, 1996. 22–35. Print.

Scodari, Christine, and Felder, Jenna L. "Creating a Pocket Universe: 'Shippers,' Fan Fiction, and *The X-Files* Online." *Communication Studies* 51.3 (2000): 238–257. Print.

Spotnitz, Frank. Personal interview. 18 Sep. 2012.

_____. "Re: Interview for a Forthcoming Book." Message to the author. 7 Aug. 2012. E-mail.

_____. "Welcome." *Big Light Productions.* 28 Sep. 2004. Web. 20 Aug. 2011. http://biglight .com/blog/2004/09/.

Wakefield, Sarah R. "Your Sister in St. Scully: An Electronic Community of Female Fans of The *X-Files.*" *Journal of Popular Film and Television* 29.3 (2001): 130–37. Print.

X-FilesNews.com. "FB: this is Sir Frankenbear speaking...." *Big Light Productions.* 6 Jul. 2009. Web. 3 Jul. 2012. http://network.biglight.com/profiles/blogs/fb-this-is-sir-frankenbear.

Alternate Reality Games, Narrative Disbursement and Canon

The Lost Experience

KENT AARDSE

The Lost Experience is an alternate reality game (ARG) that began during the second summer hiatus of the immensely popular ABC television show, *Lost* (2004–2010). Information was delivered through multiple media, from fictional (created for the purpose of the game) and real (real-world, existing web sites featuring embedded fictional information) websites, to television commercials and novels. Damon Lindelof, the head writer for *Lost* at the time, confirmed in an interview with BuddyTV that all the information delivered throughout *The Lost Experience* was canonical to the fictional world established via the television show. Not only is *The Lost Experience* important for its contribution to mainstream ARGs, but it also illustrates the importance of transmedia storytelling by incorporating canonical information into its narrative. Further, *The Lost Experience* highlights the acceptance — by marketing companies in the current media ecology — of fan-created narrative delivered in non-traditional venues. Media companies are now embracing these paratextual elements, elaborating on their own intellectual property, just as fans have long done themselves.

I use *The Lost Experience* as a case study in exploring how ARGs can complement the canon of a narrative. Furthermore, I focus on the enthusiastic online community that sprouted not only from the ARG, but from the television show in general. The tenuous relationship between fan-driven content and canonical narrative will also be examined.

Before beginning the discussion of alternate reality games, a brief background of the *Lost* television show is warranted. *Lost* is the fictional account of the survivors of Oceanic Flight 815, a flight from Sydney, Australia scheduled to arrive in Los Angeles, California. Downed somewhere in the Pacific Ocean, the survivors find themselves marooned on an uncharted island. While the first season of the show focuses primarily on the survival (building a camp, scrounging for food, etc...), it quickly becomes apparent that the island houses some intriguing mysteries, as evidenced when the castaways hear strange noises coming from the jungle and even encounter a polar bear. The second season of the show ramps up the mystery angle, as the survivors find a hatch buried in the jungle, leading to a bunker housing a mysterious man named Desmond. Desmond is in charge of inputting a series of numbers (4, 8, 15, 16, 23, 42) into a computer every 108 minutes; why exactly he is doing this remains a mystery until season four. The survivors are shown a DHARMA Initiative orientation video, which vaguely details the importance of "pushing the button." The mystery surrounding the hatch and its history was one of the most discussed topics on *Lost* message boards throughout these two seasons, leading into the third. *The Lost Experience*, then, allowed the show's developers to further contribute to the mythology introduced in the television show, while at the same time rolling out new content via hidden clues scattered around the World Wide Web. The intricacies of *The Lost Experience* will be discussed in detail, but first, a sufficient explanation of alternate reality games is needed.

The alternate reality game moniker has become somewhat of an umbrella-term, encompassing a number of divergent forms of non-traditional storytelling and gaming. Synonymous with the term, and often used alongside it, are names such as pervasive games, environmental games, location-based gaming (or locative games), mobile games, street games or big games, and transmedia storytelling. Although each name reflects a different thread in the focus of individual games, many of these forms fall under the more popular and well-known term, alternate reality game. If the list of terms above is any indication, defining exactly what makes a game an alternate reality game is a complicated venture, as is settling on a clear definition. In the interest of clarity, I would like to offer forth this definition: an alternate reality game is a game which oftentimes covertly encourages player participation, takes particular advantage of the networked, digital environment, distributes game content via multiple media channels, and transforms real-world locations by grafting fictional layers onto these spaces.

The Beast, created by Microsoft to promote the film *A.I.: Artificial Intelligence* (2001), ran in 2001 and is widely considered to be the first and most influential ARG. *The Beast*, and a majority of popular ARGs since, have largely been used as a marketing and promotional tool for other media art forms, such as movies or video games. *The Lost Experience* is no exception; however, it is worth noting that *The Lost Experience* began after the second season of the television show. Thus, *The Lost Experience* was not primarily a means of marketing. Indeed, the strength of *The Lost Experience* lies in the game's delivery of canonical narrative information for rabid fans of the show eager to uncover and solve the show's many mysteries. This purpose dovetails with the added bonus of potentially reaching new audience members who stumble across the game's many fictional websites (more on this later). In ARG parlance, these entry points are called rabbit holes (a nod to Lewis Carroll's *Alice in Wonderland*). These rabbit holes are usually covert clues leading to the first puzzle of the game, and can take the form of television commercials, unsolicited emails, websites, or viral videos. Alternate reality games are all about these clues and are, effectively, large-scale scavenger hunts designed to take the player across a wide range of different media devices.

   The Lost Experience began with a television commercial aired during an episode of *Lost* for the Hanso Foundation. The UK version of the commercial provided a phone number, whereas the U.S. version of the commercial pointed interested participants towards a website, hansocareers.com. Calling the telephone number provided a password for the website, allowing the player to access secret content. The Hanso Foundation commercial acted as the initial rabbit hole for many players, allowing them access into the game. Players are not yet aware that they are playing a game; this illusion is common in ARGs, as it is imperative to the design mandate of layering fictional elements over real life events, making for a more intriguing experience. The Hanso Foundation's website would act as the main hub throughout most of the game. Players completed small puzzles on the site, which often revealed more information about the Hanso Foundation's link to the DHARMA Initiative. The DHARMA Initiative was mentioned in season two of the television show, as it was the name connected with the orientation video shown in the hatch. In revealing pertinent information about the DHARMA Initiative in the ARG, the developers of the game sought to deliver canonical narrative through the use of transmedia storytelling. I should note that, as I write this (July 2012), all websites associated with *The Lost Experience* have been shut down and can no longer be accessed. Many of the discussed commercials and videos can be found on YouTube, though; accessing this information six years after the game concluded is itself a digital scavenger hunt that can seem quite rewarding. Further, when this author's memory has failed him, *Lostpedia*, the online *Lost* Encyclopedia, has been beyond helpful.

   In *Convergence Culture: Where Old and New Media Collide* (2006), Henry Jenkins defines transmedia storytelling as "a new aesthetic that has emerged in response to media convergence — one that places new demands on consumers and depends on the active participation of knowledge communities" (21). Put differently, transmedia storytelling is narrative delivery for the networked world. Narrative information flows across multiple media, and it is up to the active participation of the audience or players to locate the information and make sense of it. As *The Lost Experience* progressed, players were led to the blog and website of fictional character Rachel Blake, also known as Persephone. Her website included more puzzles and clues, often requiring more sophisticated encryption skills to solve, in contrast with the fairly simple click-and-reveal clues hidden on the Hanso Foundation's website. Although still located online, Rachel Blake's inclusion in the game illustrates the strength of ARGs: narrative information is not confined to one space or location. Further, as Henry Jenkins notes, transmedia storytelling "is the art of world making" (21). By creating a vast wealth of sites for the player to access, the fictional world is enriched and expanded, as the fiction is distributed through websites that are often so polished and sleek, they appear as real as any other site.

Taking transmedia storytelling one step further, *The Lost Experience* also benefited from the publication of a book in the real world. The book, titled *Bad Twin* (2006), was published by Hyperion (part of the Disney-ABC Television Group) and written by real author Laurence Shams, although it was published under the fictional moniker of Gary Troup. Throughout the course of the game, it is revealed that Gary Troup was actually a passenger on board Oceanic Flight 815. During the pilot episode of the television show, Jack Shepard is seen yelling at a man, urging him to get away from the plane's jet turbine lying on the beach; the man cannot hear Jack and is sucked into the propellors and killed. According to the game, this man was Gary Troup. On top of this, in a subsequent episode, the character Sawyer can be seen reading a manuscript entitled *Bad Twin*, which was recovered from the wreckage.

More than just a fascinating easter egg, *Bad Twin* contains valuable world-building content. The novel directly references the Widmore corporation, which has ties in the *Lost* universe to the Hanso Foundation and Paik Heavy Industries (the family company of Sun-Hwa Kwon). The Widmore corporation would become much more vital to the narrative arc of the series in season three, and players of *The Lost Experience* would have privileged information concerning the company before its full introduction into the television show. These cross-over references contribute to a greater understanding of the fictional world and, in keeping with popular design mantras, reward the players willing to thoroughly search various media and artifacts for clues.

In a move of sheer marketing brilliance (and indicative of the high operating budget for these sorts of ARGs), the Hanso Foundation ran advertisements in real-world newspapers, including *The Washington Post*, *The Philadelphia Inquirer*, and the *Chicago Tribune*. These ads publicly denounced the content of *Bad Twin*, as the novel's author does not speak kindly of the Hanso Foundation. Again, these press releases serve as rabbit holes; advertising in a major newspaper will inevitably lead to more potential players, as interested readers may take to the Internet in search of the full back story. A simple search of the Hanso Foundation should lead potential players to the company's website, in turn leading to more clues and puzzles the farther the player dives down the rabbit hole. Writing of *The Matrix* (1999) and its own ARG, Henry Jenkins (2006) states that "[t]he deeper you drill down, the more secrets emerge, all of which can seem at any moment to be *the key* to the film" (101, emphasis in original). The same no doubt applies to *The Lost Experience*. Engaging in an ARG, even without being aware that it is a game, provides the players with a vast amount of content. A well-designed ARG will provide this content, yet still keep the amount of *information* low, so as to encourage the player to forge her own connections and links with the on-going story being told.

Alternate reality gaming and transmedia storytelling are narrative delivery platforms indicative of the shift in cognition associated with "new" digital media. How digital media alters our cognition and attention has been a hot-topic issue, as evidenced by such as books as Nicholas Carr's *The Shallows: What the Internet Is Doing to Our Brains* (2010), and Maggie Jackson's *Distracted: The Erosion of Attention and the Coming Dark Age* (2008). While both somewhat sensationalist, these books highlight the growing perception that digital media are altering our ability to focus on one artifact for a sustained amount of time, and this in turn will have irrevocable consequences on our cognitive abilities. In her influential essay "Hyper and Deep Attention: The Generational Divide in Cognitive Models," N. Katherine Hayles divides this phenomenon into the two ends of the spectrum outlined in her title: hyper attention and deep attention. In a passage worth quoting at length, Hayles sums up the differences between the two "modes" of attention:

> Deep attention, the cognitive style traditionally associated with the humanities, is characterized by concentrating on a single object for long periods (say, a novel by Dickens), ignoring outside stimuli while so engaged, preferring a single information stream, and having a high tolerance for long focus times. Hyper attention is characterized by switching focus rapidly among different tasks, preferring multiple information streams, seeking a high level of stimulation, and having a low tolerance for boredom [187].

This distinction in mind, ARGs are easily viewed as a new form of narrative delivery attuned to the unique audience of the digital age. A potential audience raised on television, movies, and video games as their primary media (rather than books), is looking for constant stimulation, for a story that they have to work to uncover, and will keep them engaged and focused for brief bouts via various sources. In fact, *The Lost Experience* and the *Lost* television show are prime examples of the hyper-deep attentional divide. *The Lost Experience* encourages the player to seek out narrative and world-building information in a manner more suited to hyper attention, whereas the television show, with its complicated and branching storyline, requires more sustained, deep attention to absorb all pertinent information (cf. Steven Johnson's *Everything Bad Is Good for You*, 2005).

Attempting to complete an ARG by oneself is not an easy task. Indeed, ARGs have been lauded by theorists like Jane McGonigal for their ability to bring people together, from disparate walks of life, in order to solve the numerous and often complex, task-specific puzzles which make up the game. This phenomenon is often called "collective intelligence," a term originally coined by Pierre Lévy in his book, *Collective Intelligence: Mankind's Emerging World in Cyberspace* (1997). The connection between collective intelligence and ARGs has been well-researched and documented, particularly by Henry Jenkins and Jane McGonigal. Jenkins writes that "[n]one of us can know everything; each of us knows something; and we can put the pieces together if we pool our resources and combine our skills" (Convergence 4). Meanwhile, influential ARG designer and academic Jane McGonigal has documented the activities of collective intelligence groups, in her article, "Why *I Love Bees*: A Case Study in Collective Intelligence Gaming." Drawing on her time developing ARGs for major companies like Microsoft, McGonigal documents the collaboration of players working to solve puzzles and move the game along. McGonigal writes that this "intense collaboration provided the players with a sense of community, shared focus, and common knowledge." McGonigal sees this collective, social aspect to ARGs as being a major strength in distributed fiction.

The Lost Experience is another example of collective intelligence at work. In fact, the television show itself created a large and eager fan community, vocal on chatrooms and message boards, all discussing possible solutions or current conspiracy theories in relation to events on the show. In a sense, the ARG that followed the second season was a logical progression, both for the writers to deliver content, and to ensure that the rabid fan community remained engaged with the mythology over the course of a summer break. In his seminal work on fan communities, *Fans, Bloggers, and Gamers: Exploring Participatory Culture* (2006), Henry Jenkins explores the transition in fandom over the last twenty years or so. From being a marginalized, underground activity, fan communities have become embraced by large corporations, and now, as evidenced by ARGs, transmedia storytelling embraces the fan community and provides them with the opportunities to connect and share information. Again referencing Lévy, Jenkins sees online fan communities as "some of the most fully realized versions of Lévy's cosmopedia, expansive self-organizing groups focused around the collection production, debate, and circulation of meanings, interpretations, and fantasies in response to various artifacts of contemporary popular culture" (Fans 137). *Lost* fans were engaging in these activities even before *The Lost Experience* began; the ARG illustrates the willingness of production companies to engage more directly with their fan companies. Indeed, alternate reality games are experiences tailored for the networked, digital environment that most fans are already familiar with.

Alternate reality games are designed for players already immersed in a digital environment, willing to seek out narrative information and solve complex puzzles that often require multiple people to solve them. Further, ARGs are games and stories built for the "hyper" attentive, those less interested in only engaging with one artifact for a sustained amount of time. Building off of these features, the strength of ARGs can also be found in the fan's willingness to create content, rather than just absorb it. *The Lost Experience* only relied on a basic level of player creation; that is, the players did not actively contribute to the story, but through the playing of the game they were able to "create" the back story of the DHARMA Initiative and learn more about the world. This sort of creation hinges on a game's potential for interactivity; in other words, through the player's interaction with the game mechanics, the story is delivered in chunks, and the player can be said to "create" that content.

In addition to this basic content interaction, the creation of content by the players is a feature that must be utilized more in future ARGs. Indeed, as Christy Dena remarks in her essay "Emerging Participatory Culture Practices," the "content that players of ARGs create becomes a tier for massive audiences to experience as the work. The content ARG players create is a mix of production that is characterized by what it contributes to the fictional world of the ARG and how it enables gameplay" (44). In other words, game designers must catch on to the fact that there is a wealth of intelligence and talent housed in the players of the game. These players are already invested in the fictional world, and are oftentimes more than willing to create the content themselves. Indeed, as is evidenced in Dena's writing, the huge tomes of information often generated by ARG players become yet another rabbit-hole for potential participants to engage with the alternate reality.

I propose that a more developed and creative union emerge between the producers and the fans of mass-market entertainment properties. ARGs provide a hopeful direction for this union, as these games have the mass-appeal and ease of use that would allow for a multitude of fans to engage with their favorite works of fiction. As Dena writes, "ARGs are considered by many to be accessible because no specialist devices such as joysticks or game controllers are needed. Instead, players need only use what they are hugely likely to have already mastered: search engines, email programs, phones and postal services" (48). In this sense, ARGs are a hyperbolic, exaggerated version of the hypertext movement in literature, which was spurned on by the rise of home personal computing in the 1980s. ARGs, then, as they require the player to search both online and in the real world, can be seen as a form of hypertext writ large. This idea is discussed by Henry Jenkins in *Convergence Culture*, as it relates to the work of Manuel Castells:

> In *The Internet Galaxy* (2001) Manuel Castells claims that while the public has shown limited interests in hypertexts, they have developed a hypertextual relationship to existing media content: "Our minds — not our machines — process culture.... If our minds have the material capability to access the whole realm of cultural expressions — select them, recombine them — we do have a hypertext: the hypertext is inside us." Younger consumers have become informational hunters and gatherers, taking pleasure in tracking down character backgrounds and plot points and making connections between different texts within the same franchise [133].

Indeed, ARGs might even be a "remediated" form of hypertext, to borrow the term coined by Jay David Bolter and Richard Grusin in their book *Remediation: Understanding New Media* (1999). The book explores the nature of media, particularly its genealogy; the text posits that all media seek to improve upon older media, thus all media participate in remediation. While ARGs are crucially different, in that they consist of not just one media but a multitude of different media, the act of searching and seeking remediates clicking and linking techniques used in hypertext.

Further, ARGs are yet another example of ergodic literature, a phrase championed by Espen Aarseth in his book, *Cybertext: Perspectives on Ergodic Literature* (1997). For Aarseth, the "concept of cybertext focuses on the mechanical organization of the text, by positing the intricacies of the medium as an integral part of the literary exchange" (1). Aarseth believes that the actual organization and manipulation of the medium itself creates a work of cybertext, and this term is not necessarily reserved for only literature of an electronic nature. Cybertext is closely related to Aarseth's construction of ergodic literature, wherein cognitive reasoning is required by the reader to traverse a text consisting of multiple paths rather than a straightforward linear progression. In other words, cybertext demands a certain level of interaction between the user and the work; this interaction requires more cognitive work from the user than the traditional idea of "reading" requires. Hypertext, on the other hand, is a term coined by Theodore H. Nelson in 1965, and refers to a computer system that could implement the notion of linked lexias. George Landow and Paul Delany, in *Hypertext and Literary Studies* (1991), write that hypertext "as a term refers almost exclusively to computerized hypertext programs, and to the textual structures that can be composed with their aid" (4). Cybertext and hypertext, therefore, are much more interactive than traditional forms of narrative, as the users must forge their path through the text to construct the narrative, rather than traverse through the narrative by flipping pages. Again, ARGs essentially utilize this formula from cyber- and hypertext, requiring the player of the game to sift through multiple streams of information, locate key passages or clues, and dynamically move throughout the narrative, be it in the physical world or in an online space. This is where the large media corporations, such as those in charge of network television, see the unlimited possibility in using ARGs to augment fictional worlds created in more traditional media. As Jenkins notes, young consumers are eager to engage in these sorts of playful activities, and this is where fans of television shows can become creators.

In his dissertation "Reality Ends Here: Environmental Game Design and Participatory Spectacle," Jeff Watson takes on the world of ARGs from a slightly different perspective. Operating from outside the realm of marketing strategy, Watson prefers to think of ARGs as "environmental" gaming. For Watson, "environmental games create new spaces of possibility within lived environments by opening pathways for players to directly engage in the construction of their own realities rather than an externally-authored or simulated reality" (76). Herein lies the most influential alteration to ARGs that Watson purports: these large-scale, environmental ARGs must be driven by player-generated content, rather than the curated narrative elements delivered by puppet-masters. Watson writes that most ARGs, especially earlier experiences, "engaged the energies of sometimes quite large audiences in collective acts of narrative archeology" (18). This "narrative archeology" is essentially what is at play in *The Lost Experience*, as players work their way through various nodes and silos of information that have been pre-determined and developed with the task of discovery and retrieval in mind. Working as a practitioner as well as a theorist, Watson developed his own ARG, or environmental game, for the University of Southern California's IMAP program, entitled *Reality Ends Here*. In Watson's own words, worth quoting at length, his game attempts to eschew some of the more traditional aspects and strategies of ARG game design. The flaws that Watson observes in this system are as follows:

> 1) that ARGs are constructed as linear event-driven experiences; 2) that ARGs treat their core audiences as monadic "collective detectives" rather than groups of diversely-motivated living and breathing individuals; and, 3) that despite the decidedly playful and improvisatory character of the relationship between puppet masters and players, ARGs are ultimately not deeply generative textual systems, but rather vehicles for delivering curated story materials [25].

Indeed, the flaws that Watson sees in traditional ARG game design are evident in *The Lost Experience*. The game provided a relative linear-experience, requiring all players to perform similar acts to uncover information, and the content was not generative in any sense, as the players were simply moving through the curated story materials. This is where I see the direction of all ARGs need-ing to go: moving away from top-down storytelling strategies, and instead finding unique experiences for players to create their own content, and for that content to be embraced within the fictional world.

Axel Bruns explores this idea in his book, *Blogs, Wikipedia, Second Life, and Beyond: From Production to Produsage* (2008). Bruns writes that a "physical product ... is defined by its boundedness; it is "the complete package," a self-contained, unified, finished entity. By contrast, the "products" of the collab-orative content creation efforts ... are the polar opposites of such products: they are inherently incomplete, always evolving, modular, networked, and never finished" (22). A productive direction for ARGs, game designers should start to view their creations less as self-contained units, and more as vehicles for fans to engage and interact with story content in a meaningful way. Viewed in this light, ARGs can realize the view set out by Henry Jenkins in his book, *Textual Poachers: Television Fans and Participatory Culture* (1992). Jenkins' work has, for many years now, altered the perception of fans, from the passive fan cultures of yesteryear to the active groups of dedicated media consumers today. The uncrossed boundary between these fan cultures and the core media artifacts they are built around is that of canonization; fans produce scores of material based on their favorite intellectual properties, but this material is never fully accepted into the world, never canonized as such.

This may, in fact, turn out to be an unattainable goal, as the amount of fans producing content essentially makes canonization of content nigh impos-sible. But if game designers were open to working more dynamically with ARG players, the content generated in a story-generated environmental game can contribute to the fictional world in a very real way. I will reiterate that Jeff Watson does not see ARGs as being traditional games, and thus environ-mental games are an altogether different beast, but the parallels are there enough for him to describe best practices for game designers working in the general realm. The issue here becomes one of moving away from storytelling to that of story facilitating. Watson writes that, "[b]y moving away from the time-sensitive and event-driven structure of traditional ARGs, designers can create more open-ended games that work better as engines for participation and community building" (34). Therein lies the key for the future of ARGs, as I must concur with Watson: by working towards open-ended structures that allow for greater participation, ARG designers working in the field of marketing can encourage active involvement from the fans. As the game comes to a conclusion, the designers can then sift through the material generated by the game and work towards augmenting the main fictional world (the canon) of the television show, book, film, or video game. Here Jenkins' "textual poaching" comes full circle, as the core material used for fan content creation can be supplemented by content generated within the ARG, and canonization may be achieved.

   With the alternate reality game, designers have an opportunity to engage with a core base of motivated, passionate, active fans, eager to participate with their favorite media properties. A game like *The Lost Experience* illustrates how traditional forms of ARG design encourage the player to seek out information, solve complicated, covert riddles and clues, and create a semblance of story through their own media sifting and rearranging. Taking these core ideas to the next stratum requires media companies to eschew traditional ARG game design; rather than focus on top-down content delivery, as is the case with *The Lost Experience*, and focusing on bottom-up content creation by the fans, ARGs can begin to move away from the position of hyperbolic hypertext. In other words, ARGs have the potential to actively engage players through means other than simple hunt-and-seek gameplay. Encouraging content creation, and welcoming this content into the story world of the fictional universe, will benefit both parties involved. Fans, in theory, will be more willing and eager to contribute to the gameplay and story generation if they feel their contributions can directly impact the story (even in limited ways), and this active fan participation will lead to more pervasive knowledge of the original base artifact. Pervasive and guerrilla marketing can be a more profound experience if the receivers of these tactics have the opportunity to actively engage with the media being delivered, and this can elevate ARGs to the next level of storytelling and story-generating media.

Works Cited

Aarseth, Espen J. *Cybertext: Perspectives on Ergodic Literature*. Baltimore: John Hopkins University Press, 1997. Print.

Bolter, Jay David, and Richard Grusin. *Remediation: Understanding New Media*. Cambridge: MIT Press, 1999. Print.

Bruns, Axel. *Blogs, Wikipedia, Second Life, and Beyond: From Production to Produsage*. New York: Peter Lang, 2008. Print.

Carr, Nicholas. *The Shallows: What the Internet is Doing to Our Brains*. New York: Norton, 2011. Print.

Delany, Paul, and George P. Landow, eds. *Hypermedia and Literary Studies*. Cambridge: MIT Press, 1991. Print.

Dena, Chrisy. "Emerging Participatory Culture Practices: Player-Created Tiers in Alternate Reality Games." *Convergence* 14.1 (2008): 41–57. Print.

Hayles, N. Katherine. "Hyper and Deep Attention: The Generational Divide in Cognitive Modes." *Profession 2008*. 187–199. Print.

Jackson, Maggie. *Distracted: The Erosion of Attention and the Coming Dark Age*. Amherst, NY: Prometheus, 2008. Print.

Jenkins, Henry. *Convergence Culture: Where Old and New Media Collide*. New York: New York University Press, 2008. Print.

_____. *Fans, Bloggers, and Gamers: Media Consumers in a Digital Age*. New York: NYU, 2006. Print.

_____. *Textual Poachers: Television Fans & Participatory Culture*. New York: Routledge, 1992. Print.

Lévy, Pierre. *Collective Intelligence: Mankind's Emerging World in Cyberspace*. New York: Basic, 1997. Print.

"*The Lost Experience*." ABC Entertainment, 2006. Multiple media.

McGonigal, Jane. "Why I Love *Bees*: A Case Study in Collective Intelligence Gaming." *The Ecology of Games: Connecting Youth, Games and Learning*. MIT Press Journals. Web. 3 Dec. 2007. http://www.avantgame.com/McGonigal_WhyILoveBees_Feb2007.pdf.

Watson, Jeff. *Reality Ends Here: Environmental Game Design and Participatory Spectacle*. Diss., University of Southern California, 2012. Print.

SECTION 3: FAN-INFLUENCED CONTENT

Block Party
A Look at Adult Fans of LEGO
JENNIFER C. GARLEN

LEGO toys are widely recognized as a staple of western children's culture, particularly for boys between the ages of 8 and 12. Stroll through the toy section of any major discounter or retail toy store, and you'll find a wide assortment of LEGO products, from PRIMO and DUPLO blocks for younger children to Hero Factory figures and $400 *Star Wars* (1977) Death Star models for the older crowd. The casual shopper, struck by the themes and prices of many of these items, might be moved to wonder whether little boys really do buy these toys. Well, yes, they do, or rather their indulgent middle class parents buy the sets for them, but there's also another target group that the company has in mind. Many parents and members of the general public may not be aware of it, but LEGO products also boast a large, devoted, and well-organized adult fan base.

These adult fans of LEGO, known as "AFOLs" within the LEGO community, have a tremendous impact on the decisions made by the LEGO company, officially known as The LEGO Group. AFOLs support their hobby through local clubs, conventions, websites, user groups, publications, and even an official global ambassador program with the LEGO company, which gives adult fans a direct line of communication with the industry about product lines, prices, events, and consumer concerns. As a group, adult LEGO enthusiasts form a small but fascinating community within the larger arena of popular culture, and their reigning passions and interests give shape to the decisions made by The LEGO Group and also highlight the cultural significance of certain icons and values within the broader cultural groups to which they belong. The introduction to this community that follows is meant to give those unfamiliar with AFOLs a better sense of who they are and what they do, as well as illustrate the way in which this subgroup of "geek culture" ties into its wider community and forges connections between a diverse array of other subgroups.

First, it might be useful to offer a brief history of LEGO toys so that we can understand how they came to achieve the iconic status that they enjoy today. According to *The Ultimate LEGO Book* (1999), the company got its start in the 1930s when Danish carpenter Ole Kirk Christiansen expanded his business to include wooden toys. Named "LEGO" as a contraction of the Danish words "leg godt," or "play well," the business made its first plastic building bricks in 1949. Seeing a niche for an expandable toy system, the early LEGO company quickly capitalized on the possibilities represented by the simple brick design, with additional products and sets being developed on a regular basis. By 1959, the modern version of the LEGO brick had been created, and by 1963, the company had moved to using ABS plastic for its products, which allowed for higher quality bricks that fit together better and held their color longer (*The Ultimate LEGO Book* 10–15).

Minifigures, the iconic little LEGO people who populate the toy's worlds, appeared in 1978, and they rapidly became one of the company's most important innovations. The 30th anniversary of the LEGO minifigure in 2008 was even celebrated with the release of a special book about them, *Standing Small: A Celebration of 30 Years of the LEGO Minifigure.* The introduction describes the LEGO minifigure as "an icon that defies cultural boundaries and generational divides, consistently standing small as one of the most revolutionary and popular toys of all time" (Martell 6). The early figures were basic in design, but the company has refined them over the decades, adding increasingly elaborate hair, costumes, and facial expressions. Licensed themes gave rise to recognizable versions of film and television characters like Luke Skywalker, Indiana Jones, and SpongeBob SquarePants, and the new themes also prompted the company to start producing minifigures in more realistic and racially diverse flesh tones in addition to the familiar yellow.

LEGO eventually looked beyond sets that built towns and cars to introduce more technical product lines. According to *The LEGO Book*, the LEGO Technic theme first appeared in the 1970s to "add mechanical motion to LEGO models" (Lipkowitz 132). The Technic sets feature cranes and construction vehicles with unique parts that allow for a greater range of motion, but the advent of the robotics age brought even more innovative lines into production. In 1998, LEGO released the first MINDSTORMS robotics set, which allows users to build and program their own LEGO robots with a combination of motors, sensors, and specialty parts. MINDSTORMS proved so popular that it even spawned its own school clubs and international competitions, including FIRST LEGO League, "an annual program that culminates in a robotic technology tournament for elementary and middle school students from around the world" (Lipkowitz 139).

The product line continues to expand today, with new sets, new building elements, and other new LEGO themed items becoming available every year. LEGO video games, partnered with lucrative franchises like Rock Band, *Star Wars*, and Batman, have been tremendously successful over the last few years. According to *The LEGO Book*, "More than 30 LEGO video games have been released since the original LEGO Island in 1997" (Lipkowitz 173), including the recent releases of *LEGO Lord of the Rings* and *LEGO City: Undercover*. There are even several LEGOLAND theme parks, with two in the U.S. situated near San Diego and Orlando, and smaller facilities, called LEGOLAND Discovery Centers, in Chicago, Atlanta, Kansas City, and Dallas/Fort Worth. Global locations for the parks and centers include Canada, England, Japan, Germany, and, of course, Denmark (*LEGOLAND Parks*). The toy's increasing cultural significance is also demonstrated by the 2014 release of the first major LEGO motion picture, *LEGO: The Piece of Resistance*, featuring vocal performances from Will Ferrell, Liam Neeson, Morgan Freeman, and Elizabeth Banks.

Although the company has experienced financial ups and downs over the decades, its steady stream of product innovations and new items, coupled with the idea of a persistent toy system, means that children who begin playing with PRIMO blocks as babies can still, in theory, be using those same blocks in conjunction with their MINDSTORMS robots once they reach adolescence and adulthood. The LEGO line is quite literally designed to be a toy system that one never outgrows, which helps to explain why it has accumulated such a large, active adult fan base.

Demographically, the adult fan community tends to be comprised mainly of people who first played with LEGO toys as children, usually left the hobby during some part of adolescence or early adulthood, and then dusted off their tubs of bricks and returned to LEGO building in their twenties and thirties. As Jonathan Bender mentions in his 2010 book, *LEGO: A Love Story*, the period during which people stop playing with LEGO bricks is called "the Dark Ages" within the AFOL community. Bender's personal account depicts a more or less typical AFOL experience: he also observes that the idea of the Dark Ages is "a phenomenon that even the corporate executives at The LEGO Group have recognized by actively separating their community relations efforts into two categories: people over and people under the age of thirteen" (Bender). The LEGO Group, however, does not report numbers or data for AFOLs as a separate part of its customer base, so it is difficult to say with any real precision what the "typical" AFOL spends on the hobby, makes in terms of personal income, or gravitates toward in the way of particular themes or products.

Based on AFOL websites, club memberships, and LEGO events, however, one can sketch a rough image of the AFOL community as a whole. Typically in their twenties and thirties, American AFOLs are most likely to be male, college-educated, and white. Older hobbyists in their forties and fifties are becoming more visible, however, as the fan community and Gen Xers age. Women hobbyists are less common, especially in the ranks of the highest profile builders, but those who are active in the community are proud of their idiosyncratic interest and vocal in representing their segment of the overall group. The controversial 2012 release of the LEGO Friends line, developed specifically for a girl target audience, brought many adult, female fans into the public view as they joined the debate over gender specific toys. Because they are often at the age when young professionals marry and have children, many AFOLs participate in the LEGO hobby with their children and even their spouses, making fan activity a family affair.

AFOLs are by no means limited to the United States. The hobby has proven especially popular in Europe, not only in LEGO's native Denmark but in Great Britain, Germany, and Hungary as well. The Asian AFOL community has also been growing in recent years, with active groups in Taiwan, Japan, and Thailand. The 2012 LEGO Ambassador program, which provides an official communication forum between the company and its adult fan community, reveals the scope of the worldwide AFOL community; 88 ambassadors from 30 different countries and LEGO user groups were selected from the pool of applicants to represent AFOL interests and communicate with the company about fan activities and product development. The LEGO website offers the following definition for the program: "The mission of the LEGO Ambassadors is to work together with The LEGO Group in all areas which concern the worldwide LEGO community and be the voice of their respective LEGO user group towards The LEGO Group" ("LEGO Ambassador"). The ambassador program is just one of many ways in which the company integrates the global community of LEGO enthusiasts into its own corporate culture.

Adult LEGO hobbyists often organize themselves at the local level into clubs known as LEGO user groups, or LUGs. Groups range in size, depending on their location and their particular area of interest, but The LEGO Group surveys their members regularly and provides certain incentives that reward active groups for their efforts. The Tennessee Valley LEGO Club, based in Huntsville, Alabama, is one such LUG. As the club's website reports, the group was founded in 2008, and its members are "mostly professionals in their 30s and 40s" (*Tennessee Valley LEGO Club*). The club meets regularly, organizes several public shows each year, and even visits local school groups and children's organizations to talk about the LEGO hobby. Club members elect officers, including an official LEGO Ambassador, and the officers communicate frequently with representatives of nearby LEGO Stores and The LEGO Group. In addition to their other activities, club members volunteer at LEGO Store events in Birmingham, Alabama, and Nashville, Tennessee, which draw large crowds and require extra support beyond the stores' regular employees. In return for these efforts, club members enjoy some perks at the stores and also qualify for a special program from The LEGO Group that allows LUGs to purchase large quantities of bricks at discounted prices. The club meetings and shows help to maintain and increase members' interest in the hobby, and LUGs around the world engage in activities similar to those of the Tennessee Valley group.

Whether they're in Alabama, England, or Taiwan, most AFOLs self-identify as "geeks" or "nerds," not merely in terms of their LEGO hobby but in their larger interests, as well, and many AFOLs pursue careers in engineering and high tech fields, although the "dream job" of adult LEGO enthusiasts is most likely a coveted position as a LEGO Master Builder, a professional LEGO sculptor who works for the company and helps create the large-scale models seen at theme parks, stores, and special LEGO events. Adult builders frequently use their technological skills and experience in the service of their hobby. AFOL activity and community building depend on the Internet and on computer software programs like LDraw and MLCAD, which allow individuals to design structures digitally and create precise plans for complicated, large scale models. This dependence on technology, coupled with the large number of AFOLs employed in high tech fields, means that the AFOL community as a whole has a far more sophisticated, technologically involved approach to the hobby than the traditional child enthusiast.

This approach can be seen in the kinds of structures that AFOLs build. Original LEGO creations built by fans are referred to as "MOCs," short for "My Own Creation," to distinguish them from the kits produced by the company. In the adult community, MOCs are strongly preferred over kit designs, as they demonstrate the creativity, building skill, and collection size of the designer. Unlike children, AFOLs tend to build with an audience in mind; they design and execute MOCs for online viewing or for display at AFOL events. Websites like *The Brothers Brick*, *MOCpages*, and *Classic Castle* specialize in giving AFOLs a place to share their creations with other members of the community, while annual conventions like Brickworld, BrickFair, and Bricks by the Bay allow large numbers of builders to collaborate on huge displays for the public and for other AFOLs. The popular photography website *flickr* has also provided a venue for builders to showcase their creations and their skill at composing effective photographs of LEGO scenes. Groups like the generic LEGO pool have more than 11,000 members, while niche groups like LEGO Sci-fi, LEGO Halloween, LEGO Vignettes, and LEGO City allow members to share more narrowly focused images and creations.

The size, quality, and attention to detail of AFOL creations can be staggering, and, as a result, they often become popular Internet items, appearing on various blogs, news sites, online magazines, and Facebook feeds. *Wired Magazine, i09, Gizmodo,* and other technology and culture publications frequently feature LEGO creations or LEGO related news. A good example of the newsworthy AFOL MOC would be Sean Kenney's model of Yankee Stadium. Completed in August 2009, the re-creation uses more than 45,000 bricks and took three years to build. At six feet wide and five feet long, it is a massive structure that includes over 1,700 micro-scale people and hundreds of tiny details, from locker rooms to score boards and even *The Simpsons* (1989–present) family lined up at one of the stadium entrances ("Yankee Stadium"). Another popular MOC is Mark Borlase's huge Hoth diorama, which took four years and roughly 60,000 bricks to complete. Featured on *Gizmodo, Geekologie, The Brothers Brick* and numerous *Star Wars* fan sites, the Hoth base includes details like real lights, remote control mechanisms, and even the snowy footprints left by Snowtroopers approaching the base ("60,000 Piece LEGO Hoth Base Diorama"). In 2011, LEGO hobbyist Alex Eylar attracted attention from *Geek Tyrant, Gawker,* and *The Hollywood Reporter* for his smaller scale recreations of all ten Best Picture nominees as LEGO scenes, proving that creativity and detail matter just as much as scope when it comes to meme-worthy LEGO creations. One of the most publicized MOCs of 2012 was Adrian Drake's LEGO rendition of the spaceship *Serenity* from the cult sci-fi series, *Firefly* (2002). According to Lauren Davis at *i09,* the construction took 475 hours, 21 months, and 70,000 bricks to complete. The finished project, which included custom minifigures of the show's cast, weighed more than 130 pounds and debuted at BrickFair Virginia, which immediately launched it into Internet fame as other online outlets picked up the story and the eye-catching images.

While large scale projects like Yankee Stadium and Hoth are not necessarily typical of the average AFOL, they demonstrate the potential of the medium and encourage other adult hobbyists to design larger and more complicated MOCs of their own. AFOLs very often dedicate a whole room of their homes to their hobby, where they can lay out large, permanent structures and build entire towns, villages, or train routes. Over the course of several years, the display will change and grow as the builder adds new features, redesigns old ones, and acquires new elements from sets and kits. These efforts are less likely to draw widespread media attention, but they reveal the commitment to the hobby that AFOLs make, and many postings on AFOL websites and blogs feature photos of "LEGO rooms" and show off the elaborate organizational systems that hobbyists use to keep track of their collections of bricks. MOCs that require thousands of dollars and months or years to build require collectors to organize their materials carefully, and typical AFOLs differ from child LEGO enthusiasts in their obsession with sorting, cataloging and storing their bricks. Many adults admit that they have as much fun organizing their collections as they do building with them, and the best methods for sorting and storing bricks are much debated in AFOL circles.

The idea that adult enthusiasts enjoy sorting as much as building leads to a consideration of the other things that draw adults to the LEGO hobby. Why do grown-ups play with plastic bricks? In part, of course, the answers remain the same for any kind of adult toy collector: adults collect and enjoy toys for nostalgia, for a sense of belonging to a small but specialized group, and for a prolonged experience of the pleasures of childhood. In this regard, AFOLs have much in common with doll collectors, model train hobbyists, comic book enthusiasts, and baseball card devotees. However, AFOLs differ from these other groups because their chosen toy is an inherently and explicitly constructive one, where the collector actually builds and shapes the collection into truly unique creations. Model train clubs do some of this same work, but they generally purchase the trains, buildings, and trees that make up their displays, while a LEGO train club builds its entire layout, from engines and cabooses to water towers and depots, literally brick by brick.

The opportunity for creative expression is, therefore, a defining element of the hobby's appeal. As one AFOL interviewed for this essay pointed out, "With LEGO, anyone can be a sculptor, artist, train model builder, action-figure hero, doll house creator, spaceship designer, mechanized robot programmer ... and on and on. LEGO is a medium that unleashes everyone's creativity — no matter what object or adventure their imagination holds" (Wardlaw). In AFOL MOCs, creativity, building technique, and attention to detail matter a great deal; AFOLs also value humor and presentation quality, and a creation that combines all of these elements is sure to attract the community's admiration. These values demonstrate the qualities that adult LEGO hobbyists value in themselves as well as in their efforts; they are drawn to the hobby because it allows them to exercise their aesthetic and architectural creativity, awareness of form, eye for detail, and sense of humor, preferably all at once. Outstanding work, like Mike Doyle's incredibly detailed Abandoned House series or SoftaRae's Victorian "painted ladies" creations, shows the hobby's potential for creative self-expression and inspires other builders to expand their own vision of what can be done with the medium. Doyle specializes in building large structures showing abandoned houses in various stages of decay. LEGO fans have been especially impressed with the organic, realistic look of Doyle's work, as emphasized in a feature about the creator on *The Brick Blogger* ("Featured LEGO Artist: Mike Doyle"). SoftaRae also builds large houses, but these structures highlight the architectural detail and beautiful colors of the Victorian style, which can be seen on the builder's website, *Spontaneous Dragon*.

As Mark Borlase's Hoth diorama and Adrian Drake's *Serenity* model amply demonstrate, another important element of the AFOL community is a shared interest in certain pop culture icons and trends. AFOL interests help drive LEGO company decisions about which themes to produce, especially where licensed products are concerned, and the kinds of things that AFOLs like tend to reflect their position within the larger spheres of geek and Gen X culture. Fanboy culture has taken root over the last several years in many different media venues, and it should come as no surprise that LEGO products have also been influenced.

This element of the adult LEGO fan community's influence first became apparent in the late 1990s. LEGO *Star Wars* sets originally appeared in 1999, in conjunction with the release of *Star Wars: Episode I—The Phantom Menace* (1999), and they have been extremely popular ever since, spawning t-shirts and video games as well as a constant stream of new sets. *Star Wars* LEGO fans even have their own website, *From Bricks to Bothans*, which keeps track of all LEGO *Star Wars* news and provides a public face for that segment of the LEGO community. AFOL devotion to the LEGO *Star Wars* line allows the toy company to produce and sell remarkably expensive kits, including the Ultimate Collector Series, which features high end sets designed specifically for ages 16 and up. The AFOL fan community had direct influence on the production of one particular 2009 set, Home One, which depicts the Rebel Alliance's command center from *Return of the Jedi* (1983). The set was the winner of the 2009 LEGO Star Wars Fan's Choice Competition, and it's clearly not a set designed for the 8–12 year old fan, with its focus on a scene that is basically a committee meeting and its inclusion of obscure characters like Mon Mothma (a middle-aged woman, no less!) and General Nadine, as well as the first ever LEGO Mon Calamari minifigures (Beecroft 60–61).

The subsequent release of other *Star Wars* elements, like the long antic-ipated Tauntaun from *The Empire Strikes Back* (1980) and characters like Oola from *Return of the Jedi*, shows how much the old school, Gen X *Star Wars* fan base still influences product lines, despite younger fans' preference for the prequel trilogy's films and characters. The AFOL demand for a minifigure scale Tauntaun had been great enough that custom designed versions were popping up online and within the AFOL community, clearly sending a mes-sage to the company that money could made by providing its customers with an official model. In 2010, LEGO finally made an official version of the prized creature available in stores, thus prompting the specialty market to move on to other unfilled niches. This cycle can be seen in other LEGO lines, as well; town and castle builders had long wanted farm animal figures for their layouts, but LEGO only offered horses, so secondary suppliers like Brick Forge filled the gap by producing small, high quality runs of cows, pigs, and sheep. In

2008, The LEGO Group finally addressed some of this demand by releasing its own official cows, and in the last several years it has continued to release new animals, including goats, chickens, new dog figures, and a revamped and more articulated horse. These new additions show that the company is responding to demand from the community for a broader and more interesting collection of creatures, including really unusual specialty beasts like the Rancor included in the 2013 Rancor Pit set inspired by *Return of the Jedi*.

Other themes also demonstrate the overlaps between AFOL, Gen X, and fanboy culture. The Indiana Jones sets were markedly hot in 2010, often selling out at retail stores and LEGO Stores, but the most popular sets were those based on the original three films and not the latest installment. One set in particular seemed intended for the AFOL market; the $90 Temple of Doom set is based on a scene from a twenty-five year old movie that helped to spur the creation of the PG-13 rating, so its appeal to younger children seems uncertain at best. *Indiana Jones and the Temple of Doom* (1984) was the darkest and least popular of the original films, but among adult fans it has its devotees, and the set appeals to AFOLs through its inclusion of Mola Ram and a uniquely costumed Willie Scott as minifigures.

This trend has become even more pronounced in the last two years, as LEGO has pursued more licensing agreements with blockbuster franchises geared toward Gen X and fan culture tastes. The Harry Potter and *Pirates of the Caribbean* lines proved very popular with both children and adult collectors. Batman and Marvel's Avengers sets thrilled hobbyists of all ages and flew off shelves after their initial release. *The Lord of the Rings* and *The Hobbit* sets in 2012 and 2013 also set the AFOL community abuzz with excitement, as have the expanding Marvel and DC Super Heroes lines and the 2013 *Lone Ranger* and *Teenage Mutant Ninja Turtles* themes. While children might certainly enjoy all of these themes, their frame of reference seems to have more in common with fanboy and geek culture at large, and that has been directed by Gen Xer interests. New product lines continue to reflect this influence, with tie-in lines related to popular Hollywood films and comic book heroes premiering each year at San Diego Comic-Con. LEGO's strong presence at Comic-Con is itself an indicator of the cultural space being occupied by its perceived fans. The LEGO Group even creates exclusive sets just for the Comic-Con event, offering a different item for each day of the convention. In 2012, the rare and eagerly awaited exclusives were minifigure versions of comic book characters Shazam, Bizarro, Venom, and Phoenix, and it's a safe bet that few of those collectibles ended up in the hands of children.

As diverse as the official LEGO offerings have become, AFOLs still expand the toy's connections to popular culture by creating their own themed worlds and figures, and their passions have a way of eventually turning up in official products. During the years when *The Lord of the Rings* movies were being released, AFOL re-creations of Helm's Deep and Orthanc popped up all over the Internet, which might well have inspired the company to start work on its later licensing agreement to produce official sets. *Star Trek, Halo, StarCraft,* and *Transformers* all have their AFOL devotees, as well. Modified minifigures in particular reflect AFOLs' love for the entire spectrum of geek culture: fans make custom LEGO versions of characters from *Doctor Who, Buffy the Vampire Slayer,* and *Dr. Horrible's Sing-a-long Blog,* just to name a few. Even with its response to fan interests, The LEGO Group can never meet this kind of demand, and only a few brands have enough mass-market appeal to be really profitable, but the inherent nature of LEGO bricks and figures means that fans can make whatever they like, and what they like tends to run primarily in this vein. Even the cultural craze for zombies has not escaped the creative interest of the AFOL community; the LEGO Apocalypse, also called Apoca LEGO, is perhaps the most inventive and macabre of unofficial, AFOL-created themes, with hordes of zombies and cthuloids running amok through LEGO landscapes designed to be broken, twisted, and bizarre. The LEGO convention BrickCon even features a whole area devoted to this theme, called the Zombie Apocafest. Again, the niche group has benefited from the company's awareness of its interests. After initially releasing a single zombie figure in the wildly popular collectible minifigure series, LEGO provided the zombie builders with a huge boon when it released the Monster Fighters line in 2012, complete with a variety of zombie characters.

As the Ambassador program and new product lines demonstrate, The LEGO Group is well aware of the value of its adult fan community not only as a small but dedicated consumer group but also as volunteer representatives of the company's larger mission. Jim Foulds, The LEGO Group's Community Operations Manager for the Americas and Australia, has this to say about the adult fan community:

> The LEGO Group is very excited about the activities and growth of the Adult Fan community. We have strived to create programs and actions to support fan activities and at the same time to ensure that we don't impede them. For example, Rebrick, which is a social bookmarking site that The LEGO Group created, allows fans to highlight and share LEGO creations they find on the internet. The fan community is a great way to expose the general public to the possibilities of what can be created with LEGO elements [Foulds].

LEGO engages and even caters to its adult fan community because their club events, conventions, and online creations inspire and attract the much larger child consumer market. Even though children and adults often like different things about LEGO and gravitate toward different product lines, the adult community generates a huge amount of public interest in the toy line. Far from shutting down fan activities and secondary outlets like some corporations, The LEGO Group encourages them because it makes adult fans happy to keep spreading the good word about the fascinating possibilities inherent in little plastic bricks.

The most exciting evidence of LEGO's attention to its AFOL community is the development of the LEGO CUUSOO project, which allows individual fans to submit ideas to the company and other fans for possible production. Fans create ideas for LEGO sets and post them to the site. Other fans vote for the projects that appeal to them, and LEGO reviews ideas for production once they acquire 10,000 votes. If the concept eventually becomes an official LEGO set, the designer earns royalties from the company. Once again, the proposed sets reflect the cultural identity of the LEGO fan community. The first set to be produced as a result of CUUSOO was inspired by *Minecraft*, a popular building blocks computer game with obvious parallels to LEGO bricks. Other proposed sets recreate *Ghostbusters*, *The Legend of Zelda*, *Back to the Future*, *Portal*, and *EVE Online*. Licensing difficulties for such sets can prevent them from actually being made, but fans clearly have a very specific preference for gamer, Gen X, and geek culture productions. Even the license-free design for a Western modular town series, which proved very popular with CUUSOO users, reflects an AFOL interest in detail and the legacy of the classic movie genre rather than the tastes of the average ten year old boy (*LEGO CUUSOO*).

Overall, the AFOL community is defined by its creativity and commitment to its medium for self-expression. As the Internet has become a dominant tool for communication and public display, adult LEGO enthusiasts have become more visible to the world at large, and millions of people around the globe can see and appreciate their efforts. The strengthened coherence of the AFOL community has also given it greater sway with The LEGO Group, allowing lifelong, serious fans the opportunity to influence commercial decision-making in an unprecedented way. Most importantly, however, increased visibility and community power help LEGO devotees enjoy their hobby more fully. At the end of the analysis, after all, adults who play with LEGO know that it's really just about having fun.

Works Cited

Beecroft, Simon. *LEGO Star Wars: The Visual Dictionary*. New York: DK, 2009. Print.
Bender, Jonathan. *LEGO: A Love Story*. Hoboken, NJ: Wiley, 2010. Kindle file.
Davis, Lauren. "Seven-Foot Long Minifig-Scale Serenity Model is a LEGO Masterpiece." *i09.com*. 4 Aug. 2012. Web. 5 Nov. 2012. http://i09.com/5931903/seven+foot+long-minifig+scale-serenity-model-is-a-lego-masterpiece.

"Featured LEGO Artist: Mike Doyle." *The Brick Blogger*. 30 Sep. 2011. Web. 28 Dec. 2012.
    http://thebrickblogger.com/2011/09/mike-doyle-lego-artist/.

Foulds, Jim. Personal Interview. 14 Dec. 2012.

From Bricks to Bothans: A LEGO Star Wars Community. From Bricks to Bothans, 2009–2012.
    Web. 30 Dec. 2012. http://www.fbtb.net/.

"LEGO Ambassador." *LEGO*. The LEGO Group, 23 Oct. 2012. Web. 28 Dec. 2012. http:
    //aboutus.lego.com/en-us/lego-group/programs-and-visits/lego-ambassador/.

LEGO CUUSOO. CUUSOO System, 2008–2012. Web. 28 Dec. 2012. http://lego.cuusoo.com/.

LEGOLAND Parks. Merlin Entertainments Group Attraction, 2010. Web. 28 Dec. 2012.
    http://www.legoland.com/.

Lipkowitz, Daniel. *The LEGO Book*. New York: DK, 2009. Print.

Martell, Nevin. *Standing Small: A Celebration of 30 Years of the LEGO Minifigure*. New York:
    DK, 2009. Print.

"60,000 Piece LEGO Hoth Battle Diorama." *Geekologie*. 23 Dec. 2008. Web. 28 Dec. 2012.
    http://www.geekologie.com/2008/12/60000-piece-lego-hoth-battle-d.php.

Spontaneous Dragon. SoftaRae, 2012. Web. 28 Dec. 2012. http://www.softarae.com/.

Tennessee Valley LEGO Club. Tennessee Valley LEGO Club, 2008–2012. Web. 30 Dec. 2012.
    https://sites.google.com/site/tvbricks/.

The Ultimate LEGO Book. New York: DK, 1999. Print.

Wardlaw, Scott. Personal Interview. 14 Sep. 2009.

"Yankee Stadium." *Sean Kenney: Art with LEGO Bricks*. 2009. Web. 28 Dec. 2012. http://www
    .seankenney.com/portfolio/yankee_stadium/.

A New Kind
of Pandering

Supernatural and
the World of Fanfiction

ANISSA M. GRAHAM

The Internet has offered fans of literature, television, film, and music a variety of ways to respond to and in some cases affect the plots and dynamics of the sources of their devotion. While fan-created webpages collect news and images, and Wikias offer opportunities to share esoteric knowledge, it is the dissemination of fan-generated fiction that has evoked some of the strongest responses from creators. Fanfiction writers often see themselves as participants in world building, adding to the wealth of stories about their favorite characters. The original copyright holders, on the other hand, may see these writers as poachers and hacks profiting (whether monetarily or through Internet notoriety) from the intellectual property of another. Hostility could define the relationship between fanfiction writers and their inspirations; however, some creators, like Eric Kripke and the writing staff for *Supernatural* (2005–present) openly acknowledge the work of their fans. Episodes like "The Monster at the End of this Book" (4:18), "Sympathy for the Devil" (5:1), and "The Real Ghostbusters" (5:9) offer a layered look at fandom, introducing an author whose works based on the adventures of Sam and Dean Winchester have spawned fan conventions and fanfiction of their own. While "The Monster at the End of this Book" and "Sympathy for the Devil" examine fan culture as a sidebar to the main plot, "The Real Ghostbusters" is an important part of the main plot. These episodes place in the foreground slash fiction (fiction centered on same-sex pairings) as a means to explore one type of fanfiction writer, but other sorts of fans appear as well, including the oft-mocked LARPer (or Live Action Role Player) and the fangirl. Such episodes exist in part because creators and fans are able to use the Internet not only to absorb new information, as is the case of show-sponsored websites, but also to examine the multiple readings the episodes invite.

Fandom Before the Internet

Discussions of fandom before the Internet typically begin with the self-published and distributed fanzines (fan-created magazines) that grew out of the desires of fans who wanted to share their observations of and creative responses (fanfiction, fanart, and music) to the objects of their devotion. These fanzines do not appear out of the ether, however. As Francesca Coppa points out in her essay on media fandom, the origins of fan publishing can be seen in the letters column of *Amazing Stories,* a magazine begun in 1926 and devoted to publishing works of science fiction: "by publishing fans' addresses, *Amazing Stories* allowed science fiction fans to contact each other directly" (42) and thus helped to create a community that would grow to write and produce material of their own. Created *by* fans *for* fans, these fanzines took from their pulp magazine predecessors a focus on the supernatural, adventure, and mystery; also like the pulps, they had low production values. Fanzines were often produced on mimeograph machines and sold either at conventions or through mailing lists. Although science fiction fans had works published in genre-specific magazines to spark their discussions, the popularity of two early television shows — one a spy series, the other "*Wagon Train* to the stars"— inspired some of the earliest fanzines (Gibberman).

In the late 1960s two series, *The Man from U.N.C.L.E.* (1964–1968) and *Star Trek* (1966–1969), stood out in terms of fan devotion. While *The Man from U.N.C.L.E.* had strong ratings and featured science fiction writers like Harlan Ellison, it was *Star Trek* with its more precarious position in the ratings that created a more vocal fan base. When faced with the show's cancellation after its second season, that fan base, lead by Bjo and John Trimble, launched a letter writing campaign that convinced studio executives to shoot a third season (*StarTrek.com* Staff). These pro-active Trekkers became the model, for good or ill, for fans to come.

While *Star Trek*'s science fiction elements are often touted as the roots of fan devotion, an equal case can be made for the draw of the character inter-actions, in particular the friendship of James T. Kirk, the very human captain, and Spock, his half–Vulcan second-in-command. The apparent intensity of that relationship inspired some early fanfiction writers to posit a potential amorous relationship between the two. This interest in intense relationships caused some fans in the late 1970s to turn to *Starsky and Hutch* (1975–1979) and *The Professionals* (1977–1983), cop shows that relied on the dynamic of close partners (Coppa 48). The era also saw more science fiction on television thanks to the success of *Star Wars* (1977). Series like *Battlestar Galactica* (1978–1979) and *Blake's 7* (1978–1981) featured ensemble casts on quests in the great wide spaces of the galaxy (Coppa 49). These shows, like *Star Trek* before them, allow fan writers to comment on concepts of gender and power.

Coppa points out that in the 1980s fandoms emerged centered on *Doctor Who,* which had been around since 1963 in the U.K. but only caught on in America around 1978. Other fandoms to evolve at the same time included *The Hitchhiker's Guide to the Galaxy* (appearing in various incarnations on radio, in print, and on television from 1978 until 1982), *Hill Street Blues* (1981–1987), and *Cagney & Lacey* (1982–1988) (Coppa 51). Each of these series sparked fanzines devoted solely to them; however, fanzines don't always focus on a single media phenomenon. Crossovers, a blending of two fandoms, became popular in the late 1980s (52), and early Internet resources like "Usenet and bulletin boards" (53) became part of the fan experience widening their reach.

The 1990s saw fans utilizing online mail lists; these lists were often split into two groups, "one for distributing fiction, and one for hosting discussion" (Coppa 54). Distributing fiction and generating discussion are still the two major features of online fandom. Series like *Quantum Leap* (1989–1993) and *The X-Files* (1993–2002) continued the trend of science fiction and cop shows as the heart of fandom, while *Highlander* (1992–1998) and *Hercules: The Legendary Journeys* (1995–1999) brought in a more strictly fantasy/supernatural element (54). The late 1990s and the new millennium saw the blending of traditional fandom source texts (television and film) with "comics, celebrities, music, and anime" (55). These fandoms make full use of the Internet, creating and releasing their own collections of episode guides (*Wikias*) and their own videos via YouTube as well as interacting with the producers of the source material via discussion boards on official show-sponsored websites or through social media like Facebook and Twitter.

The early 2000s brought to fans content that re-envisioned earlier stories like Superman in *Smallville* (2001–2011), Tolkein's Middle Earth in The Lord of the Rings film trilogy (2001–2003), and *Battlestar Galactica* (2004–2009). These media phenomena continue to inspire fan webpages, collections of fanfiction posted to archives like *Fanfiction.net,* and the creation of LiveJournal pages. Each new webpage, archive, and LiveJournal page encourages the same kind of connection via texts and web conversations (thanks to programs like Skype) that those addresses published in *Amazing Stories* once did.

Fan Fictions: Rewriting the Source

In *Textual Poachers: Television Fans and Participatory Culture,* Henry Jenkins outlines the many ways and reasons why fans interact with texts. Chapter

Five of his book focuses particular attention on the interaction between fans as consumers and as creators. Discussing a group of female *Quantum Leap* fans who meet to create fanfiction and other types of fan-texts like videos and art, Jenkins notes "writing becomes a social activity for these fans, functioning simultaneously as a form of personal expression and as a source of collective identity (part of what it means to them to be a 'fan')" (154). This blending of public and private mirrors the experience of watching television itself. A largely private activity becomes public when discussed around the water cooler or the message board online. Fan narratives often emerge from fan desires filling in perceived gaps in storylines or rewriting entire episodes when they do not fit into the fan's conception of the show's dynamic; Jenkins calls this type of writing recontextualization (162–163). Jenkins outlines other methods of engaging texts in fanfiction: these stories can expand the series' timeline, refocus attention on minor characters, realign the morals of villains, shift genres, create stories that merge two fandoms (e.g., *Buffy the Vampire Slayer*, 1997–2003 and Harry Potter, 2001–2011), dislocate characters, insert the fan-author into the story, intensify emotions, or create erotic scenes where none existed before (163–177). These classifications are rather broad and often overlap in practice. It is worth noting that while certain fan products are dismissed as "pretty poor stuff," many authors began as fan writers (qtd. in Coppa 43). The hit *Fifty Shades* series of novels began life as a series of fanfiction stories set in the world of Stephenie Meyer's *Twilight* series (Alter). Young adult authors Meg Cabot and Cassandra Clare started out writing *Star Wars* and Harry Potter fanfiction respectively (Alter).

When fan writers become successful professional writers, it is tempting to see the writing of fanfiction as a kind of apprenticeship, a testing ground of a writer's skills. If writers are really that good, they will be able to create their own universe, populate it with their own characters, and write the next great American novel, or so goes the logic. However, having written fanfiction labels an author as an opportunist who profits from the creative energy of others in the eyes of many members of the traditional publishing community. Authors like Anne Rice (*The Vampire Chronicles*), Diana Gabaldon (*Outlander* series) and George R. R. Martin (*Game of Thrones* series) are resistant to the appropriation of their work by fans; Gabaldon has been quoted as saying, "They're [fanfiction authors] stealing an audience they're not entitled to" (qtd. in Alter). Such reactions often lead to lawsuits because the rules defining fair use of creative works are nebulous. Rebecca Tushnet of the Organization for Transformative Works (OTW) is working with scholars of fan culture to carve out a safe legal space for fan works. Grace Westcott in an article for the *Literary Review of Canada Online* summarizes the OTW's stance on fair use this way: fan-created texts (art, fiction, song) "[take] the source material as raw material and creatively [transform] it in ways that copyright law is meant to encourage — for example, by expanding covert meanings perceived to be present or implicit in the original text, presenting new interpretations and viewpoints or reflecting critically on the original content." Such an interpretation of fan-created texts would protect both works published on *Fanfiction.net* and their publishing house sanctioned brethren, such as Geraldine Brooks' *March* and Gregory Maguire's *Wicked* (Alter). Brooks' book refocuses the attention of the *Little Women* story onto Mr. March, while Maguire's text in some ways realigns the character of the Wicked Witch of the West from *The Wizard of Oz*. Those practices mimic the practices of fanfiction writer as outlined by Jenkins (165–169).

While some creators wish to discourage fan appropriation, others see fan texts as a way to reach a wider market. For instance, in a case of expanding the possibilities of fanfiction, Sony Music contracted fanfiction writer Leah Crichton to construct a Valentine's Day story around the boy band, One Direction (LDCrichton Profile Page). As of late November 2012, the story posted on wattpad.com has been read over 1.5 million times (Crichton). Orson Scott Card, author of the science fiction fan favorite, *Ender's Game,* was once an outspoken opponent of fan-created texts. In an article by Alexandra Alter for *The Wall Street Journal,* Card is quoted as saying "Every piece of fan fiction is an ad for my book. What kind of idiot would I be to want that to disappear?" which seems to reverse his earlier stance; the article also mentions a fanfiction contest sponsored/sanctioned by the author to be held in the fall of 2012, but an examination of his website in November of that year did not turn up any such contest.

In spite of the mixed responses to the creation of content by fans, fanfiction is alive and well on the Internet. Fans can post to fandom-specific archives, like FictionAlley.blogspot.com, a Harry Potter fandom site, crossover archives like *Twisting the Hellmouth* (www.tthfanfic.org), a *Buffy the Vampire Slayer* crossover site, general fanfiction sites like fanfiction.net or wattpad.com, or sites devoted to adult themes like adultfanfiction.net. Fans can recreate and reinvent characters and plotlines and receive feedback from a range of readers; they can choose to use their real life identities or use pseudonyms. Chatrooms and forums offer spaces for writers to discuss pacing, character design, and plot twists. While the Internet and Internet publishing can be the site of commercial success for writers thanks to the feedback given by other fans and the exposure of their work to a large audience, fan work published on the Internet seems to function in the same way as fanzines as envisioned by Henry Jenkins: "Fanzines are not commercial commodities sold to consumers; they are artifacts shared with friends and potential friends" (160). Jenkins' emphasis on friendship brings to the foreground the way fans see themselves. They are members of a larger community which can be accessed from anywhere and at any time through the auspices of the Internet. This sense of community implies a sense of safety and belonging, making online spaces the perfect environment for writers of slash fiction, that subgenre of fanfiction that features same-sex pairings.

Slash fiction as a segment of fanfiction texts offers scholars a challenge in terms of creating a stable definition. Jenkins refers to it as "not so much a genre about sex" but rather a "genre about the limitations of traditional masculinity and about reconfiguring male identity" (191). Other critics, like Sara Gwenllian Jones, see slash not as a resistant form but instead as an outgrowth of cult television itself with cult television typically being defined as any series that deals with elements outside the norms of real experience. For Jones and other critics, "Slash arises out of cult television's intrinsic requirement of distance from everyday reality, its related erasure of heterosexuality's social process, and its provision of perceptual depths that invite and tolerate diverse speculation about characters' 'hidden' thoughts and feelings" (Jones 89). In other words, because cult television often creates universes that only *seem* to be like our own, the characters that populate those universes are freer to explore their sexuality since the restraints placed upon them by their culture do not necessarily match our own. Conventional wisdom still has slash fiction written largely by heterosexual women for heterosexual women; the need for such writing is often explained as a kind of wish fulfillment: "A lot of male slash fiction is written by heterosexual women for whom eroticization of intertwined male bodies is erotic in and of itself and also as an expression of utopian desire for a fulfilled egalitarian sexuality" (Kaveney 245). In all these readings of slash fiction, one finds a common thread; the texts seem to ask that we as readers revisit and revalue notions of sex and power and who has the right to determine what in a relationship.

Wincest and Other Supernatural Fanworks

The CW has a track record of creating shows that inspire a devoted fandom. Before becoming CW, its component parts (WB, CBS, and UPN) featured fandom-inspiring series like *Buffy the Vampire Slayer, Gilmore Girls* (2000–2007), *Smallville, Star Trek: Enterprise* (2001–2005), and *Veronica Mars* (2004–2007). Launched in 2006, The CW has made a name for itself in the industry as a network that courts very specific audiences; for instance, *The Vampire Diaries* (2009–present), based on a series of books by L. J. Smith, taps into the market of female viewers who were captivated by the world of *Twilight*. Since the fantasy/horror series *Supernatural* features two hard-traveling heroes who battle demons in a classic 1967 Chevrolet Impala, one might assume the series targets the advertiser-coveted 18–49 male demographic. However, if fan output is any indication, the series has a strong following among women; a look at the regular writers for the fansite *The Winchester Family Business* highlights women in the fandom. Of the twenty writers listed, only one author is clearly identified as male. The CW hosts an impressive official website for the series which allows fans to watch episodes, follow official news, and purchase music and DVDs. *Supernatural* also has an official presence on Facebook and Twitter. Beyond the official venues, the Internet offers the fan encyclopedias, *Supernatural Wikia* and *SupernaturalWiki,* as well as the fansite *The Winchester Family Business* and a *Supernatural* page on the site *BuddyTV* among others. These sites feature episode guides, discussion boards, videos, and games: content designed to fill the perceived need for information regarding the show outside the boundaries of the television broadcast.

Eric Kripke, along with McG and Peter Johnson, pitched *Supernatural* to executives at the WB in 2005. In an interview during the show's third season with TV.com's Tim Surrette, Kripke offered fans a version of the show's origins. After discussing his own interest in urban legends and Americana, Kripke outlined the evolution of the series' pitch this way:

> At one point I wanted to do an anthology show. Another time, I wanted to do a series about a reporter who works for a tabloid magazine, pretty much a rip-off of the original *Kolchak: The Night Stalker.* And then, finally, just through development with the studio, settled on this idea of telling these stories in the format of this Route 66: Great American Road Trip with these two brothers [qtd. in Surrette].

Still later near the 100th episode of the series, Kripke would refer to the series as "*Star Wars* in truck-stop America" (Knight). The series mixes stand-alone, monster-of-the-week episodes with massive series-long story arcs all the while exploring the nature of family and brotherhood through the characters of Sam and Dean Winchester. This blending of stand-alone and series-long story arcs places *Supernatural* in a category with other fan favorites like *Buffy the Vampire Slayer* and *The X-Files.* The basic set-up of series like *Supernatural* invites fan creation as episodes allude to events viewers never see on screen.

One way the Internet assists in the creation of fanfiction is through sites like *The Winchester Family Business* and *SupernaturalWikia.* Posted interviews with actors, writers, and producers help the fanfiction writer flesh out character motivation or expand a perceived gap in the story. A Google search in November of 2012 using the search terms "supernatural television series fan fiction" pulled up over two million hits. Fanfiction inspired by *Supernatural* can be found on sites like *Supernatural Fanfiction, The Hunters Tomb* which also features *Blue Bloods* fanfiction, *Rock Salted — Supernatural Fanfiction,* and *Fanfiction.net.*

A perusal of the sites' homepages makes clear that much of the fanfiction is driven by relationships presented on the show, in particular the relationships between brothers Sam and Dean but also between the brothers and their surrogate father, Bobby Singer, and between the brothers and their angel guardian, Castiel. Sometimes these stories mirror the episodes upon which they draw inspiration, exploring characters and their interactions in much the same way as the show's creators and writers do. For instance, HikaKiti's "Merry Christmas, Castiel!" posted on *Fanfiction.net*, features Sam and Dean celebrating Christmas with an Earthbound Castiel. The story features a more playful sort of interaction than usually seen on the show as the brothers and Castiel choose to pick out a Christmas tree instead of going out hunting. The story uses show elements as a kind of shorthand to illustrate the character's feelings; beef jerky and loud music remind us that Dean is the emotionally distant one, Sam's puppy dog eyes label him as the sensitive one, and Castiel's stilted speech reminds us that human emotions are still quite new to him.

Other stories, often posted to sites like *The Sam/Dean Slash Archive*, focus on the relationship between Sam and Dean as a potentially incestuous one. These Wincest (a portmanteau of Winchester and incest) stories often use incest as a way to intensify and deepen the homosocial bond established through the characters' familial link. Other slash pairings in the *Supernatural* fandom focus on Castiel, the angel, typically paired with the surly Dean. These stories, like a lot of slash fiction, do not always focus on the mechanics of sex as another subgenre of fanfiction, PWP (Plot? What Plot? or Porn without Plot) might. Instead, "a lot of both male slash and femslash is less about sexual acts than about the process of relationships, plots that are intended to bring characters together" (Kaveney 245). While many premises of slash fiction mentioned by Jenkins (in particular, "the movement from male homosocial desire to a direct expression of homoerotic passion") (186) exist within *Supernatural* slash, this focus on the emotional quality of the relationships marks the fiction as being more in line with the show's themes than the fiction's alternative representation might imply.

As might be expected, Wincest fiction is often treated with hostility by outsiders and sometimes by fans. *The Sam/Dean Slash Archive* even posts a warning regarding its content: "Most fic in this archive contain [sic] brotherly incest. If you are underage or if you don't like the idea of slashing the Winchester brothers (Wincest), please go somewhere else." Such warnings remind us of the seriousness with which fans take their source texts. Fans may now be more willing to accept as part of the mainstream discussion of fanfiction works that focus on Kirk/Spock, Angel/Spike (from the *Buffy* and *Angel* fandoms), and even Holmes/Watson — a pairing inspired not only by Sir Arthur Conan Doyle's original stories but by the BBC's *Sherlock* (2010–present) and the films starring Robert Downey, Jr. and Jude Law; however, incestuous fiction, whether heterosexual or homosexual in nature, still moves in taboo territory. Here we see the mores of the real world intruding upon the mores of the fictional one.

Beyond writing and sharing fiction, fans also interact face-to-face through convention attendance. Like fansites, conventions offer writers an opportunity to explore their fandom in a more immersive way through discussion panels on writing, autograph sessions with actors and writers, and role playing. *Supernatural*'s pilot was previewed at San Diego Comic-Con in July of 2005, and in October of 2006 both Nashville, Tennessee, and York, England, held WinchesterCon or WinCon (WinConUK in York) devoted to conversations about the show which had only been on the air for a single season. WinCon continues to be held annually in the U.S.; it was held in Dallas in 2012 and in Las Vegas in 2013. Fan-created and operated conventions tend to be smaller affairs focused on fan-organized and fan-featured discussions and fan vendors. Conventions like San Diego Comic-Con and Dragon*Con in Atlanta appeal to a variety of fandoms and feature appearances by actors, producers, directors, writers, and musicians important to the fandom. Both official and fan-made merchandise are also available. The opportunity to acquire artifacts from the show or to speak with the actors who embody the characters they write about provide fanfiction authors tangible evidence that the object of their devotion is real. While the Internet allows for instant and sometimes overwhelming access to content, such content often shifts, changes, and sometimes disappears. Purchasing a replica of the Winchesters' Colt or having a conversation with Misha Collins (the actor who portrays Castiel) at a convention provides a sense of the permanence of the spaces fanfiction writers navigate.

Fans Become the Source

Thanks in part to official channels like The CW's page devoted to *Supernatural* and the Facebook and Twitter feeds as well as fan interaction at conventions, producers and writers of series television have greater opportunities to take the measure of fan's devotion. Fans can live tweet responses to an episode as it airs. Producers no longer have to wait on public relations departments to filter through fan mail; a simple web search pulls up a plethora of information from trade publications like *Variety* to fan blogs. Because Internet searches often use algorithms that track popularity only, the *Variety* story may be listed in close proximity to that fan blog, making the fan content in some ways equal to that of the professional commentator. Being able to access fan responses to their text allows series producers to alter texts, acknowledging the importance of their fans to the life of the show. While it is true that "television ... has had the closest reciprocal relationship with fan fiction — sometimes being influenced by the view of relationships taken by fan writers in later canonical episodes of the show, and sometimes, almost certainly, playing consciously with the expectations of an audience that includes fan writers and their readers" (Kaveney 243), rarely do television producers and writers explicitly acknowledge the work of fans. Seasons Four and Five of *Supernatural* featured episodes that brought fan content and fanfiction in particular to the foreground of the show.

Season Four's "The Monster at the End of this Book" explores several aspects of fandom from the creation process of source texts to the devoted fangirl and potential Live Action Role Players (LARPers). Sam and Dean discover early in the episode, thanks to a helpful comic book store employee, that a series of books called *Supernatural* written by Carver Edlund has been in circulation and has something of a cult following. While Dean reads the books, Sam searches online and discovers a fan page devoted to the series. Here Sam and Dean learn about the perils of a strong fan following as evidenced by one post that referred to a storyline as "craptastic," and then the boys discover that there are "Sam girls and Dean girls." Dean then wonders "What's a slash fan?" Sam explains the concept of slash which leads Dean to shut the computer in disgust when he recognizes that the sibling relationship is no impediment to fan tinkering.

The brothers meet their first real life fan when they track down the publisher of Edlund's books. She gushes about how wonderful the brothers in the books are, citing their ability to cry as part of their appeal. After she quizzes the real *Supernatural* brothers regarding the small details about their book counterparts, she allows them to question her about Edlund. She balks at revealing Edlund's true name until Sam and Dean show her their tattoos proving their fan devotion. She too has a tattoo apparently on the back of her right hip, which she shows to the boys. She gives the boys an address and claims that Chuck Shurley, Edlund's real name, is "a genius" ("The Monster").

Shurley is a scruffy fellow who composes in his bathrobe. When he first meets Sam and Dean, he assumes they are overzealous fans and even goes so far as to encourage them to "get a life" ("The Monster"). Once they reveal their last names, however, a detail never included in the books, Shurley believes that the Winchesters are who they claim to be. He then leaps to the conclusion that he must be a god, one who creates through the act of writing. When the angel Castiel appears, Shurley discovers that he is a prophet of God and that his works will be considered the Winchester Gospel.

This episode, with its focus on writing and creation, examines the dilemmas not only of the series' creators who function as gods creating and destroying characters for entertainment but also of fanfiction writers who wish to interact with the text. The episode questions the concept of ownership of a story. Sam and Dean feel that their lives are their own, and yet Shurley knows more about them than they do. In turn, Shurley does not own the story, for he is merely a conduit for God. God, the creator, owns the story. But who is God in the context of *Supernatural* the series? The layered ownership in this episode places fanfiction writers in the continuum of creation, for if Shurley is writing what will become the Winchester Gospel, then potentially fanfiction writers are creating parallel narratives, ones that might someday be included or excluded from a Winchester canon just as the Apocrypha was once included and now has been excluded from the Bible.

In Season Five's opening episode "Sympathy for the Devil," series creator Eric Kripke returns as a writer. The episode also sees the return of Chuck Shurley (aka Carver Edlund) and a new fan character, Becky Rosen, who serves as the webmistress for the fansite "Morethanbrothers.net." When we first see her, she is composing a Wincest story which is interrupted by a web call from Shurley. Initially Becky is insulted when Shurley asks her to get a message to Sam and Dean, saying "Yes, I'm a fan, but I really don't appreciate being mocked. I know that *Supernatural* is just a book, okay. I know the difference between fantasy and reality" ("Sympathy for the Devil"). Becky is gleeful and quick to believe him when Shurley explains that it is all quite real. She becomes Shurley's voice, bringing messages to Sam and Dean regarding a prophecy. A devoted Sam girl, Becky goes so far as to make Sam quite uncomfortable with her need to touch him. Becky appears in two other episodes, "The Real Ghostbusters" and "Season 7, Time for a Wedding" (7:8); each episode builds on Becky's obsession with the Winchester brothers, Sam in particular. While she accepts Shurley as a substitute for Sam in "The Real Ghostbusters," her desire for Sam leads her to make a deal with a Crossroads demon in "Season 7, Time for a Wedding."

Becky is the clichéd fangirl taken to its most ridiculous ends. While she claims to be able to separate fantasy from reality, she cannot. Her need to touch Sam in her first appearance is telling as it illustrates a desire for the two concepts, fantasy and reality, to merge. She wants the Sam she created to be the Sam in front of her. Becky embodies the fears outsiders have of what fanfiction writers might become, individuals so immersed in their fantasies that reality disappoints them as Dean's appearance disappoints Becky. Her later appearances emphasize the potential damage done to Becky because of her exposure to and obsession with *Supernatural*. In "The Real Ghostbusters," she lies to bring Sam to her even though she and Shurley are apparently involved in a relationship; in "Season 7, Time for a Wedding" she makes a deal with a Crossroads demon in order to get Sam to love and marry her. The only relationships Becky has are those she consciously manipulates and constructs through a fantasy (the lie) and the supernatural (the demon). Becky also has a presence online, publishing on LiveJournal as samlicker81; here the series' producers themselves are merging the realms of fantasy and reality (Rosen).

One final episode, "The Real Ghostbusters," is worth discussing when exploring fanfiction and *Supernatural* the series. In this episode, Sam and Dean rush to Chuck Shurley's side to help with a matter of life and death. Unfortunately, Becky has deceived them and actually summoned the brothers to the First Annual *Supernatural* Convention. Sam and Dean are confronted by varied images of themselves and of the monsters they fight as they enter the convention space which is filled with LARPers. Sam and Dean stand in the back of a meeting room as Chuck in his Carver Edlund persona answers fans questions regarding the series and announces that a wealthy Scandinavian investor is making it possible for the series to continue. As the evening wears on, a scavenger hunt turns deadly as real ghosts begin to threaten convention attendees. As the real Sam and Dean work on tracking down the cause of the hauntings, Dean must come to terms with the fact that thanks to Shurley his entire life is on display. In a rant to two Sam and Dean LARPers, Dean announces that he thinks the *Supernatural* stories "suck" and that Sam and Dean's "pain is not for [their] amusement" ("The Real Ghostbusters"). In response, one of the LARPers points out that the stories are just fiction and that Dean should not take them so seriously — a message commonly voiced by those outside of fan communities to those inside those communities. When confronted with the real ghost of Leticia Gore (a woman suspected of murdering her son and three orphaned boys in her care in the early part of the twentieth century), the LARPers discover that what was once entertainment is a very real life and death struggle. Chuck comes into his own when he must protect the conference attendees from the ghosts of the three orphaned boys Gore murdered; in fact, his heroic actions against one murderous ghost cause Becky to switch her loyalties from Sam to Chuck. The plot is eventually resolved when Sam and Dean embrace the fan community and vanquish the ghosts.

"The Real Ghostbusters" makes for interesting viewing for scholars of fan culture as it both mocks and empowers fans of the show. Much of the mockery occurs early in the episode as the clichés about fans and their conventions play out in the parade of costumed figures, at the Q&A session with the author, and on the scavenger hunt. Of particular interest are the fans dressed like Sam and Dean; as at a real convention, participants adopt and drop personas freely, even personas that would not ordinarily be assigned to them. Several women appear as characters from the *Supernatural* books, including a Sam and Dean pair and a woman in drag as Bobby Singer complete with glued on beard. The fans are treated like overgrown children by the hotel staff, and Dean even remarks by the end of the episode that he was glad that the *Supernatural* fandom offered Demien and Barnes (two Sam and Dean LARPers) a chance to get out of their parent's basements ("The Real Ghostbusters"). All of these images work to highlight the potential weirdness inherent in fandom.

Lurking underneath the mockery is the potential for hostility, as is evidenced by Dean's discomfort with the trappings of fandom — the fanfiction, the roleplaying, the obsessive need to know. His issues with fanboys stem from his anger at having his life on display and manipulated for the amusement of others. A character driven by a need to control the world around him as best he can, Dean sees the intrusion of fans as a violation of his life, *his text*. Similarly, one can see in Dean's reactions the potential responses of the show's producers, writers, and perhaps the actors themselves. As Kripke said, this episode allows everyone involved to "explor[e] some of the uneasy issues and conflicts that arise between fictional subjects, their creators and the fans who enjoy the work" (Jester). Dean's anger and resentment could be an echo of the frustration creators feel when fans begin reworking and rewriting their texts.

While Dean may resent the fans, it is the obsessive knowledge of the fans that saves his and Sam's lives at the close of the episode. Because they have followed Sam and Dean both in real life and on the page, Demien and Barnes know what to do once they find the bones of the ghosts that need banishing. Becky's close reading of the *Supernatural* books allows her to pass on vital information about their beloved Colt to Sam. Demien and Barnes offer Dean a way to look at his life that emphasizes its possibilities, not its responsibilities. In the end, the episode affirms the fans' right to be caretakers of the creations of others as they often see what the creator cannot.

The Road from Here

Emily Turner points out in her article for *In the Hunt: Unauthorized Essays on Supernatural* that the work of Kripke and his fellow writers is not that different from that of fans. Referring to the series' relationship to classic horror, Turner claims: "This blatant celebration and transformation of the countless other horror texts being appropriated is not that different from fans' transgression of *Supernatural*'s boundaries as a TV show" (155). Rather than seeing fans as hacks who borrow from texts without permission, the episodes discussed here seem to indicate that the writers and producers of the series see fans as a creative force of their own, one to be listened to at the least and offered respect at the most. For fans, acknowledgment of their work "within the series' narrative" means their "discourses are now canonical" (Cherry 216). Of the characters in these fan-centered episodes, oddly it is the creator of the *Supernatural* book series, Chuck Shurley/Carver Edlund, that best represents the fan author. At the end of Season Five, Shurley disappears, leaving viewers to wonder about his status within the *Supernatural* universe. It is easy to read Shurley as the surrogate for the show's creators; certainly his pen name hints at that link, as it is a blending of the names of the writers and later producers (Jeremy Carver and Ben Edlund). Several theories circulate regarding just who or what Shurley is. A human prophet, an avatar for Eric Kripke, or God — all these options are possible readings of the character. Whether Shurley is all these things or none is tangential to the greater point his presence makes within *Supernatural* and its fandom. He is both a creator of wholly original material (Kripke's avatar or God) and a re-creator inspired to make the texts of other creators new (a prophet) and as such represents the show's creators and fans at work together trying to get the ending right. Collaboration between creators and fans would not have been possible in the early days of fandom when a fanzine or a chance appearance at a fan convention might lead months later to changes in scripts based on audience response. Internet fandoms, and especially online fanfiction, encourage fans to see their favorite shows in a new way and push show creators, like those on *Supernatural*, to realize not only their visions of a series but the visions of their fans as well.

Works Cited

Alter, Alexandra. "The Weird World of Fan Fiction." *The Wall Street Journal.* 14 Jun. 2012. Web. 25 Nov. 2012. http://online.wsj.com/article/SB100014240527023037342045774644 11825970488.html.

Cherry, Brigid. "Sympathy for the Fangirl: Becky Rosen, Fan Identity, and Interactivity in *Supernatural.*" *TV Goes to Hell: An Unofficial Road Map of Supernatural.* Eds. Stacey Abbot and David Lavery. Toronto: ECW Press, 2011. 203–218. Print.

Crichton, Leah. "LDCrichton Profile Page." *Wattpad.com.* 2011. Web. 25 Nov. 2012. http://www .wattpad.com/user/LDCrichton.

_____. "What Makes You Beautiful." *Wattpad.com.* 16 Feb. 2012. Web. 25 Nov. 2012. http:// www.wattpad.com/3427535-what-makes-you-beautiful.

Coppa, Francesca. "A Brief History of Media Fandom." *Fan Fiction and Fan Communities in the Age of the Internet: New Essays.* Eds. Karen Hellekson and Kristina Busse. Jefferson, NC: McFarland, 2006. 41–59. Print.

"Dragon*Con." *Supernatural Wiki: A Supernatural Canon and Fandom Resource.* 21 Sep. 2011. Web. 25 Nov. 2012. http://www.supernaturalwiki.com/index.php?title=Dragon*Con.

Gibberman, Susan. "Gene Roddenberry." *The Museum of Broadcast Communications.* 2012. Web. 25 Nov. 2012. http://www.museum.tv/eotvsection.php?entrycode=Roddenberry.

HikaKiti. "Merry Christmas, Castiel!" *Fanfiction.net.* 26 Nov. 2012. Web. 26 Nov. 2012. http://www.fanfiction.net/s/8741594/1/Merry-Christmas-Castiel.

Jenkins, Henry. *Textual Poachers: Television Fans and Participatory Culture*. New York: Routledge, 1992. 152–222. Print.

Jester, Alice. "Supernatural Breaks Down Fourth Wall." *Variety.* 14 Apr. 2010. Web. 9 Nov. 2012. http://www.variety.com/article/VR1118017744/.

Jones, Sara Gwenllian. "The Sex Lives of Cult Television Characters." *Screen* 43.1 (2002): 79–90. Web. 9 Nov. 2012. http://screen.oxfordjournals.org/content/43/1/79.extract.

Kaveney, Roz. "Gen, Slash, OT3s, and Crossover — The Varieties of Fan Fiction." *The Cult TV Book: From* Star Trek *to* Dexter*, New Approaches to TV Outside the Box*. Ed. Stacey Abbott. London: I.B. Tauris, 2010. 243–247. Digital file.

Knight, Nicholas. "*Supernatural*'s Devilish Evolution." *Variety.* 14 Apr. 2010. Web. 9 Nov. 2012. http://www.variety.com/article/VR1118017745/?refCatId=14.

"The Monster at the End of This Book." *Supernatural: The Complete Fourth Season*. Writ. Julie Siege and Nancy Weiner. Dir. Mike Rohl. Warner Home Video, 2009. DVD.

"The Real Ghostbusters." *Supernatural: The Complete Fifth Season*. Writ. Eric Kripke and Nancy Weiner. Dir. James L. Conway. Warner Home Video, 2010. DVD.

Rosen, Becky. Home Page. *LiveJournal*. 2009. Web. 25 Nov. 2012. http://sam-licker-81.livejournal.com/.

"The Sam/Dean Slash Archive." *The Sam/Dean Slash Archive*. 16 Jan. 2006. Web. 25 Nov. 2012. http://samdean.archive.nu/index.php.

StarTrek.com Staff. "Bjo Trimble — The Woman Who Saved Star Trek — Part 1." *StarTrek.com.* 31 Aug. 2011. Web. 25 Nov. 2012. http://www.startrek.com/article/bjo-trimble-the-woman-who-saved-star-trek-part-1.

Surette, Tim. "TV.com Q & A: *Supernatural* creator Eric Kripke." *TV.com.* 10 Jan. 2008. Web. 25 Nov. 2012. http://www.tv.com/news/tv-com-q-and-a-supernatural-creator-eric-kripke-10682/.

"Sympathy for the Devil." *Supernatural: The Complete Fifth Season*. Writ. Eric Kripke. Dir. Robert Singer. Warner Home Video, 2010. DVD.

Turner, Emily. "Scary Just Got Sexy: Transgression in *Supernatural* and Its Fanfiction." *In the Hunt: Unauthorized Essays on Supernatural*. Ed. Supernatural.tv. Dallas: Benbella, 2009. 155–164. Kindle file.

Westcott, Grace. "Friction Over Fan Fiction." *The Literary Review of Canada Online*. 8 Jul. 2008. Web. 17 Jun. 2012. http://reviewcanada.ca/essays/2008/07/01/friction-over-fan-fiction/.

Desiring the Tangible
Disneyland, Fandom and Spatial Immersion
MEYRAV KOREN-KUIK

From the moment of its conception, Disneyland theme park embodied not only the spatial manifestation of Walt Disney's vision but also the desire of fans of Disney's films to engage with their favorite fictional worlds. The park became a utopian haven where mundane everyday reality could be forgotten and a multi-generation celebration of childhood and nostalgia could be purchased and enjoyed at will. Disneyland's space denotes, in a tangible manner, the reciprocal relationship between fandom and a fictional world. Moreover, the space of the amusement park is constructed as a mosaic of all the narratives created by Disney and his successors: a unique spatial arrangement that enhances fans experiences and makes it all the more substantial. Fans' and theme park are tied into a reciprocal relationship marked by immersion.

Composed of the words imagination and engineering, the term "Imagineering" (Marling 30), coined by Walt Disney to describe how the space of the park was designed and brought to life, suggests a process of creation and development which cannot function without fandom input and participation. Disney Studios may come up with new layers to add to their fictional world's palpable cocktail, but the success of new Disney ventures, and thus the ways in which these will be conjured and engineered into Disneyland's physical space, is in direct proportion to the extent these new additions manage to engage fans' fancy.

Frequently, both in scholarly and news related examinations of Disney, the enormous financial success of the conglomerate is attributed solely to ingenious marketing, merchandising, branding, and franchising strategies. This view marks consumers, and thus fans, as simpletons easily influenced by the postmodern culture of the image who willingly purchase and adulate any cleverly marketed product. However, Disney's perpetual success with consumers cannot be exclusively attributed to shrewd marketing and merchandising strategies; it must include Disney's illustrated ability to repeatedly create enticing invitations for immersion within an array of products across numerous media, a model that ensures wide consumer appeal. Disney encourages participatory fandom in its most complex and wide range form, inviting fans not only to watch movies and television shows but also play, sing, learn, and experience. The jewels in the crown of this participatory fandom construct are Disney's theme parks. The theme parks offer the consumer/fan a spatial platform which brings "all the elements together in the experience of walking or riding through narrativised space" (Budd 14). The land of Disney relies on two elements to ensure its success: a particular kind of utopia and a special type of fandom.

Within the scope of contemporary popular culture, fandom is closely tied to consumerism; whether buying merchandise based on one's favorite television show, watching movies, playing computer games that showcase one's preferred fictional world, or sharing with a community a blog that centers on a favorite book series, comic strip or anime show, fans are essentially consumers. Describing the average Disney fan is impossible, as the body of Disney fandom does not consist of a specific demographic but encompasses a multigenerational global community. Two major strategies, which were practiced by Disney Studios from the moment the company was established, marked Disney as a force in the consumer market with a vision that was ahead of its time: connecting between film and merchandising and continuously re-releasing each of the company's animated features every seven years. These strategies are examples of Walt Disney's innate understanding that cultivating an audience and preserving audience interest in the brand are essential elements for the realization of his vision. As researcher Dick Hebdige notes, "As early as 1937, long before it became standard business practice, Walt was linking merchandising to movie promotions, launching a line of toys and clothing to coincide with the release of *Snow White*" (39).

Initially, Disney re-released its animated features in order to financially justify the films. Surprisingly, many movies that we now recognize as brand-making classics such as *Dumbo* (1941), *Alice in Wonderland* (1951) and *Peter Pan* (1953), were not initially profitable. As Disney enthusiast Tim Hodge notes, "during Walt's lifetime only a few of his animated features made a profit at the box office." Recirculating these films in theaters in seven year intervals (initially domestically but later on worldwide) had several advantages and positive outcomes for the company. It ensured that eventually each movie made money, but more importantly, it introduced the Disney produced narratives and fictional worlds to new generations of viewers, thus increasing the company's audience range by marketing the movies as family-oriented consumer products. Additionally, multiple generations of viewers were exposed to the aesthetically enticing Disney arsenal of character. Nostalgia became a strong factor in the process of fandom acquisition, as parents and grandparents took children to see the movies they enjoyed in their youth. Gradually, in the period between the release of *Snow White and the Seven Dwarfs* (1937) and the opening of the first theme park in 1955, Disney acquired a wide consumer/fan base eager to partake in a tangible immersion experience based on their favorite animated features.

Walt Disney's vision of giving life to his imaginary universe and sharing it with others was not limited to the production of films and promotional merchandising. In 1954, Disney linked its film adaptation of Jules Verne's *20,000 Leagues Under the Sea* to a budding initiative in television broadcasting as part of the series *Disneyland* (1954–2008), which aired on ABC. A special episode of *Disneyland* called "Operation Undersea" was produced in what researcher J.P. Telotte calls, "an elaborate attempt to promote the film's success through what we might term a convergence aesthetics" (70). Telotte is referring to the term "media convergence" coined by theorist Henry Jenkins. Jenkins explains "convergence" as "the flow of content across multiple media platforms, the cooperation between multiple media industries and the migratory behavior of media audiences who will go almost anywhere in search of the kinds of entertainment experience they want" (2). Thus, as a phenomenon, convergence accounts not only for the ubiquitous nature of content within different media platforms, but also for the ability of this model to satisfy audiences who are both consumers and fans. In linking film to merchandising and television, Walt Disney began to construct his own encompassing model of convergence, one which strategically positioned the content of the fictional world he created. In this model, merchandising became the connecting agent between content and media, fans and imaginary spaces. Merchandising entices not only a content-related connection between different media by which a particular fictional world can be experienced; it also encourages an engagement with narrative that is personal and free from temporal and spatial constraint. Scholar Marc Steinberg refers to this as the "anytime, anywhere" (113) engagement opportunity that merchandise promotes.

In his article "Anytime, Anywhere: Tetsuwan Atomu Stickers and the Emergence of Character Merchandizing," Steinberg describes the first time a connection was made between merchandise (stickers) and an animated character (Tetsuwan Atomu, known to English speaking audiences as Astro Boy) in the Japanese animation (anime) market. Steinberg observes, "Tetsuwan Atomu is not only commonly regarded as the first instance of what is now known as 'anime'; it is also regarded as the point of emergence of the commercial phenomenon of character-based merchandizing" (113). Steinberg demonstrates the ability of merchandise to entice consumers/fans to immerse themselves in a fictional world by forming a connection with other related contents through integrated mixed-media, and argues that we must expand our notion of media to include merchandising. Walt Disney understood this synergetic nature of merchandising, only his strategy in promoting his vision was not limited to character-based merchandising. Instead, Disney connected it to narrative and created narrative-based merchandising. Eventually, out of each film came a plethora of narrative related items: not just characters but costumes, artifacts, vehicles, books, and sweets. Essentially, any item that could induce participation, by retelling and reliving the narrativized experience of the visual creations, was produced and marketed to fans. Disney manufactured in audiences the desire to physically participate and become part of his imaginary world. Disney parks provide fans with an opportunity to experience that which (at least for the duration of immersion) turns the imaginary into the real. As theorist Marie-Laure Ryan aptly articulates, "the appeal of a pictorial space imaginatively open to the body is hard to kill off" (4). Fans desire the tangible, and Disney parks offer a palpable experience of the most coveted order — that of utopia.

The space of Disney parks and the pastiche of various Disney-produced narratives they are composed of represent a kind of utopia that hinges on sentimentality and nostalgia — a sentimental utopia. They build upon the desire of participants and fans not only to physically engage with their favorite fictional world but also to do so, more often than not, as a part of a group: a family outing, a romantic couple's voyage, or a bonding experience between parents/grandparents and children. The aspect of nostalgia takes on a dual meaning within the theme parks' environments and denotes both communal and individual forms of nostalgia; communal nostalgia is manifested in the parks by the idealized early 20th century urban setting, and individual nostalgia is evoked by the onslaught of images recognizable by patrons of all age groups from their own childhood.

In his book *Archaeologies of the Future: The Desire Called Utopia and Other Science Fictions*, theorist Fredric Jameson states, "Utopian space is an imaginary enclave within real social space" (15). Jameson refers to utopian spaces as they are represented by the concepts created by Thomas Moore and Tommaso Campanella; Moore's utopia is an island and Campanella's is a monastery. Both these utopian models represent spaces separated from "real social space" (15) not only by the nature of their own spatiality but also by the ideology they represent that negates that by which a "real social space" operates. In order to become a construct of desire, sentimental utopias must retain the separation from "real social space" and at the same time diffuse (or at least seem to diffuse) the ideological conflict with consensus reality. In other words, a sentimental utopia must be unbound by the political ideology that underlines utopias subscribing to the Moore/Campanella formula. Consequently, the only possible way to achieve at least a semblance of an ideology-free utopian construct is by creating a simulacrum of one. The type of sentimental utopia represented by Disneyland's space is by definition a simulacrum of what Baudrillard terms "the third order," one residing in the realm of the hyperreal without a tangible origin within consensus reality.

In his book *Simulacra and Simulation*, Baudrillard states:

> The imaginary was the alibi of the real in a world dominated by the reality principle. Today, it is the real that has become the alibi of the model, in a world controlled by the principle of simulation. And, paradoxically, it is the real that has become our true Utopia — but a utopia that is no longer in the realm of possible, that can only be dreamt of as one world dream of a lost object [122–123].

Baudrillard's observation encapsulates both the idea of contemporary utopian spaces as the sentimental product of longing for an idealized past and the principle that these simulations of utopia are representations of hyperreality — a virtual construct. The appeal of Disney parks' version of sentimental utopia is so strong and the effects of the utopian enclave so consuming that the parks are perceived by patrons as spatially as well as temporally removed from everyday reality. The parks are true enclaves of the imaginary where the cares of the outside world are temporarily put aside and forgotten, a practice which includes the monetary. Park goers often overlook or forget that a ticket to utopia is expensive; nourishing oneself in utopia is pricey, and the latest version of Buzz Lightyear's ray-gun they just bought their offspring costs a ridiculous amount of money. The park's enchantment induces suspension of financial disbelief as the spatial immersion in the fantastic and the fictional is celebrated.

The spatial immersion experience Disneyland offers is marked by the connection between desire and fictional world. This connection supports both spatial and temporal dimensions and projects a unique chronotope — a unique space/time construct of immersion experience. Theorist Mikhail Bakhtin defines chronotope as "the intrinsic connectedness of temporal and spatial relationships that are artistically expressed in literature" (15). The chronotope of immersion hinges on spatiality, on the physical aspect of interaction with the narratives Disney's parks encompass. The temporal aspect of the chronotope of immersion is connected to nostalgia; participants in the Disney park immersion model desire the simplicity of the past that the park's architecture projects and look forward to a future of family unity which the immersion experience promises. Thus, immersion and narrative desire go hand-in-hand within the Disney consumer/fandom model and understanding the connection between desire and narrative is therefore useful.

In his essay "Narrative Desire," Peter Brooks examines narrative as a play of desire in time. He stresses the role of plot as "an embracing concept for the design and intention of narrative" (130) and as a device that cuts across the story/discourse construct to enable a process of logical reconstruction of the order of events in the reader's perception. In Brooks' own words, "plot ... animates the sense making process" and "the reading of plot" is therefore "a form of desire that carries us forward, onward, through the text" (132). Consequently, according to Brooks, narrative desire encapsulates both the play of desire within the narrative itself— the conflicts and passions presented by the plot — and desire generated by the reader which is a result of the "experience of reading narrative" (132).

While Brooks explores the play of desire in narrative as a temporal experience, Susan Stanford Friedman expands the scope of interaction to include space. For Friedman, who advocates "spatialization" as "a strategy for reading narrative," a narrative is "the play of desire in space as well as in time" (217). Although both Brooks' and Friedman's essays refer to the interaction of desire within written narratives, the mechanisms they propose are both suitable and useful as a departure point for the examination of the play of desire within the framework of spatial narratives similar to those represented in the array of spatial narratives which Disney parks introduce.

One aspect that separates a written narrative from a spatial one is the corporeality of the experience. Written narratives offer an opportunity for interaction and immersion which is in essence passive. The play of desire is an intellectual construct involving the reader's (or the participant's) imagination as a reaction to a string of written words. Even interactive narratives, involving a computer as an agent affording a prefabricated visual dimension, do not elevate the level of physical involvement beyond the effort required for the movement of one's wrist upon a computer's mouse. Experiencing spatial narratives, on the other hand, requires a physical presence. It employs the complete array of our corporeal senses. This prerequisite has a profound impact on the interaction between narrative and audience. The desire in this interaction is no longer limited to the realm of action within narrative and the reaction to it; it also includes the personal perspective of individuals as they bring their own internal play of desire into the physical space they occupy.

The physical aspect of spatial narratives therefore consists of two elements coming together at a specific temporal point: the physical objects occupying a given space (buildings in a city, for example, or the rides, merchandise and Imagineered architecture within Disneyland) and the manner in which the space is experienced and perceived by the people occupying it. The physical arrangement of objects in a given space can thus be viewed as the spatial narrative's diegetic level, the level of the concrete physical world and the placement of objects within it. Accordingly, the individualized interaction and the subsequent personalized narratives that are the results of such interaction may be viewed as part of the spatial narrative's extradiegetic level, the level consisting of the additions that are not strictly tangible within the immediate spatial environment: musing about related past experiences, feelings of nostalgia, particular familial dynamics, contribute layers to the creation of a personalized spatial narrative. The play of desire occurs through the process of absorption and manufacturing of individualized narratives that is a result of the dynamics of these two levels of the spatial narrative.

The mechanism which enables the construction of individualized interactive spatial narratives is what Hayden White calls "emplotment" (193). White defines emplotment as "the encodation of the facts contained in the chronicle as components of specific kinds of plot structures" (193); he argues that this process is a product of a "constructive imagination" process (194). Emplotment represents an innate need for order and coherency which is in itself a representation of a mode of desire — a desire for meaning. Within the space of the Disneyland utopia the desire for meaning — the creation of individual fans' inner narratives — is a result of spatial immersion that is discursive in nature and closely relates to convergence. As Henry Jenkins observes, "convergence occurs within the brains of individual consumers ... each of us constructs our own personal mythology from bits and fragments of information extracted from the media flow and transformation into resources through which we make sense of our everyday life" (3–4). Within the confines of the Disney theme park, this very process of convergence allows fans to position themselves and establish personal narratives that reaffirm who they are in relation to the momentary experience of immersion, as well as establish and enhance their individuality outside the framework of the Disney utopia. Consequently, fandom becomes a tool in the exploration of subjectivity and the construction of identity.

The Disney Fandom model relies heavily on reciprocity for its success; moreover, the reciprocal component is crucial for the overall commercial success of the Disney conglomerate. The parks operate as an elaborate laboratory for the manufacturing of data regarding fans' predilections. The parks are essentially platforms that allow fans a selective physical engagement with those sections of the Disney spatial mosaic that most take their fancy. In turn, the element of freedom-of-choice provides feedback regarding consumers/fans preferences; it gives fans the power to influence by being selective. The success of Disney hinges on taking fans and consumer preferences seriously. Convergence and influence emerge as two vital components of the Disney reciprocal fandom construction as content finds its way into different media in accordance with fans' inclination; illustrations of this dynamics are numerous.

The "Pirates of the Caribbean" ride, the last Imagineering vision of Walt Disney before his death, opened in Disneyland in 1967. Since then it has enjoyed over forty years of immense popularity with park visitors. The attraction is a log flume-type ride that offers participants a thrilling boat journey through a pirate-themed setting. It transports fans to another space and another time allowing them to partake in the adventure that is a pirate's life. In an attempt to capitalize on the popularity of the theme park's ride, the Disney company decided to turn "Pirates of the Caribbean" into a motion picture; the film *Pirates of the Caribbean: Curse of the Black Pearl* was released in 2003, and was followed by *Pirates of the Caribbean: Dead Man's Chest* (2006), *Pirates of the Caribbean: At World's End* (2007), and *Pirates of the Caribbean: On Stranger Tides* (2011).

Working to enhance the movie's chance of favorable reception, Disney's film and television production division, Buena Vista, contracted popular A-List actors (such as Johnny Depp) to play major roles in the films. Fans were enthusiastic about the movies, which directly translated into enormous box office profits. However, when Disney decided to branch the franchise into Internet and video gaming, fans' responses were less than favorable, as *Newsweek's Daily Beast* reports: "Based on the box-office hit trilogy *Pirates of the Caribbean*, Disney launched a Web-based game called Pirates of the Caribbean Online and released several videogame titles as well. Despite such big-name games, the interactive division lost $130 million" (Tracy).

The failure of the digitalized versions of *Pirates of the Caribbean* to entice fans to immerse in the fictional world was clear; it wasn't just a financial debacle, it was a signal from Disney's fans and consumers that something was wrong. It forced Disney to take a step back and re-evaluate its course of action. In an attempt to improve the quality of the company's digital offerings to consumers/fans, Disney acquired Playdom, a company apt in producing popular online social games. *The Pirates of the Caribbean* example demonstrates the feedback mechanism that exists between Disney and its fandom — fans' choices are not taken for granted, and while corrections in business strategies translate into more revenue for the company, they also benefit consumers. Moreover, acquisition of intellectual knowledge, which companies like Playdom represent, enriches and enhances the quality of the fictional world that Disney offers its fans.

Rides that turn into films represent but one strategy of transferring content from one medium to another in order to enhance the possibility of immersion; another version of content sharing between media are films that are turned into rides in order to offer an opportunity to physically immerse and engage with one's favorite narratives. The animated feature *Snow White and the Seven Dwarfs* was made into a Disney park attraction ("Snow White's

Scary Adventures") as early as 1955, and versions of the ride still exists in Disney parks worldwide. *Peter Pan* is another example. Based on the much beloved narrative of J.M. Barrie's book, the movie depicts the adventures of a group of children in an imaginary land were children do not age. The ride "Peter Pan's Flight" takes participants on an aeronautic magical journey through the movie's narrative; it flies them out of Wendy's nursery window into the nighttime London skies and on to Neverland and the adventures which await them there. Disney ultimately capitalized on the success of both ride and film and transferred the narrative into another emerging market segment — DVD releases. Now people could relive not only the adventures of Peter Pan, but also those of scores of other Disney characters from the comfort of their own living room. However, the real heroine of this franchising story is a little fairy named Tinker Bell.

The character of Tinker Bell, Peter Pan's friend and confidant, was popular with Disney fans due to her spunky portrayal and her charming visual depiction as a little winged fairy. Tinker Bell became a Disney icon, representing the ideas of imagination and magic with her fairy dust-sprinkled flight toward the screen as part of Disney's animated logo. Because of the popular response among fans, Tinker Bell eventually spawned her own franchise, revealing an approach to character development that might best be described as spin-off franchising. Spin-off franchising utilizes a character belonging to one narrative to create a separate fictional world. This strategy allows the flow of content from one narrative to another, as well as from one medium to another and thus increases choice. Fans that are indifferent to the original Peter Pan narrative but are immensely fond of Tinker Bell can now chose to partake in her imaginary universe rather than engaging that of Peter Pan; diversity promotes choice and thus increases fans' willingness to participate and immerse.

"Disney Princesses" represents another version of Disney's ingenuity in the realm of diversification. This innovative Disney franchise capitalizes on existing characters and gathers them under one umbrella; Snow White, Belle, Sleeping Beauty, the Little Mermaid and all the other pretty princesses from the Disney animation productions are included in this prestigious royal group. Mainly aimed at attracting the interest of young girls, engaging with a Disney princess offers the illusion of being a princess, and walking the paths of a Disney theme park dressed as a Disney princess further enhances this feeling and increases the level of immersion. The "Disney Princesses" are represented in the parks by merchandise (stickers, books and sweets), and the princesses roam the park ready to meet and greet young fans. Within Disneyland's utopian enclave, every girl is a princess and taking a Disney princess home ensures that the engagement will continue even after leaving the park. Moreover, little girls have power and can influence the decisions of a billion-dollar media by choosing one Disney princess over another. To a certain extent, taking into account the wishes and tastes of young girls also forced Disney to take into consideration ethnic diversity and, as a result, dark skinned princesses were featured in the films *Aladdin* (1992) and *The Princess and the Frog* (2009).

Disney's partnership with Pixar animation, which began in 1991, marks the beginning of a new age at Disney for both convergence strategies and fandom relationship. It launched a period of what may be termed as instant franchising. In 1995 the movie *Toy Story* was released, and Disney simultaneously marketed *Toy Story* related merchandise in both Disney stores and Disney parks worldwide. Soon after, an array of *Toy Story* related attractions and rides sprouted in the Disney theme parks, an animated television series *Buzz Lightyear of Star Command* (2000–2001) was produced, *Toy Story* computer games for Sega and Nintendo were developed, and *Toy Story* sequels for the big screen were made. *Toy Story*'s instant franchising success, both as a financial venture and as a venture that captured the imagination of Disney enthusiasts, served as a model for future undertakings, and the mechanism of instant franchising/instant convergence became standard operation procedure in other Disney-Pixar productions; *Monsters Inc.* (2001), *Finding Nemo* (2003), *Cars* (2006), and *Brave* (2012) are examples of this pattern of operation. With the acquisition of Pixar in 2006, Disney added to its arsenal both the company's intellectual property and its expertise ensuring further enrichment of the Disney mosaic.

The establishment of *The Lion King* (1994) as a desirable commodity, owing to the animated feature's success at the box office, inspired Disney to diversify their commodity model to include live theater productions. As Mike Budd recounts in *Rethinking Disney*:

> Disney hired experimental theatre artist Julie Taymor to direct the stage version of the Lion King, opening at the New Amsterdam in November 1997. The show was not only a huge financial success but a critical one as well, adding greatly ... to Disney's cultural capital, revaluing the company's image upward ... by demonstrating that a definitively middlebrow culture producer could impress with conspicuous displays of aesthetic distinction [19].

The artistic distinction of the production, or rather the efforts taken to ensure a quality end product, may be viewed solely as efforts to preserve and ensure the commodity's commercial success; however, it also can be attributed to Disney's understanding of the reciprocal relationship the company enjoys with their consumer/fan base. Ensuring a quality product may be interpreted as a sign of Disney's recognition of fans' intelligence, and the fact that the conglomerate's continuous financial success depends on respecting fans by producing the type of convergence and immersion opportunities that exhibit aesthetic and content quality.

Disney's strategy in adding theater to its immersion opportunity arsenal stemmed from the understanding that even a stage musical should be presented to fans as an opportunity to partake in a fictional world. Scholar Maurya Wickstrom notes, "an ad in the program for *The Lion King* ... reads, 'enjoy your audience with the King. And remember, even in the jungle American Express helps you do more'" (99). This note within the program directly denotes *The Lion King*'s connection to the market; nevertheless, it also, as Wickstron remarks, "places audience members bodily inside the fiction of the musical. They are not merely an audience watching the lion king Mufasa on stage; they are in the play enjoying his audience" (99). A half-hour version of the musical is continuously staged within the Disney theme parks, with tickets booked in advance by park patrons who crave the experience of becoming part of this grand romantic/heroic narrative, and sharing the stage with Mufasa, Simba, Pumbaa and Timon. Thus, adding musical theater to the array of spatial immersion opportunities within the Disney theme parks represents Disney's understanding of the reciprocal relationship they enjoy with their fans.

The fact that Disney is a conglomerate, a financial entity designed to generate revenue, is obvious. Nevertheless, Disney is also the encompassing imaginary vision of Walt Disney and his successors that manages to consistently and continuously entice consumers and fans to engage the Disney fictional universe. Though the Disney model of operation may be viewed as exclusively relating to contemporary commodity culture, this view is narrow as it neglects to take into account the reciprocal cultural-social interaction that the relationship between a commodity and consumer expresses. The Disney model does not take consumers/fans for granted; the recognition that fandom, as a collective, possesses both astuteness and the power to influence is an important component of Disney's reciprocal and interactive fandom model.

In offering platforms for an encompassing spatial immersion, the Disney theme parks emerge as a core component of the reciprocal fandom model. The parks offer a comprehensive array of engagement opportunities, with every segment of Disney's fictional universe in every possible medium; from merchandising to rides to musical theater, physical engagement is hedonistically enjoyed and celebrated. The parks are established as utopian enclaves, disengaged from outside reality, and immensely attractive in their continuous inducement of longing and nostalgia for the pleasures of childhood, the simplicity of the past, and the imaginings of idyllic family harmony.

The spatial mosaic of the Disney theme parks, composed of elements representing various Disney narratives, offers an immense degree of choice. The freedom to choose which sections of the fictional universe to select, for the purpose of immersion, allows fans and patrons to signal preference in a feedback mechanism that influences Disney's marketing decision making process. Freedom of choice in this context is a realization of the connection that exists between the politics of consumerism and that of culture. Recently the Disney company diversified its fictional universe further by acquiring Marvel Comics and Lucasfilm, thus adding to its arsenal of brands and commodities two of the most successful franchises of all times: The Avengers and Star Wars. Physical immersion opportunities to engage with these popular narratives/fictional worlds will no doubt be added to the Disney parks worldwide. These latest acquisitions will further fortify Disney's financial portfolio, but at the same time they offer fans ample chances to partake in much beloved fictional worlds. Princess Leia has finally joined the prestigious club of Disney princesses.

Works Cited

Bakhtin, M. M. "Forms of Time and of the Chronotope in the Novel: Notes Toward a Historical Poetics." *Narrative Dynamics: Essays on Time, Plot, Closure, and Frame*. Ed. Brian Richardson. Columbus: Ohio State University Press, 2002. 15–24. Print.

Baudrillard, Jean. *Simulacra and Simulation*. Ann Arbor: University of Michigan Press, 1994. Print.

Brooks, Peter. "Narrative Desire." *Narrative Dynamics: Essays on Time, Plot, Closure, and Frame*. Ed. Brian Richardson. Columbus: Ohio State University Press, 2002. 130–137. Print.

Budd, Mike. "Introduction: Private Disney, Public Disney." *Rethinking Disney: Private Control, Public Dimensions*. Eds. Mike Budd and Max H. Kirsch. Middletown, CT: Wesleyan University Press, 2005. 1–33. Print.

Friedman, Susan Stanford. "Spatialization: A Strategy for Reading Narrative." *Narrative Dynamics: Essays on Time, Plot, Closure, and Frame*. Ed. Brian Richardson. Columbus: Ohio State University Press, 2002. 217–228. Print.

Hebdige, Dick. "Dis-Gnosis: Disney and the Re-Tooling of Knowledge, Art, Culture, Life, Etcetera." *Rethinking Disney: Private Control, Public Dimensions*. Eds. Mike Budd and Max H. Kirsch. Middletown, CT: Wesleyan University Press, 2005. 37–52. Print.

Hodge, Tim. "Top 10 Ridiculous Disney Movie Flops" *Listverse*. 5 Nov. 2012. Web. 24 Jan. 2013. http://listverse.com/2012/11/05/top-10-ridiculous-disney-movie-flops/.

Jameson, Fredric. *Archaeologies of the Future: The Desire Called Utopia and Other Science Fictions*. New York: Verso, 2005. Print.

Jenkins, Henry. *Fans, Bloggers and Gamers: Exploring Participatory Culture*. New York: New York University Press, 2006. Print.

Marling, Karal Ann, ed. *Designing Disney's Theme Parks: The Architecture of Reassurance*. New York: Flammarion, 1997. Print.

Telotte, J.P. "Science Fiction as 'True Life' Adventure: Disney and the Case of 20,000 Leagues Under the Sea." *Film and History* 40.2 (2010): 66–79. Print.

Tracy, Rayn. "The Business of Magic: How the Disney Marketing Machine Generates Billions." *The Daily Beast*. 3 Nov. 2010. Web. 15 Nov. 2012. http://www.thedailybeast.com/newsweek/2010/11/03/disney-s-powerful-marketing-machine.html.

Ryan, Marie-Laure. *Narrative as Virtual Reality*. Baltimore: John Hopkins University Press, 2001. Print.

Steinberg, Marc. "Anytime, Anywhere: Tetsuwan Atomu Stickers and the Emergence of Character Merchandizing" *Theory, Culture and Society* 26:2–3 (2009): 113–138. Print.

White, Hayden. "The Historical Text as Literary Artifact." *Narrative Dynamics: Essays on Time, Plot, Closure, and Frame.* Ed. Brian Richardson. Columbus: Ohio State University Press, 2002. 191–210. Print.

Wickstrom, Maurya "The Lion King, Mimesis, and Disney's Magical Capitalism." *Rethinking Disney: Private Control, Public Dimensions.* Eds. Mike Budd and Max H. Kirsch. Middletown, CT: Wesleyan University Press, 2005. 99–121. Print.

Chuck Versus the Advertiser

How Fan Activism and Footlong Subway Sandwiches Saved a Television Series

Kristin M. Barton

In February of 2011, actor Nathan Fillion was interviewed by *Entertainment Weekly* and asked about his feelings regarding the short-lived science fiction series that jump-started his career, *Firefly* (2002). During the interview, Fillion stated, "If I got $300 million from the California lottery, the first thing I would do is buy the rights to *Firefly*, make it on my own, and distribute it on the Internet" (Hibberd). Within days, fans of the series took Fillion's comments as a call to arms and launched a website called HelpNathanBuyFirefly.com (later renamed UnstoppableSignals.com) where, within the span of three weeks, fans pledged to donate $1 million to purchase the rights for the show from Fox (Bierly 44). With momentum gaining quickly, Fillion and others close to series creator Joss Whedon cautioned fans that their proposed purchase of the series was impossible and warned fans against sending money to anyone for the purposes of bringing back the show. As this example illustrates, fan communities, acting on behalf of the shows they love, are willing to undertake drastic measures and go to extreme lengths to preserve or revive a beloved television series.

After five seasons on the air, the NBC series *Chuck* (2007–2012) had its series finale on January 27, 2012. While 91 episodes is certainly a respectable run for any series, for *Chuck* it represented an almost improbable feat, one that was made a reality through the continuing efforts of cast members, crew, and fans who fought to keep the show on the air following its second, third, and fourth seasons. Nowhere within the landscape of contemporary television is the heart-felt love of a particular television series (and deep-seated loathing of a network) more apparent than during rumors of cancellation, which was certainly evidenced with *Chuck*. The cancellation of a television series is never something taken lightly by any of the parties involved; networks struggle with issues like the bottom line and profitability, cast and crew enjoy the stable work environment and satisfaction of producing quality television, and fans anguish over the loss of beloved characters and the dissolution of future storylines. But beyond the traditional letter writing campaigns that have become the mainstay of grassroots fan campaigns in the past, devoted fans of *Chuck* began a different kind of campaign, one that could potentially change how fans make their voices heard and revolutionize fan campaigns in the future. Instead of appealing to the network (in this case, NBC), the fans literally put their money where their mouths were and targeted one of the show's biggest advertisers: Subway.

Following a highly successful campaign initiated by fans and strengthened by support from the cast and crew of *Chuck*, the "Finale & Footlong" campaign sought to prevent the cancellation of the series by demonstrating to Subway that if the company helped preserve their beloved series, fans would reciprocate by making sure to buy plenty of sandwiches from the fast food chain. But in addition, fans of *Chuck* would also willingly subject themselves to blatant and sometimes off-putting product placements for Subway, including entire scenes taking place inside Subway restaurants. Casual viewers may have scoffed at the shameless mention and incorporation of Five-Dollar Footlongs during the show's final three seasons, but die-hard fans willingly accepted the arrangement in exchange for more episodes. This type of tacit approval of Subway's integration into *Chuck* could end up being the first in a new model of advertising and sponsorship in the age of the DVR. While this degree of product integration may seem foreign and discordant in modern narrative television, this type of partnership between sponsor and series has roots that go back as far as the development of the medium itself.

Product Placement on Television

Product integration is certainly nothing new to the television industry. In fact, after television began flourishing following World War II, many shows were created and put on the air with the specific purpose of serving as vehicles for advertisers' messages (Cantor and Cantor 18). In an effort to enhance name recognition and favorability among consumers, many sponsors even included their names in the shows' titles, including popular series like *Kraft Television Theatre* (1947–1955), *Texaco Star Theater* (1948–1956), and *The Colgate*

Comedy Hour (1950–1955). Unlike the current spot commercial system in place today, these shows were almost always exclusively paid for by a single sponsor, which entitled them to have their company and products favorably mentioned throughout the show. The thinking behind this approach to advertising was that viewers who enjoyed the program would develop a favorable attitude towards the company that made the show possible, translating into product sales and increased revenues. Even news programming was not completely immune to product placement, as demonstrated by NBC's *Camel News Caravan* (1949–1956). As Turner notes, each nightly news broadcast of the *Camel News Caravan* opened with the proclamation, "The makers of Camel cigarettes bring the world's latest news events right into your living room. Sit back, light up a Camel, and be a witness to the happenings that made history in the last 24 hours. Produced for Camel cigarettes by NBC" (12).

As the single-sponsor system continued to grow during the 1950s, so did the influence the sponsors exerted. This type of advertiser-produced content was so rampant that, "By 1957, more than a third of television programs were created and controlled by advertisers and their agencies" (Turner 11). This system came crashing down in the late 1950s after the revelation that sponsors of popular game shows (most famously *Twenty One* (1956–1958)) were feeding answers to well-liked contestants in order to keep viewers tuning in. Reaction to the now-infamous quiz show scandal was so strong that many people began boycotting the companies that sponsored the corrupt game shows, and by 1960, Congress had passed amendments to the Communications Act of 1934 establishing strict guidelines for how televised game shows could operate. This quickly allowed networks to reassert control over their programming by introducing the current spot commercial system, whereby advertisers would each pay for individual spots to be run during shows rather than paying for entire episodes. However, despite this retooling of the television industry, sponsors continue to exert an immense amount of control over media content, often limiting what kind of content can appear in proximity to their ads and threatening to withhold sponsorship if changes aren't made to objectionable content. Media scholar Mary-Lou Galician notes, "The purported influence is so great that product placement's detractors have sought federal regulation of the practice" (1).

This reemergence of product placement within contemporary primetime television programming (like *Chuck*) can be traced to two distinct events taking place over the last decade. First, with the proliferation and wide-spread dissemination of digital video recorders (DVRs), viewers have taken to zipping past the commercials that, in essence, pay for the program to be broadcast. With DVR penetration reaching over forty-three percent of homes (Stelter), advertisers know their messages are being quickly passed over. To combat this, more and more advertisers are looking to have their products incorporated directly into the shows they sponsor. Some of these product placements have been incorporated subtly and naturally into network shows (all of the computers seen on *The Office* are from HP, one of the show's big sponsors), while others have been more overt, calling attention to themselves by playing at the absurdity of product integration (perhaps most famously in the NBC sitcom *30 Rock*, including a first season episode "Jack-Tor" (1:5) that is rife with Snapple references and the season two episode titled "Somebody to Love" (2:6) when, after discussing the popularity of Verizon phones, Liz Lemon [Tina Fey] looks into the camera and asks, "Can we have our money now?").

The second reason for the increased prevalence of product placement has to do with viewers' overexposure to advertising. Joe Cappo argues in his book *The Future of Advertising* that commercials have less impact today because viewers have begun to mentally filter out advertisers' messages. His argument rests on the notion that media consumers are so inundated with advertisements that we've reached a point of saturation, and as a result, advertising has become less effective because of our overexposure. This means that all advertising begins to blend together and look the same, causing nothing to stand out and viewers to forget the messages being presented. When a novel or innovative idea to advertising emerges, other advertisers are quick to adopt it, leading to more similar-looking commercials. As Cappo succinctly states, this copycat approach to creative ads ultimately leads to the point where "advertising has become more or less homogenized" (88).

In-program product placement serves to eliminate both of these issues at the same time. Obviously, since the products are incorporated into the show, fast-forwarding past them would mean having to miss parts of the story taking place in the episode. In some cases (as with *Chuck*), entire scenes may take place inside an advertiser's store, making exposure to the ads necessary for understanding the events unfolding. Similarly, these ads eliminate the concern that ads begin blending together since, as many television critics and viewers have noted, the incorporation of Subway into *Chuck* gained significant attention. One would be hard pressed to forget the blatant corporate tie-ins that were worked into the storylines over three seasons. While it may be obtrusive and remove viewers from their immersion into the show, it certainly achieves the goal of being memorable.

These issues have brought about a return to advertiser-sponsored content and product placement within primetime network television, most notably and seamlessly over the last few years among reality-based programming. The incorporation of a Snickers bar on *Survivor* or watching the *Extreme Makeover: Home Edition* designers shopping for bedding at Sears seems like a much more natural fit than the heavy-handed type of product placement that *Chuck* became infamous for. While Subway's presence on *Chuck* was undeniably overt, many may be surprised to find that the number of mentions was relatively minimal compared to many other shows on television at the time. In an article titled "Is TV Selling Out?" in the February 6, 2012 issue of *TV Guide*, Schneider reports that *Chuck* wasn't even in the top ten shows with the most instances of product placement in 2011 (6). The article reveals that *American Idol* contained the most instances of product placement (577 instances), with *The Amazing Race* rounding out the top ten with 161 instances. In fact, of the top ten shows featuring product placement, nine fall under the Reality TV genre (the NBC drama *Friday Night Lights* was the only scripted program to make the list at number eight with 201 instances). In many cases, the exuberant number of product mentions has been the impetus that has kept faltering series on the air when traditional methods could not.

The Evolution of Fan Campaigns for TV Shows

While not always effective, letter writing campaigns have served as the cornerstone for grassroots fan movements to save endangered television series since the medium's debut. In the 1960s, fans of the original *Star Trek* series (1966–1969) launched what could be considered one of the first successful fan campaign to save a television show by rousing support from thousands of loyal Trekkers to help campaign for the show's third season. As Cochran notes, "Probably the first fan activists, Trekkers took to the streets and also flooded the network with letters when the show was slated for cancellation" (245). *Star Trek* creator Gene Roddenberry even helped orchestrate some early guerrilla marketing tactics by supplying one fan with bumper stickers to distribute in the NBC offices at 30 Rockefeller Center after helping the fan sneak into the building (Shatner 251–253). Another example of a successful fan campaign, the CBS crime drama *Cagney & Lacey* (1981–1988) was brought back from cancellation by fan support and a letter writing campaign initiated by the show's executive producer Barney Rosenzweig. After initially being cancelled and revived following its first season, the series was cancelled a second time following its second season in 1983 due to low ratings and mixed audience reaction to having two female leads. The fans' letter writing campaign (coupled with Tyne Daly's Emmy win) convinced CBS to bring the show back from cancellation again in 1984.

But television fans have become savvier over time and understand that the letter writing campaigns of old no longer have the effect they once did, as executives can't possibly sit down to read every piece of mail that lands on their desks. With that knowledge, fans have had to adapt and become creative in how they enact their campaigns to save faltering television series. Indeed, some fans have come to recognize that the media attention garnered from their efforts can have a larger effect than if the executives actually read their letters at all. To explore this phenomenon further, there are a number of examples from the past decade that have highlighted the innovative approach fans have taken (with mixed degrees of success) to avert cancellation.

In the fall of 2002, fans of the Fox series *Firefly*, sensing cancellation was inevitable for the fledgling show, began what could be seen as a traditional fan campaign, encouraging anyone who loved the series to send letters and postcards to Fox President Gail Berman letting her know how important the show was to them. But as the situation became more dire and fans (along with cast and crew) sensed the end approaching, a new fan campaign was started that aimed at raising money to promote the show to a wider audience. Fans responded with open wallets, and their efforts paid for an ad to be run in the trade magazine *Variety* on December 9, 2002, which specifically thanked the show's creative team, Fox executives, and acknowledged forty three individual sponsors by name. This type of ad, reminiscent of similar "For Your Consideration" ads that populate entertainment trade magazines during award seasons, was intended by the fans to raise awareness of both the show itself and the dedication of its fans. The show was officially cancelled four days later on December 13, 2002, but the fans' enthusiasm was instrumental in getting the film sequel *Serenity* (2005) made at Universal three years later. While unsuccessful in keeping *Firefly* on the air, their coordinated efforts showed that passionate fans could mobilize and act quickly, a practice that would become more prominent in many fan campaigns to come. This new, non-traditional type of fan campaign, intended to get network executive's attention, would become a trend that many fan communities would emulate over the coming years, including fans of the CW series *Veronica Mars* (2004–2007) who paid to fly a banner over the CW's Los Angeles headquarters on May 9, 2006 (the same day that the second season's finale aired), fans of the vampire-themed *Moonlight* (2007–2008) who organized blood drives across the country, and the *Everwood* (2002–2006) fan community, which rented a Ferris wheel and positioned it near the WB's offices. While these publicity stunts generated a fair amount of press, they ultimately proved largely ineffective at convincing network executives to renew the series (of the above, only *Veronica Mars* remained on the air). Other fan communities attempted similar non-traditional campaigns that sought to demonstrate a more tangible benefit to the network, like fans of the ABC series *October Road* (2007–2008), who donated DVD sets of the show's first season to libraries across the country in an attempt to attract more fans by making the first season more accessible as well as increase DVD sales in order to justify a third season (which would never come to be).

What these publicity stunts on behalf of the shows taught fans was that they needed to appeal to the networks' biggest concern (the bottom line) and that the various public relations campaigns were having minimal effects. With this awareness, fan campaigns began devising new ways to reach executives *directly* with their message. To this end, a simple question was put forth in many fan circles: If sending letters wasn't having an impact on keeping a series on the air, what could the fans send that *would* have an impact? To bring more attention to their campaigns than letters alone could provide, many campaigns began mailing products representative or symbolic of their shows to network executives, the thinking being that the effort required to purchase a product and ship it to the network indicated a higher level of both consumerism (on behalf of the show) and devotion. What follows is a by no means an exhaustive list, but it highlights the creativity and determination of some fan groups.

Roswell (1999–2002)
  In 2000, following declining ratings, fans sent 6,000 mini bottles of Tobasco sauce (a favorite of *Roswell*'s resident aliens) to UPN executives. The series remained on the air for two additional seasons.

Farscape (1999–2003)
  When the formerly-named Sci-Fi Channel announced it would not renew the popular Friday night series because of high production costs and declining ratings, female fans sent cookies and bras to the network to highlight the show's appeal to women as well as men. While ultimately cancelled, the network did produce a four-hour miniseries to wrap up lingering storylines.

Veronica Mars (2004–2007)
  After the "Cloud Watching" flyover campaign of the previous season and other campaigns (which included sending CW executives postcards and Photoshopped two-dollar bills), the final *Veronica Mars* campaign consisted of sending approximately 10,000 Mars bars to the network after the third season. The CW cancelled the show shortly afterward.

Arrested Development (2003–2006)
  Despite its critical acclaim, the Fox comedy had difficulty finding an audience and saw fewer episodes produced each year during its three seasons on the air. Following its cancellation in 2006, loyal fans sent fake bananas to Fox (a reference to the banana stand owned and operated by the show's main characters). Fox did not renew the series, but in 2011 Netflix announced that it would begin production on new episodes of the series as part of their entry into the original programming market.

The 4400 (2004–2007)

The USA Network series was cancelled after its fourth season despite a cliffhanger, leaving fans unsatisfied and with unanswered questions. Fans sent 6,000 bags of sunflower seeds (regularly consumed by one of the show's popular recurring characters) to USA Network and NBC executives, but the series remained cancelled.

Jericho (2006–2008)

In honor of the proclamation "Nuts!" made by the show's main character in the season one finale, fans of the CBS drama sent more than twenty tons of nuts to CBS Entertainment president Nina Tassler after word came down that a second season would not be produced. In response, Tassler released a statement announcing the show's return, thanking fans for their dedication, and concluded with the line, "P.S. Please stop sending us nuts :)"

Kyle XY (2006–2009)

After ABC Family announced that the teen science fiction series would not return for a fourth season in 2009, a fan campaign was started to send Sour Patch Kids (the titular character's favorite treat) to the network. The campaign proved unsuccessful, and the show remained cancelled.

Journeyman (2007)

In perhaps one of the more far-reaching campaigns to date, boxes of Rice-A-Roni were sent to NBC executives as a reference to the show's setting (San Francisco). But with a fifty percent drop in ratings over the course of its initial thirteen episode run, the campaign did not manage to change the network's cancellation order.

Reaper (2007–2009)

Following the Writers Guild strike of 2007–2008 and mediocre ratings during its first season, series lead Bret Harrison encouraged fans to send socks to the CW offices (in honor of the show's comedic standout character, Bert "Sock" Wysocki). Although the series was not officially cancelled at the time the campaign was launched, the preemptive campaign had a positive effect and the CW announced the show would return for a second season the following year.

These examples stand out against a field of similar campaigns, ultimately producing mixed results. But as these types of campaigns become more and more common, executives have started to become numb to the deluge of symbolic products that fans send. As noted on the website TelevisionWithout Pity.com, "After *Jericho*, networks have basically ignored campaigns that involve food as a plea" (Bellotto). And while fan campaigns for *Chuck* arose that attempted to mirror previous campaigns (sending letters, donating money to the American Heart Association on behalf of NBC, and calling for fans to send Nerds candies to executives), it was ultimately an idea sparked by an episode late in the show's second season that would prove to be the series' saving grace. The idea was simple: get a message to the show's sponsors that their advertising was working. If the point of advertising is to reach customers and increase sales in exchange for their sponsorship, then fans were willing to make it explicit that they would hold up their end of that bargain. After seeing Subway featured prominently in an episode of the show, fans rallied together and launched the "Finale & Footlong" campaign, where fans would descend upon Subway shops across the country (and globe) on April 27, 2009 (the night of *Chuck*'s second season finale) to show their support by actively and publicly purchasing Subway sandwiches. As *Time* columnist James Poniewozik noted, "Four million people who watch a show *really hard* are still just four million people to an ad buyer. Unless they spend money."

Fans used social media to schedule meet-ups and arrived together *en masse*, often documenting their experiences and uploading them to social networking sites and YouTube. At the most publicized of these events, Chuck himself (actor Zachary Levi) led over 300 fans to a Subway in Birmingham, England, where he was appearing at a convention. Levi even jumped behind the counter to help the beleaguered and overwhelmed Subway employees prepare sandwiches for the hundreds of fans in tow, ensuring that photos and videos would be uploaded to hundreds of fan sites before the night ended. While Levi may have been the face of the campaign, other members of the cast and crew rallied support for the cause as well. Three days before the season two finale, series co-star Ryan McPartlin (who played Chuck's eventual brother-in-law Devon Woodcomb) wrote to GiveMeMyRemote.com founder and editor Kath Skerry, saying in part that, "you guys are the best fans ever and personally, I'm going to put your ideas into action on Monday and have a "SAVE CHUCK" party with a bunch of $5 footlongs from Subway." Even series co-creator Josh Schwartz commented that the campaign "shows a real sophistication on the part of the viewer" (Flint). While those involved with making the show certainly had an easier time getting their message to the public, the fans continued to make it known that they were willing to become loyal consumers in exchange for a third season. TV entertainment websites like the aforementioned GiveMeMyRemote.com encouraged viewers to "Fill out a comment card and let Subway know you support them because they support Chuck." Fans were also encouraged to take photos of themselves with footlong subs and send them in to an online gallery, which collected and displayed hundreds of photos from fans across the country and around the world.

To the credit of everyone involved, *Chuck* was officially renewed for a thirteen-episode third season by NBC on May 17, 2009, which was eventually expanded to nineteen episodes. Not only did the campaign work as intended, but it actually resulted in a sharp spike in sandwich sales for the fast food chain. As reported on TVWeek.com, "According to two people familar [*sic*] with the situation, Subway's internal tracking of the *Chuck* promotion was off the charts. One source labeled it the best such product placement the restaurant chain has done 'in several years'" (Adalian). In what may have been the clincher that ultimately saved *Chuck*, the website also notes that Subway marketing officer Tony Pace "was so impressed with *Chuck*'s impact on sandwich sales, he actually called a top NBC ad sales executive to let him know just how much Subway loved the Chuckster. What's more, Pace told NBC the company hoped the network decided to renew *Chuck* for another season."

The Results of a Successful Fan Campaign

Even with all the attention focused on product placement in the show, it still pales in comparison to the volume advertisers' products have been appearing in other shows. As mentioned above, *Chuck* didn't even crack the top ten shows in 2011 in terms of amount of product tie-ins contained in a network series. For *Chuck*, the instances of product placement were less concerned with *quantity* (the number of times the Subway logo appeared on screen), and more concerned with *quality* (the reverence Subway products were awarded by the characters in the show). Rather than pepper the Buy More set with Subway cups in the background, *Chuck* brought the sandwich shop to the forefront, often writing entire scenes around Subway products. In the episode "Chuck Versus the Final Exam" (3:11), after Buy More employees Jeff (Scott Krinsky) and Lester (Vik Sahay) are physically assaulted by undercover spy John Casey (Adam Baldwin), the store's manager arranges a meeting that he hopes will prevent the litigious duo from suing Casey. When the location for the meeting is revealed as a Subway restaurant, angelic music plays as the camera lingers on the storefront logo, beginning an almost two-and-a-half-minute scene that takes place in the restaurant, adorned with multiple Subway logos appearing in every shot and culminating with Casey enjoying a bite of a freshly made sandwich.

The above example brings the discussion to one of the more obvious (but easily overlooked) aspects of Subway's incorporation into the series: the storylines that contained mentions of Subway were the more comedic aspects of the show, and never the more serious dramatic or action-intensive threads (never was there an episode where Chuck was sent to a starving third world country, only to save the day by bringing Meatball Marinara subs to the masses). Since the Subway mentions were unabashedly silly and done almost tongue in cheek, the scenes most prominently featuring Subway products were naturally the humorous parts of the show revolving around the comic-relief characters that inhabited the Buy More. For example, when a computer virus threatens to erase every hard drive in the world, Chuck's best friend and *de facto* spy Morgan Grimes (Joshua Gomez), along with Casey, offer the computer-savvy Buy More employees Jeff and Lester anything they want in exchange for their help stopping it ("Chuck Versus the Santa Suit," 5:07). After Jeff and Lester's initial reluctance to get involved, the scene plays out as follows:

MORGAN: Name your price.
LESTER: (To Jeff) I got this. (To Morgan) I would like a ... (pause) ... six inch Classic Italian BMT from Subway. Boom!
JEFF: I was going to say a trip to the Bahamas.
MORGAN: Subway. Done. I'll make it a footlong.
LESTER: Nice! Make mine flatbread, boys!

When the story returns to Jeff and Lester less than four minutes later, a Subway employee is serving the duo sandwiches and coffee at their Buy More work-space. This scene serves as a coda to the Subway commercial within the episode, with the two exchanging a few last comments before they get to work on the virus:

JEFF: (Being handed his sandwich) Mmm. Twelve inches of bubbly cheese, spicy pepperoni and ham.
LESTER: You really should try the Fresh Fit option. No offense.

While this example may seem extreme, it actually serves as fairly representative of the type of mentions Subway was given during the show's latter three seasons. When Big Mike (Mark Christopher Lawrence) is kidnapped by the Buy More's retail rival (Large Mart), he attempts to assuage his employees' fears during a phone call ("Chuck Versus the Muuurder" 4:19). After confirming he's fine, Big Mike tells Morgan:

BIG MIKE: And anyway, I'm having a nice time. They brought in Subway flatbread breakfast sandwiches.
MORGAN (on the phone): Steak, Egg & Cheese ones?
BIG MIKE: With chipotle southwest sauce.

As the series wrapped up, *Chuck* made sure to include one last plug for the sandwich chain in the series finale, "Chuck Versus the Goodbye" (5:13). With less than eight minutes to go before the series ended forever, a lighted Subway sign is raised within the Buy More and Big Mike casually notes that a "new owner's moving in," a less-than-subtle nod to the relationship the restaurant had with the show for the past three seasons. Not surprisingly, despite the sign appearing on screen for only four seconds, it managed to get mentioned in a majority of the reviews and summaries the following day, once again highlighting how impactful these product placements proved to be.

These instances of incorporation into the series may have seemed jarring and even absurd, but they were unquestionably effective in promoting the fast food franchise. Every mention of "delicious Footlongs" and Fresh Fit meals served to expose the audience to an ad that very likely would have been skipped were it a traditional commercial. As *Ad Age* columnist Brian Steinberg observed, "Getting a character to repeat the company's ad slogan is tantamount to turning "Chuck" for even the briefest of moments into a bona fide Subway commercial" ("Subway Places"). The show came up with interesting ways to incorporate products into episodes, and could almost be seen as a pioneer in the field of blatant product placements. It was even thought for a while that *Chuck*'s leading lady Sarah (Yvonne Strahovski), who is seen on the show for a time working undercover at a fast food restaurant called Wienerlicious, might spend at least one season as a sandwich artist as a more natural way to incorporate Subway into the series. Alas, Sarah never donned the Subway uniform.

Conclusion

While it is important to acknowledge the tremendous impact that fans of *Chuck* had in keeping their show on the air, that isn't to say that other factors weren't involved in NBC's decision to keep the show running as long as it did. Linda Holmes, columnist for NPR.org, suggests that shows like *Chuck* and *Friday Night Lights* remained on the air as an altruistic gesture from NBC, who needed all the goodwill they could get following fans' outrage at the 2010 *The Tonight Show* debacle that resulted in Conan O'Brien's firing. Holmes also notes that the failure and cancellation of *The Jay Leno Show* in 2010 left five hours of primetime network airtime empty each week, suggesting that keeping an under-performing show like *Chuck* was a numbers game: it was better for NBC to stick with a show that a modest number of fans liked than replace it with a show with the potential to flop.

While not many in number, the fans of *Chuck* utilized every weapon at their disposal to let the television industry know that there were people out there who cared and that they were willing to buy plenty of Subway sandwiches to prove it. This type of creative approach to fan campaigns has the potential to revolutionize how fans interact with the shows they love and how networks approach product placement for shows on the verge of cancellation. TV editor for *Advertising Age* Brian Steinberg notes of this type of in-program product placement, "TV networks have seemed more willing to break old conventions in recent years, but their experiments don't always bear fruit" ("Why the Subway"). Only time will tell if this new model will prove more effective at keeping shows on the air than earlier letter writing campaigns, but one thing is certain: fans are becoming more astute at figuring out how the television industry works and how to take a measure of control when it comes to the shows they love.

Works Cited

Adalian, Josef. "Subway: Good Night, and Good 'Chuck.'" *TVWeek.com*. 27 Apr. 2009. Web. 12 Apr 2012. http://www.tvweek.com/tvmojoe/2009/04/subway-good-night-and-good-chu.php.

Bellotto, Rebecca. ""Save Our Show: Fan Campaigns That Worked (And Lots That Didn't)." *TelevisionWithoutPity.com*. 28 Apr. 2009. Web. 6 Mar. 2011. http://www.televisionwithoutpity.com/brilliantbutcancelled/2009/04/save-our-show-fan-campaigns-th.php.

Bierly, Mandi. "Nathan Fillion: Geek God." *Entertainment Weekly* 25 Mar. 2011: 38–45. Print.

Cantor, Muriel G., and Joel M. Cantor. *Prime-Time Television: Content and Control*, 2d ed. Beverly Hills: Sage, 1992. Print.

Cochran, Tanya R. "The Browncoats Are Coming! *Firefly, Serenity*, and Fan Activism." *Investigating* Firefly *and* Serenity: *Science Fiction on the Frontier*. Eds. Rhonda V. Wilcox and Tanya R. Cochran. London: I.B. Tauris, 2008. 239–249. Print.

Flint, Joe. "Can Twitter and Subway save 'Chuck'?" *Los Angeles Times*. 22 Apr. 2009. Web. 16 Mar. 2012. http://latimesblogs.latimes.com/showtracker/2009/04/can-twitter-and-subway-save-chuck.html.

Galician, Mary-Lou. "Introduction: Product Placements in the Mass Media: Unholy Marketing Marriages or Realistic Story-Telling Portrayals, Unethical Advertising Messages or Useful Communication Practices?" *Handbook of Product Placement in the Mass Media: New Strategies in Marketing Theory, Practice, Trends, and Ethics*. Ed. Mary-Lou Galician. Binghamton, NY: Best Business Books, 2004. 1–8. Print.

Hibberd, James. "'Firefly' Returning to Cable; Fillion Says He'd Play Mal Again." *Entertainment Weekly*. 17 Feb. 2011. Web. 7 Mar. 2012. http://insidetv.ew.com/2011/02/17/firefly-returns/.

Holmes, Linda. "Farewell to an Unlikely Hero: Why 'Chuck' Packed Such A Potent Punch." *NPR.org*. 27 Jan. 2012. Web. 18 Feb. 2012. http://www.npr.org/blogs/monkeysee/2012/01/27/145986575/farewell-to-an-unlikely-hero-why-chuck-packed-such-a-potent-punch?sc=tw.

Poniewozik, James. "Saving Chuck: Don't Applaud, Throw Money." *Time.com*. 23 Apr. 2009. Web. 18 Mar. 2012. http://entertainment.time.com/2009/04/23/saving-chuck-dont-applaud-throw-money/.

Schneider, Michael. "Is TV Selling Out?" *TV Guide* 60.7 (2012): 6–7. Print.

Shatner, William. *Star Trek Memories*. New York: HarperCollins, 1993. Print.

Skerry, Kath. "CHUCK's Ryan McPartlin Is ... Awesome!" *GiveMeMyRemote.com*. 24 Apr. 2009. Web. 12 Apr. 2012. http://www.givememyremote.com/remote/2009/04/24/chucks-ryan-mcpartlin-isawesome/.

Steinberg, Brian. "Subway Places More Than Just Product in NBC's 'Chuck.'" *Advertising Age*. 16 Apr. 2009. Web. 18 Feb. 2012. http://adage.com/article/madisonvine-news/subway-places-product-nbc-s-chuck/136036/.

_____. "Why the Subway-'Chuck' Deal Doesn't Rewrite TV Formula." *Advertising Age*. 8 Jan. 2010. Web. 18 Feb. 2012. http://adage.com/article/mediaworks/television-chuck-subway-deal-point-tv-model/141345/.

Stelter, Brian. "On Sundays, the DVR Runneth Over." *New York Times*. 19 Apr. 2012. Web. 23 Apr. 2012. http://www.nytimes.com/2012/04/20/arts/television/on-sundays-the-dvr-runneth-over.html.

Turner, Kathleen J. "Insinuating the Product into the Message: An Historical Context for Product Placement." *Handbook of Product Placement in the Mass Media: New Strategies in Marketing Theory, Practice, Trends, and Ethics*. Ed. Mary-Lou Galician. Binghamton, NY: Best Business Books, 2004. 9–14. Print.

"Guys, where are we?"

Podcasts, Online Video and
Lost's Participatory Culture

Michael Graves

Premiering in 2004, the ABC television series *Lost* focused on a group of plane crash survivors stranded on an enigmatic island inhabited by warring demigods, a group of nefarious island natives, and a defunct scientific research organization. In response to the mysterious qualities of the island depicted in the series' pilot episode, one of the survivors ominously asks his fellow castaways, "Guys, where are we?" ("Pilot, Part 2"). Given that *Lost*'s six-year run (2004–2010) coincided with a confluence of significant technological, industrial, and cultural shifts challenging, reconfiguring, and even reinforcing normative understandings of producer-audience relationships, producers and fans may be asking themselves the same question. Capitalizing on the engagement potentials afforded by new media technologies, producers now actively invite fans to participate in the production of media properties. Yet courting audiences through participatory strategies can have consequences seemingly unintended by media producers, ultimately giving way to conflict when fans perceive that their participation is not valued by producers. This essay examines two *Lost* podcasts, *The Official Lost Podcast* and *The Transmission*, in order to explore the often uneasy relationship between producers and participatory fans fostered by the advent of podcast technology, shifting post-network era engagement strategies, and the rise of an increasingly communicative relationship between media producers and fans.

Beginning in the mid–2000s, the post-network era is characterized by a fragmentation of the television audience due to a substantial increase in content choices as well as a gradual shift toward more self-determined viewing behaviors facilitated by digital technologies (Lotz 15–19). As such, podcasts are now a crucial component of post-network era engagement strategies, in which the creation of a producer-audience dialogue serves producers' economic aims in a fractured and competitive televisual marketplace. For instance, *Lost*'s executive producers, Damon Lindelof and Carlton Cuse, used *The Official Lost Podcast* as a way to communicate with fans in an effort to build and maintain a fan base. By encouraging fan feedback and responding directly to fans, Lindelof and Cuse facilitated the creation of a participatory culture as well as a heightened connection between producers and fans. However, Lindelof and Cuse's validation of fan feedback on *The Official Lost Podcast* fostered notions of fan agency in *Lost*'s television series, prompting fans to challenge producers and even dictate the direction of the narrative.

In addition, the use of online narrative extensions is becoming integral to televisual storytelling in the post-network era, as by 2006, television networks expanded media properties over an average of four digital and analog platforms (Johnson 67). Original, online content functions as a way to simultaneously promote a television series and strengthen the text-audience bond by providing viewers with prolonged access to a storyworld. Yet as the boundary of a television series expands, so too, does the potential for tension between producers and fans. For example, among fans of *The Transmission*, the inconsistencies present in *Lost*'s transmedia narrative fostered feelings of being exploited or duped by the producers. Produced by husband and wife *Lost* fans Ryan and Jen Ozawa, *The Transmission* became one of the most popular *Lost* podcasts as ranked by iTunes. In fact, *The New York Times* profiled the Ozawas in 2010, highlighting their status within *Lost*'s fan culture (Wilson). *The Transmission* focused on comprehending *Lost*'s transmedia storyworld, with the discourse frequently centering on the notion of canon formation in a manner reflecting notions of trust (or lack thereof) in Lindelof and Cuse's ability to provide fans with a satisfying experience.

Thus, as television producers and fans use podcasts as a way to engage with audiences outside of a series' broadcast and extend the fan experience, they increasingly become the platform on which these groups negotiate the value of participation in fan cultures. Whereas previous scholarship (Benkler, 2006; Jenkins 2006; Bruns, 2008) often forwards an optimism regarding the utopian and democratic potentials offered by audience participation and new media technologies, an examination of *The Official Lost Podcast* and *The Transmission* highlights the often disruptive qualities of online, participatory cultures.

Podcasts as an Engagement Strategy

The use of podcasts as engagement tools is indicative of a larger transformation within the media industries toward an increasingly communicative producer-audience relationship. From television producers and filmmakers to novelists, communicative audience outreach through new media technologies provides producers with opportunities to strengthen affinity bonds with consumers (Shefrin, 2004; Murray, 2004; Andrejevic, 2008; Weber, 2009). In particular, "dialogue branding"—the creation of a producer-audience oral discourse as part of a brand experience—has become an effective strategy for media producers. Dialogue branding strengthens audience loyalty by forging an intimate bond that extends the brand identity beyond a media property and onto the producer as well. For instance, in a 2011 *New Yorker* article, Random House editor Anne Groelle contends, "Outreach and building community with readers is the single most important thing you can do for your book these days. You need to make them feel *invested* in your career" (qtd. in Miller 32). Groelle's declaration highlights the economic benefits of producer-audience communication. As my analysis of *The Official Lost Podcast* will illustrate, an investment is given in the hopes of a return, with fans anticipating that their participation will be valued and rewarded by producers.

Beginning during the second season of *Lost* in 2005, ABC debuted *The Official Lost Podcast*, hosted by executive producers Damon Lindelof and Carlton Cuse. In *The Official Lost Podcast*, Lindelof and Cuse emphasized significant details of previous episodes, responded to fan-submitted questions, and previewed upcoming episodes. In addition, the producers shared exclusive details about *Lost*'s creative development, including frank discussions about the difficulties of producing the television series. ABC's use of *The Official Lost Podcast*, therefore, is an example of an "increasing willingness to disseminate usually highly guarded production information ... in the interests of sophisticated viral marketing and audience development schemes" (Murray 8). By responding to submitted feedback—often addressing fans by name—and by sharing behind-the-scenes details centering on the production of *Lost*, Cuse and Lindelof facilitated the perception of an intimate producer-audience bond. Consider for example, the following exchange between a fan and Cuse on *The Official Lost Podcast* in regards to a storyline inconsistency:

> NICK: [C]an you tell us whether that was intentional or a "whoopsie?"
> CARLTON CUSE: I mean, we don't do this thing in the abstract. J.K. Rowling has the great luxury and privilege of being utterly in control of all the characters in her universe, but we do our show in collaboration with four hundred other people, and for a variety of reasons ... that story branch ... kind of fell out of the tree [11 May 2009].

Hence, listeners of *The Official Lost Podcast* were privy to secret "insider" information otherwise unknown to the general audience. Lindelof and Cuse furthered an insider/outsider dynamic with fans through a series of recurring in-jokes, code words, and references featured in the podcast. Two frequent in-jokes, for instance, centered on Cuse's alleged banjo-playing skills and the notion that Cuse did not wear pants during the recording of the podcast. The producers also used secret code words when discussing the season finales with fans and playfully referenced the production of a seventh "zombie season" of the television series.

While this participatory culture was economically advantageous to ABC and *Lost*'s producers, with *Lost*'s audience increasing by seventeen percent from the previous year after Lindelof and Cuse began podcasting and ABC made previous episodes available on iTunes (Grossman), Lindelof and Cuse's validation of fan feedback on *The Official Lost Podcast* fostered notions of fan agency. As early as the fifth episode of *The Official Lost Podcast* in 2005, fans questioned their role in influencing the production of the series, as the following exchange between a fan and Lindelof suggests:

> LOSTCASTS: How much does the speculation from your fans ... change or affect the writing of the show?
> DAMON LINDELOF: We are very interested ... in what the fans are thinking about the show, and ... what theories they come up with and what they're responding to [28 Nov. 2005].

Lindelof's response is noncommittal, expressing a vague "interest" in what fans are "responding to" but stopping short of specifically addressing how fan speculation influences *Lost*. Moreover, Lindelof's response is unsurprising given that fans increasingly relate to television programs through the social networking facilitated by the Internet and new media technologies (Ross 174). The validation of this feedback, therefore, represents an audience-building strategy by forging a producer-audience bond as well.

By directly addressing fans on *The Official Lost Podcast*, Lindelof and Cuse promote a more sustained and personal producer-fan-text connection. In this way, reinforcing the notion that fan discussion and speculation are important to *Lost*'s producers can be seen as a strategic move — one in which dialogue branding provides Cuse and Lindelof with greater insight into a wide range of audience data. Yet, *Lost*'s producers went beyond simply paying lip service to participatory fans. Later in the same podcast, for example, Lindelof explicitly acknowledges how fan feedback influences creative decisions on *Lost*, offering the following analogy:

> DAMON LINDELOF: The equivalent is imagine if ... I critiqued everything that you did in the course of a day: "I can't believe you got a double-latte at Starbucks! That's idiotic! Those things are bad for you!" That's probably going to affect your purchases the next day [28 Nov. 2005].

Lindelof's frank declaration was the first indication, within the discourse of *The Official Lost Podcast*, of fan feedback's power to directly affect the production of the series. Interestingly, while highlighting how fan feedback — specifically negative criticism — influences future decision-making, Lindelof's remarks also, in effect, reinforced the voicing of such complaints. In short, *The Official Lost Podcast* functioned as a feedback loop in which fan speculation, evaluation, and criticism worked its way back into the television series. The more "noise" or "interference" made by fans, the more significantly fans could affect the television series' signal.

The issue of fan influence persisted throughout *Lost*'s second season, culminating with the following exchange at the 2006 *Lost* Comic-Con panel:

> FAN 2: [B]ecause of how huge your internet following is, you guys pretty much have immediate access to a ton of fan feedback. And I was just wondering how much influence, if any, you feel that should have on the creative process.
> CARLTON CUSE: You know ... *it does have influence....* [W]e tried to answer more questions in the season two finale, and *that was in direct response to internet feedback* [31 July 2006, emphasis added].

Lindelof continued:

> DAMON LINDELOF: *[T]he fans always determine the barometer.* You know, it's the Goldilocks thing — where the porridge is always either too hot or too cold, but it's never just right. And the fans are really there to tell us, you know, to temperature gauge it, because we're wrapped in our little cocoon in the show, and there's no one there to say, "Stop! Go back" other than *the most loyal fans, who are on the Net* [31 July 2006, emphasis added].

Cuse and Lindelof attempt to create a sense of belonging and community — one engineered by Internet and podcast technologies — by empowering "loyal" fans to actively communicate with the producers and thereby maintain the series' high artistic quality. However, this empowerment ultimately resulted in the contestation of the producers' authorial power centering on the narrative of the television series. As a result, the participatory cultures of both *The Official Lost Podcast* and *The Transmission* became "cultures of complaint" in which fan criticism reflected a desire to intervene in the production of *Lost* (Rowe, Ruddock, and Hutchins 298–299).

The negative fan reaction centering on the introduction of two new characters, Nikki and Paulo, in *Lost*'s third season illustrates how the creation of a producer-audience discourse ultimately allows fans to challenge producers when a narrative is not presented in a satisfying fashion. Whereas the previous two seasons of *Lost* focused almost exclusively on a core group of characters, *Lost*'s producers introduced Nikki and Paulo in an effort to shed light on the other survivors who were previously depicted only in the background. Notably, Nikki and Paulo's very appearance on the series resulted from fan feedback, as Lindelof explained on *The Official Lost Podcast*: "People were kind of curious about ... the other castaways that we never heard from ... so we basically came up with this idea for Nikki and Paulo" (21 Sept. 2007). Although the appearance of Nikki and Paulo sprung from a desire to satisfy audience curiosity for stories centering on characters outside of *Lost*'s principal cast, the fan reaction to Nikki and Paulo was overwhelmingly negative. Fans derided Nikki and Paulo's clumsy introduction as well as the narrative focus on storylines that had little to do with the series' main characters or core mythology — what Jason Mittell defines as a "highly elaborate plot that endlessly delays resolution and closure" (33). One fan expressed her dissatisfaction with the new characters in the following way on *The Official Lost Podcast*:

> MS. DIANE: I don't understand the purpose of [Nikki and Paulo].... [S]eriously, *what does this have to do with anything?* I am so frustrated [16 Apr. 2007, emphasis added].

As this response suggests, fans expressed contempt for Nikki and Paulo stemming from the characters' irrelevance to the core characters, as well as their tangential connection to the television series' central storylines. Additionally, Nikki and Paulo did not meet the taste standards of *The Official Lost Podcast* and *The Transmission*'s fan cultures. Whereas fans generally lauded *Lost* as a series with compelling characters, fans regarded Nikki and Paulo's characterization as significantly weaker. One of the co-hosts of *The Transmission* perhaps best conveyed the fan reaction to Nikki and Paulo.

> JEN OZAWA: [i]nstantly, the most hideous, awful, annoying characters [in] the history of TV ["Season Three: Episodes 1–3"].

Ozawa's assessment was indicative of the larger fan response to Nikki and Paulo. For instance, fans regarded Nikki and Paulo as "unlikable," "obnoxious," "dull," "jokey," and "a waste" ("Season Three: Episodes 1–3"). Using the participatory potentials provided by *The Official Lost Podcast*, fans demanded Nikki and Paulo's removal from the series:

> I LIKE LOCKE: If you're too busy trying to decide, just write Paulo's death and make it a quick one.... *In fact, we don't even need to see how he dies. Just let us know if he did die* [12 Feb. 2007, emphasis added].

Summing up the fan response to Nikki and Paulo on *The Official Lost Podcast*, Lindelof noted, "[T]he moment that we introduced them, you know, the fan community and audience at large basically cried foul" [21 Sept. 2007].

Lost's producers responded to Nikki and Paulo's negative reception during the same season in which the characters first appeared, and the swiftness of Nikki and Paulo's removal from the television series was indicative of the power of the participatory producer-audience relationship. The backlash centering on Nikki and Paulo coincided with ABC's new scheduling strategy for *Lost*, splitting the third season into two parts separated by a three-month gap between the sixth and seventh episodes. The implementation of this strategy stemmed from a desire to eliminate the frequent reruns that annoyed fans during the first and second seasons of *Lost* (Littleton). ABC's scheduling strategy also had the unexpected outcome of allowing Cuse and Lindelof to effectively revise their plans for Nikki and Paulo, during the production of the third season, based on the response from fans. Bowing to fan pressure, Cuse and Lindelof abruptly ended Nikki and Paulo's arc on *Lost*, as they indicated in *The Official Lost Podcast*:

> CARLTON CUSE: You know, we had sort of bigger plans for what we were gonna do with them, but then, you know ... *we heard a lot* [from fans] *about how we were neglecting our regular characters.*
>
> DAMON LINDELOF: So we began to come up with an *alternate plan* to basically cram all the story we had come up with them, and deal with it and resolve it in a faster and more timely manner.
>
> CC: And by "alternate plan," he means *back-pedaling.*
>
> DL: *We're not too proud of ourselves to know when something that we tried didn't work exactly* (21 Sept. 2007, emphasis added).

Cuse and Lindelof's discussion suggests "the replacement of the controlling author with a regulating community" of participatory fans (White 136). Although such a move may appear, on the surface, to erode the producers' power, the creation of an "alternate plan" for Nikki and Paulo resulting from fans' negative feedback also represents a savvy business move. As Alan Wexelblat maintains, producer-audience communication is a way to cater to fans while simultaneously reinforcing "old models of authorial power" (225). In other words, although Lindelof and Cuse frequently couched fan feedback within the rhetoric of audience empowerment and quality control, the roots of such a strategy lie in the economic sphere. For example, in an interview with *The New York Times*, Cuse discussed Nikki and Paulo's death as "an acknowledgment of the audience" and fans' power to "influenc[e] the course of the narrative" ("Looking Back on 'Lost'"). However, responding to negative fan feedback pertains more to producers' desire to maintain fan interest and cater to an energized fan base by not undermining trust in the producer-audience relationship.

Tellingly, the manner in which the producers removed Nikki and Paulo from *Lost* was emblematic of both fans' regulatory power and the animosity centering on the two characters. In "Exposé" (3:14), Nikki and Paulo fall victim to the bite of a Medusa spider, resulting in a state of paralysis and lowered heart rates. Believing Nikki and Paulo to be dead, two of *Lost*'s main characters shockingly bury the duo alive, with Nikki's paralysis subsiding just as dirt is cast onto her face. The two maligned characters, however, never regain enough power to escape, and the episode concludes with a shot of the freshly covered graves. The power of Nikki and Paulo's exit from the show was clear: *Lost*'s producers literally and figuratively buried two of *Lost*'s most unpopular characters. Shortly after "Exposé" aired, the producers again addressed the issue of fan influence on *The Official Lost Podcast*, indicating the torrent of negative responses to Nikki and Paulo played a direct role in their deaths:

> DAMON LINDELOF: We introduced [Nikki and Paulo], [and] *the backlash was instantaneous and unanimous....* The good news is ... Nikki and Paulo are buried and dead, and *they will not be back* [16 Apr. 2007, emphasis added].

The narrative treatment of Nikki and Paulo illustrates the shifting producer-audience relationship — one in which the implementation of dialogue branding strategies reinforces the sense that fans wield power over a television series. The resulting struggle between fans who wanted *Lost's* narrative to focus on the series' main characters and the producers who attempted to concentrate on secondary characters illustrates the disruptive qualities of participatory cultures.

The tension surrounding Nikki and Paulo also points to a larger issue at work in regards to participatory fandom and producer-audience communication. Fans repeatedly questioned executive producers Lindelof and Cuse about the presence of a master narrative plan. Despite continual reassurances from the producers that, as Cuse noted at the 2006 *Lost* Comic-Con panel, "We have an endpoint for the show. We have an overarching mythology for the show," the "master plan" question persisted (31 July 2006). This sentiment appears at odds with fans' preoccupation with the notion of fan influence and the desire for a producer-audience "feedback loop," as the reaction and subsequent narrative treatment of Nikki and Paulo illustrates. The tension between producer-audience participatory storytelling and a singular, uncompromising vision was best summed by one of the co-hosts of *The Transmission*:

> RYAN OZAWA: I'm not sure, though, that I want [*Lost's* producers] to always be so responsive to the fans, because I like to think that, for the most part, *they're giving us the show they want to give us and not the show that we want* ["Season Three: Episodes 1–3," emphasis added].

Although these two desires appear inherently contradictory, the balance between producer-audience responsiveness and *Lost* producers' control of a pre-plotted master narrative is similar to audience participatory strategies dating as far back as the 1800s with authors such as Charles Dickens (Rose 166). While this "authorship-sharing" has a long history, what is unique about contemporary participatory cultures is producers' use of new media technologies to interactively engage with fans (Rose, "Deep Media"). As Angie Knaggs argues, "Small groups of tech-savvy fans are no longer being courted and cultivated by producers; they are now invited into the text itself in small but significant ways" (409). This invitation to participate represents a culturally significant shift — and not solely a technological transformation — in which the new technologies simultaneously empower fans while reinforcing producers' role as cultural gatekeepers. Hence, *The Official Lost Podcast* and *The Transmission* became sites of contestation in which this contradictory negotiation between producers and audiences was continually challenged and reconfigured. This struggle continued as *Lost*'s producers implemented engagement strategies involving online video.

Online Video as an Engagement Strategy

In addition to the use of dialogue branding strategies facilitated by *The Official Lost Podcast* during the television season, *Lost*'s producers screened original content during ABC's *Lost* panels at the San Diego Comic-Con in an effort to maintain audience engagement during the television series' hiatus periods. The production and distribution of one such video, *The Orchid Video*, reflects the current industrial logic regarding the use of online content. As Michael Curtin astutely observes, "Online video may represent a grand opportunity for television companies, but executives are nevertheless aware that they cannot simply recirculate broadcast programming onto the web. They must develop dedicated material that is conducive to web viewing" (17). By releasing original content encouraging fan-text interactivity and producer-audience communication during *Lost*'s hiatus periods, ABC and *Lost*'s producers both promoted *Lost*'s television series and sustained fan interest. The use of *The Orchid Video*, therefore, represents an engagement strategy involving the use of online video to promote a range of participatory activities.

Starting in 2004, ABC began cultivating a fan base with panels consisting of *Lost* cast members and creative staff. Lindelof and Cuse played central roles in these panels, discussing the production of the series and answering questions from Comic-Con attendees. At the close of several panels, ABC screened original content that depicted character back stories, offered narrative clues, and foreshadowed future storylines in an effort to sustain audience engagement by providing "additive comprehension" or additional narrative insights (Perryman 33). Released in July 2007 after the conclusion of *Lost*'s third season, the first video screened for a Comic-Con audience, *The Orchid Video*, featured a character explaining the scientific purposes of The Orchid research station — one of many such stations located on the island. In contrast to other orientation films, as they were known within *Lost*'s diegesis, *The Orchid Video* consisted primarily of outtakes. As such, many of the most integral parts of *The Orchid Video* were missing, fueling speculation from fans regarding both the missing footage and the narrative significance of the events depicted in the outtakes. ABC's scheduling of *Lost*'s fourth season, in particular, presented a significant economic incentive for such an engagement strategy. In contrast to more traditional summer hiatus periods, ABC opted for scheduling strategy in which an eight-month gap separated the end of *Lost*'s third season, in May 2007, and the beginning of the fourth season, in January 2008 (Ryan). Providing new content in the form of *The Orchid Video* allowed *Lost*'s producers to maintain the series' relevance by offering fans a cryptic look at the series' fourth season — one that would keep fans communicating and speculating about the video's significance during *Lost*'s extended hiatus.

Although first screened at Comic-Con in July 2007, *The Orchid Video* appeared on YouTube and *Lost*-related websites, such as the *Lost*-themed wiki Lostpedia, shortly thereafter. When *Lost*'s fourth season began, Cuse and Lindelof further directed fans to watch *The Orchid Video* in order to more fully understand events taking place on the television series. For instance, in the episode "Confirmed Dead" (4:02), the unexpected discovery of an island-originating polar bear in a desert prompted the following exchange on *The Official Lost Podcast*:

> BEN NEVER LIES: How does a polar bear with a Dharma collar get in the middle of the desert?
>
> DAMON LINDELOF: You know ... there are properties of the island ... that are potentially capable of ... transporting things from the island off the island.
>
> CARLTON CUSE: *It might be helpful actually for those viewers who are interested in this question to go online and find the training film for The Orchid station* [15 Feb. 2008, emphasis added].

Lindelof and Cuse's discussions on *The Official Lost Podcast*, therefore, established a canonical link between *The Orchid Video* and the television series — a connection reinforced by the eventual appearance of The Orchid station in the season four finale "There's No Place Like Home" (4:13). This revelation was significant in that previous narrative extensions, such as *The Lost Experience* alternate reality game and the *Lost: Via Domus* video game, detailed events that were never directly referenced in the television series. In their final podcast before the conclusion of the fourth season, Lindelof and Cuse hinted that the narrative elements established by *The Orchid Video* in July 2007 would finally surface on the television series in May 2008:

> CARLTON CUSE: We've seen tantalizing bits of The Orchid station ... last year at Comic-Con.... *Would it be possible that we might be seeing more of that orientation film*, Damon?
>
> DAMON LINDELOF: If we saw the bloopers [from] the orientation film at Comic-Con, I would hope that we actually get to see the real deal in the finale. *I'd feel pretty ripped-off if we didn't* [19 May 2008, emphasis added].

In addition to discussing the use of an engagement strategy involving original, video content to "tantalize" fans during *Lost*'s hiatus period, the producers also established a precedent for the use of such an engagement strategy. Lindelof, for instance, notes that he would feel "ripped off" — a point that will be further examined in the following section — if *The Orchid Video* was not relevant to events occurring on the television series, thereby firmly establishing the intertwined relationship between the narratives of the videos screened at Comic-Con and the television series.

While *The Orchid Video* and *The Official Lost Podcast* provided ABC with new methods for sustaining an audience by promoting fan-text interactivity and producer-audience communication, such engagement strategies presented potential pitfalls as well. ABC's screening of a subsequent video at the 2008 *Lost* Comic-Con panel resulted in tension and conflict between producers and audiences when the canonical relationship between the Comic-Con videos and the television series became unclear.

Podcasts, Online Video and the Struggle Over Lost's Canon

Beginning largely during the hiatus period between *Lost*'s second and third seasons, *Lost*'s producers expanded the television series' storyworld through an array of paratexts, including websites, mobisodes, online videos, a novel, a video game, and jigsaw puzzles. As such, debates centering on the notion of a *Lost* canon — the body of texts constituting *Lost*'s official narrative — were a recurring theme within the discourses of *The Official Lost Podcast* and *The Transmission*. The notion of canon is an expression of a text's "integrity" in relation to an existing storyworld (Milner 723), and the inconsistency and even outright contradiction between canonical and non-canonical texts fostered tension between Lindelof, Cuse, and fans centering on the value of fan participation and interactivity. In particular, the struggle over the canonical nature of *The Dharma Booth Video*, the video screened at the 2008 *Lost* Comic-Con panel, provides a potent example of how participatory and interactive engagement strategies can actually undermine the integrity of the producer-audience relationship, thereby illustrating the often uneasy relationship between participatory producers and fans.

The Dharma Booth Video— a name originating from the video's initial exhibition location inside a Dharma Initiative booth at the 2008 Comic-Con — featured Dr. Pierre Chang, the same character from *The Orchid Video*, delivering a message from the 1970s to people thirty years into the future. In the video, Dr. Chang speaks directly to the camera and interacts with an unseen character operating the camera. After revealing that he was able to send the videotaped message into the future by using the unique properties of the island, Dr. Chang declares that he will die shortly after recording the message. *The Dharma Booth Video*'s most shocking detail, however, was the voice of Daniel Faraday, a character arriving on the island in 2004, as the person operating the camera. Although Faraday never appears on camera in *The Dharma Booth Video*, it was clear to the hosts of *The Transmission* that the character was, in fact, present in the 1970s ("Comic-Con in Review"). *The Dharma Booth Video*, therefore, proved an effective engagement tool, sparking speculation and discussion during the hiatus period between *Lost*'s four and fifth seasons, as fans debated how Faraday could be present on the island in both the 1970s and the 2000s. However, after Faraday died in the season five episode "The Variable" (5:14) before taking part in the events depicted in *The Dharma Booth Video*, fans struggled with the relationship between the television series and the video.

Informed by *The Orchid Video*, fans expected *Lost*'s transmedia narrative to be internally consistent, especially among the videos screened at Comic-Con. As such, *The Transmission*'s participatory fans incorporated a range of interpretive strategies in order to reconcile the two texts. One strategy, for example, involved positing that the events of *The Dharma Booth Video* occurred off-screen:

> SCOTT: Could Daniel [Faraday] have gone to Dr. Chang before visiting the meeting at Sawyer's? Well, how [else] could he have convinced Chang ... that he's going to die in only a few hours? ["The Variable"].

Because Faraday died in the scenes following the meeting at Sawyer's residence, the conjecture that Faraday filmed Dr. Chang's message to the future before this event is not altogether unlikely given that, at this point in the television series, *Lost*'s narrative structure included flashbacks and flash-forwards. It was not unreasonable, then, to speculate that the events of *The Dharma Booth Video* might be featured in a subsequent episode.

However, when Faraday's meeting with Dr. Chang was not depicted in the subsequent episode, fans crafted elaborate theories accounting for both Faraday's death in the television series and his appearance in *The Dharma Booth Video*. Based on the events depicted in *The Orchid Video*, in which two identical rabbits appear, one popular theory centered on cloning:

> DOUGLAS: Originally this theory spawned from [*The Orchid Video*] with [the] two rabbits.... I think that back in Ann Arbor, Daniel [Faraday] figured out a way to harness this ... so he could use it and come back more than once. So this allows for him to actually shoot the [*Dharma Booth*] video of Dr. Chang ... after having been killed.... *There has to be another Daniel* ["Follow the Leader," emphasis added].

This conjecture demonstrates fans' desire to validate their interactive and participatory activities by rendering *The Dharma Booth Video* as a meaningful, relevant extension of *Lost*'s television series. Another strategy for further rectifying the apparent discrepancies between *The Dharma Booth Video* and the television series involved time travel, a plot device introduced in the television series' fifth season. In the following theory, a fan sees Faraday's background as a physicist researching time as a way to resolve the narrative incongruity:

> NAILS: What if Dan [Faraday] has traveled back into the time multiple times and perhaps this is his last trek back.... [W]hat if the video shown at Comic-Con was indeed Dan making that video as a backup plan in case he failed further in the past to stop the Incident ["The Variable"].

By developing a range of increasingly complicated interpretive strategies that avoid the apparent contradiction between *The Dharma Booth Video* and "The Variable," *Lost* fans displayed a desire to retain the canonicity of both the television series and *The Dharma Booth Video*. Despite these efforts, however, the explanation for the storyline inconsistencies was actually quite simple: *Lost*'s producers regarded the video primarily as a promotional text for the following season — one which they did not feel obligated to honor with treatment in the television series.

For *Lost*'s producers, the power of online video lay in its promotional capacity, thereby representing the paradoxical desire to capitalize on the power of interactive and participatory engagement strategies to maintain fan interest yet an unwillingness to consistently reward such engagement. As Cuse suggested on *The Official Lost Podcast*, the producers felt no obligation to adhere to the narrative established in *The Dharma Booth Video*: "*We don't consider what goes on in Comic-Con canon. I mean, we try to make it tie into the show, but the only thing that really is canon is the show for us*" (11 May 2009, emphasis added). In other words, after serving its purpose during *Lost*'s hiatus period between seasons four and five, the producers abandoned the storyline involving Faraday filming Dr. Chang's message to the future. While *Lost*'s producers privileged promotion over storytelling, *Lost* fans placed a different value on their interactive and participatory engagement. Encouraged by the prior use of online video as well as by Cuse and Lindelof's own words regarding the importance of *The Orchid Video*, fans engaged with *The Dharma Booth Video* in an effort to gain a deeper understanding of *Lost*'s narrative. The producers' failure to integrate *The Dharma Booth Video* into *Lost*'s television series, therefore, constituted a breach of the "canonical contract," in which interactive and participatory engagement is rewarded with official storyworld insights. Lindelof attempted to assuage the widespread frustration expressed by fans, noting on *The Official Lost Podcast*, "[W]e feel like we get a little bit of leeway when it comes to material that we generate for Comic-Con and the Internet and stuff like that" (11 May 2009). Despite this plea for "leeway," fans felt cheated, and the resulting disappointment surrounding *The Dharma Booth Video* illustrates the often fluid and contradictory qualities of interactive and participatory engagement strategies.

The Dharma Booth Video's failure to honor the "canonical contract" undermined the producer-audience bond established by *Lost*'s producer's prior dialogue branding strategies. Consider the following statements from the hosts of *The Transmission* after Lindelof and Cuse indicated that *The Dharma Booth Video* was non-canonical:

> RYAN OZAWA: [I]t's been demonstrated that the Comic-Con video was what [the producers] thought was going to be coming into the story, but it turns out they couldn't write it that way. *Now* [it is] *just non-canon, non-timeline, and it's something we thought a little bit too much about.*
>
> JEN OZAWA: *Well, it really makes me feel ripped-off, in that case* ["Follow the Leader," emphasis added].

Jen Ozawa's use of the phrase "ripped-off" is telling, as a consumer gets ripped-off by overpaying for a service or commodity (Massoud and Bernhardt 96–98). Clearly, Ozawa feels as if she invested too heavily in an inauthentic or non-canonical text. Significantly, Lindelof's own comments on *The Official Lost Podcast* support such feelings. When discussing *The Orchid Video* in May 2008 — two months before the release of *The Dharma Booth Video*— Lindelof noted that he would "feel pretty ripped-off" if the video and the television series did not ultimately align (19 May 2008). Hence, both producers and audiences use the transactional metaphor to describe *Lost*'s transmedia canon.

Moreover, a consumer gets "ripped-off" by the seller — not the item being sold. Therefore, while the notion of canon is tied to the integrity of the text (Milner, 2010), canon formation is also keenly linked to the producer of the text as well. By not honoring the "canonical contract" established by *The Orchid Video*, Lindelof and Cuse betrayed fan expectations surrounding *The Dharma Booth Video*'s value, thereby depreciating what Joshua Green and Henry Jenkins regard as the "moral economy" between participatory producers and fans (214). As Green and Jenkins maintain, "[M]edia companies are being forced to reassess the nature of consumer engagement and *the value of audience participation* in response to a shifting media environment characterized by ... the increased power and capacity of consumers to shape the flow and reception of media content" (214). Simply put, *Lost*'s fans did not engage with online content for its promotional potentials; rather, interactive and participatory engagement represented a way for fans to gain official narrative insights. The failure to reward this engagement in accordance with fan's desires consequently diminished the integrity of *Lost*'s participatory producer-audience bond.

The disappointment surrounding the non-canonical nature of *The Dharma Booth Video* was still fresh in fans' minds at the final *Lost* Comic-Con panel in 2009. Since ABC debuted Comic-Con videos the previous two years, fans expected the 2009 *Lost* panel would include a similar screening. Yet, when the hosts of *The Transmission* questioned Comic-Con attendees about their expectations for the *Lost* panel, one fan remarked:

> JACK: I don't want anything — no video that's going to turn out to be meaningless ["Comic-Con Day 2"].

ABC did, in fact, screen a new video — a series of diegetic commercials featuring *Lost* characters — at the 2009 *Lost* Comic-Con panel. However, reflecting the tension and sense of disappointment surrounding *The Dharma Booth Video*, Cuse and Lindelof refused to answer questions about this latest video. Instead, after debuting the video, Lindelof and Cuse simply instructed fans to "trust us" about the video's canonical nature ("Comic-Con *Lost* Panel"). As this appeal demonstrates, the process of canon formation functions as an expression of trust in the producer-audience relationship. *The Official Lost Podcast* and *The Transmission*, therefore, became sites of struggle between producers and audiences as these notions of trust were continually negotiated.

Conclusion

So, then, where are we? A confluence of technological and industrial shifts involving the rise of podcast and online video technologies as well as shifting post-network era engagement strategies has created new terrain on which media producers and fans regularly evaluate the value of participatory fandom. Although engineered by new media technologies, these engagement strategies represent a culturally significant shift that simultaneously empowers fans while reinforcing producers' role as cultural gatekeepers. Hence, although the ability to engage directly with a producer during the production of a television series does invite the possibility for a more democratic form of creation, the participatory producer-audience relationship is often fraught with tension and conflict.

While *The Official Lost Podcast* was part of a savvy audience-building strategy in the crowded and increasingly competitive post-network era landscape, Lindelof and Cuse's dialogue branding and validation of fan feedback fostered notions of fan agency in *Lost*'s television series, thereby encouraging fans to vocalize their discontent with the series. Hence, *The Official Lost Podcast* functioned as a feedback loop in which fan evaluation and criticism worked its way back into the television series. In the case of Nikki and Paulo, two characters widely maligned by *Lost* fans, the "noise" or "interference" introduced into the feedback loop by participatory fans resulted in producers bowing to fan pressure and removing the characters in a manner emblematic of the negative reception. On the one hand, the fan reaction and narrative treatment of Nikki and Paulo illustrates the regulatory and even disruptive power of participatory fandom. On the other hand, *The Official Lost Podcast*'s participatory culture enabled *Lost*'s producers to exploit an abundance of fan feedback for their own economic gains. Nevertheless, the communicative channel of *The Official Lost Podcast* proved to be a space for the expression of contestation and tension where fans challenged the producers' power and the producers attempted to re-establish authority.

Similarly, *The Transmission* fan-produced podcast functioned as a participatory platform on which *Lost* fans challenged producers regarding the formation of *Lost*'s transmedia canon. Although *The Orchid Video* proved to be an effective tool for prolonging audience engagement by foreshadowing a future storyline while *Lost*'s television series was on hiatus, this engagement strategy ultimately backfired when the narratives of the subsequent video, *The Dharma Booth Video*, and the television series contradicted each other. Whereas Lindelof and Cuse presented *The Dharma Booth Video* to fans as a canonical extension of *Lost*'s television series, the video's status ultimately shifted, functioning more as a promotional text than an official, relevant paratext.

The use of *The Dharma Booth Video* failed to honor the producer-audience "canonical contract," thereby undermining the bond established by *The Official Lost Podcast*. When coupled with the producer-audience communication afforded by official podcasts, discourses of canon formation extend the notion of integrity beyond the text and onto the producer as well. In addition to the violating qualities of the text, non-canonical or inconsistent texts threaten the integrity of the producer-audience bond by undermining the audience's investment of trust in the producer. Among *The Transmission*'s *Lost* fans, for example, the discrepancy between *The Dharma Booth Video* and *Lost*'s television series fostered feelings of being exploited or duped by the producers — not the text itself. The resulting disappointment surrounding *The Dharma Booth Video* illustrates that fans largely valorize participatory activities when producers reward this participation with significant canonical insights. Thus, although participatory strategies offer the lure of a more democratic approach to creation, these logics can actually have the reverse effect when producers do not validate producer-audience participation and fan-text interactivity.

Works Cited

Andrejevic, Mark. "Watching Television Without Pity: The Productivity of Online Fans." *Television and New Media* 9.1 (2008): 24–46. Print.

Benkler, Yochai. *The Wealth of Networks: How Social Production Transforms Markets and Freedom.* New Haven: Yale University Press, 2006. Print.

Bruns, Axel. *Blogs, Wikipedia, Second Life, and Beyond: From Production to Produsage.* New York: Peter Lang, 2008. Print.

Curtin, Michael. "Matrix Media." *Television Studies After TV: Understanding Television in the Post-Broadcast Era.* Eds. Graeme Turner and Jinna Tay. New York: Routledge, 2009. 9–19. Print.

Green, Joshua, and Henry Jenkins. "The Moral Economy of Web 2.0: Audience Research and Convergence Culture." *Media Industries: History, Theory, and Method.* Eds. Jennifer Holt and Alisa Perren. Chichester, West Susex: Wiley-Blackwell, 2009. 213–225. Print.

Grossman, Ben. "The New Deal: How TV Executives Will Find Digital Dollars in the Coming Year." *Broadcasting and Cable.* 31 Dec. 2005. Web. 1 May 2012. http://www.broadcasting cable.com/article/102252-The_New_Deal.php.

Jenkins, Henry. *Fans, Bloggers, and Gamers: Exploring Participatory Culture.* New York: New York University Press, 2006. Print.

Johnson, Derek. "Inviting Audiences In: The Spatial Reorganization of Production and Consumption in 'TVIII.'" *New Review of Film & Television Studies* 5.3 (2007): 61–80. Print.

Knaggs, Angie. "*Prison Break* General Gabbery: Extra-Hyperdiegetic Spaces, Power, and Lana, Identity in *Prison Break.*" *Television and New Media* 12.5 (2011): 395–411. Print.

Lindelof, Damon, and Carlton Cuse. *The Official Lost Audio Podcast.* Rec. 28 Nov. 2005. ABC, 2005.

_____. *The Official Lost Audio Podcast.* Rec. 31 Jul. 2006. ABC, 2006.

_____. *The Official Lost Audio Podcast.* Rec. 12 Feb. 2007. ABC, 2007.

_____. *The Official Lost Audio Podcast.* Rec. 16 Apr. 2007. ABC, 2007.

_____. *The Official Lost Audio Podcast.* Rec. 21 Sep. 2007. ABC, 2007.

_____. *The Official Lost Audio Podcast.* Rec. 15 Feb. 2008. ABC, 2008.

_____. *The Official Lost Audio Podcast.* Rec. 19 May 2008. ABC, 2008.

_____. *The Official Lost Audio Podcast.* Rec. 11 May 2009. ABC, 2009.

Littleton, Cynthia. "*Lost*: The Weight of the Wait." *Variety.* 12 Oct. 2007. Web. 1 May 2012. http://www.variety.com/article/VR1117974014/.

Lotz, Amanda. *The Television Will Be Revolutionized.* New York: New York University Press, 2007. Print.

Massoud, Nadia, and Dan Bernhardt. "'Rip-off': ATM Surcharges." *RAND Journal of Economics* 33.1 (2002): 96–115. Print.

Miller, Laura. "Just Write It!: A Fantasy Author and His Impatient Fans." *The New Yorker.* 11 Apr. 2011. 32–37. Print.

Milner, Ryan M. "Negotiating Text Integrity: An Analysis of Fan-Producer Interaction in an Era of Digital-Connectivity." *Information, Communication, and Society* 13.5 (2010): 722–746. Print.

Mittell, Jason. "Narrative Complexity in Contemporary American Television." *The Velvet Light Trap* 58 (2006): 29–40. Print.

Murray, Simone. "'Celebrating the Story the Way It Is': Cultural Studies, Corporate Media and the Contested Utility of Fandom." *Continuum: Journal of Media and Cultural Studies* 18. 1 (2004): 7–25. Print.

Ozawa, Ryan and Jen Ozawa. "Comic-Con Day 2." *The Transmission.* Rec. 24 July 2009. Ryan Ozawa and Jen Ozawa, 2009.

_____. "Comic-Con in Review." *The Transmission.* Rec. 10 Aug. 2008. Ryan Ozawa and Jen Ozawa, 2008.

_____. "Comic-Con *Lost* Panel." *The Transmission.* Rec. 25 July. 2009. Ryan Ozawa and Jen Ozawa, 2009.

_____. "Follow the Leader." *The Transmission.* Rec. 10 May 2009. Ryan Ozawa and Jen Ozawa, 2009.

_____. "Season Three: Episodes 1–3." *The Transmission.* Rec. 6 Sept. 2009. Ryan Ozawa and Jen Ozawa, 2009.

_____. "The Variable." *The Transmission.* Rec. 3 May 2009. Ryan Ozawa and Jen Ozawa, 2009.

Perryman, Neil. "*Doctor Who* and the Convergence of Media: A Case Study in 'Transmedia

Storytelling.'" *Convergence: The International Journal of Research into New Media Technologies* 14. 1 (2008): 21–39. Print.

"Pilot, Part 2." *Lost*. ABC. 29 Sep. 2004. DVD.

Rose, Frank. *The Art of Immersion: How the Digital Generation is Remaking Hollywood, Madison Avenue, and the Way We Tell Stories*. New York: W.W. Norton, 2011. Print.

_____. "'Deep Media,' Transmedia, What's the Difference? An Interview with Frank Rose (Part Two)." *Confessions of an Aca-Fan: The Official Weblog of Henry Jenkins*. 28 Jan. 2011. Web. 1 May 2012. http://henryjenkins.org/2011/01/deep_media_transmedia_whats_th_1.html.

Ross, Sharon Marie. *Beyond the Box: Television and the Internet*. Malden, MA: Blackwell, 2008. Print.

Rowe, David, Andy Ruddock, and Brett Hutchins. "Cultures of Complaint: Online Fan Message Boards and Networked Digital Media Sport Communities." *Convergence: The International Journal of Research into New Media Technologies* 16.3 (2010): 298–315. Print.

Ryan, Maureen. "Lost's Fab Start to Season 4, and a Chat with Co-Creator Damon Lindelof." *Chicago Tribune*. 29 Jan. 2008. Web. 27 May 2012. http://featuresblogs.chicagotribune.com /entertainment_tv/2008/01/lost-shockers-a.html.

Shefrin, Elana. "*Lord of the Rings, Star Wars*, and Participatory Fandom: Mapping New Congruencies between the Internet and Media Entertainment Culture." *Critical Studies in Media Communication* 21.3 (2004): 261–281. Print.

"Times Talks: Looking Back on 'Lost.'" *The New York Times*. 20 May 2010. Web. 1 May 2012. http://www.nytimes.com/video/2010/05/21/arts/television/1247467896476/times-talks-looking-back-on-lost.html.

Weber, Larry. *Marketing to the Social Web: How Digital Customer Communities Build Your Business*. Hoboken, NJ: Wiley, 2009. Print.

Wexelblat, Alan. "An Auteur in the Age of the Internet: JMS, *Babylon 5*, and the Net." In *Hop on Pop: The Politics and the Pleasures of Popular Culture*. Eds. Henry Jenkins, Tara McPherson, and Jane Shattuc. Durham: Duke University Press, 2002. 209–226. Print.

White, Michele. *The Body and the Screen: Theories of Internet Spectatorship*. Cambridge: MIT Press, 2006. Print.

Wilson, Michael. "Finding Themselves in 'Lost.'" *The New York Times*. 2 Apr. 2010. Web. 1 May 2011. http://www.nytimes.com/2010/04/04/arts/television/04lost.html?pagewanted=all& _r=0.

Afterword
The Past and Future
of Fandom Studies

JONATHAN MALCOLM LAMPLEY

The preceding essays represent what my co-editor and I feel are some of the most exciting and insightful investigations into the complex world of fandom, an area of inquiry once marginalized (if not wholly ignored) by the academic community and generally denigrated by society at large. We are very proud to present these pieces in a volume that appeals to both academic and popular audiences, for we believe it is important that the field of fandom studies be familiar and accessible to both the scholar and the fan. As we wrap up what we hope will be the first of many such collections, we think it is important to consider where fandom comes from and where it seems to be going.

We opened this book with an introduction in which my co-editor recounted his personal introduction to fandom thanks to his exposure to *The Monkees* and Davy Jones. What particularly interests me about Kris's experience is that it occurred long after the "Pre-fab Four" enjoyed their greatest popular success; indeed, I recall the sudden re-emergence of "Monkees Mania" that developed in the late 1980s and remember being somewhat surprised by it. Many contemporaneous musical acts had completely disappeared, some of which had far higher critical reputations, so I wondered what it was about The Monkees that contributed to their revival. At the time, I didn't understand that many young Monkees fans of the 1960s were parents of their own teenagers by the 1980s and therefore wanted to share their interest with a new generation. Now there are three generations devoted to the group, and given the substantial media attention that surrounded Davy Jones's death in 2012, I suspect a fourth generation is being introduced to the band even as I write this. Monkees devotees, then, constitute yet another cult following similar to the ones explored in this book.

My own introduction to fandom predates Kris's by several years and parallels the growing complexity of the hobby (or lifestyle, if you prefer). From the age of four, I was a comic book fanatic, particularly of Batman and the Justice League of America, an obsession almost certainly sparked by reruns of the Adam West TV show, which I was too young to see when initially broadcast. By the time I started elementary school, I was a "dinosaur kid" — a subgroup of fandom that I am very glad to see is alive and well today — and became interested in movies and TV shows that featured dinosaurs and other prehistoric creatures. Not surprisingly, I started watching Godzilla and King Kong movies, which led to the point of no return in 1975. In that year, my parents bought me a copy of *Movie Monsters*, one of several "kiddie books" about horror, science fiction, the occult, and related subjects written by Thomas G. Aylesworth, a man whose influence on fans of a certain age I suspect is probably more profound than anybody today fully realizes. I wanted Aylesworth's book because it included chapters on King Kong and Godzilla, but my interest in monsters and horror grew when I read the other chapters, which introduced me to the historic, literary, and cinematic origins of Dracula, the Frankenstein Monster, and other Halloween staples.

In particular, I was fascinated by the men behind the monsters; I already knew the name of Vincent Price, but now I was introduced to the likes of Bela Lugosi, Boris Karloff, Christopher Lee, and Peter Cushing. My fascination grew, particularly after I saw Cushing in *Star Wars* (1977), a film that changed my life, and the lives of all fantasy fans, and indeed the way movies are made and marketed. It seems impossible to overstate the influence of *Star Wars* not just on fantasy lovers, but on movies and popular culture in general. If nothing else, it certainly cemented Cushing's status as my favorite actor of all time, a status the late English actor retains today.

At about the same time that *Star Wars* changed everything, I stumbled across my first issue of *Famous Monsters of Filmland* (or *FM* as it was often abbreviated), the legendary monster magazine that for nearly 20 years had been bringing horror lovers from across the country together. I didn't know it at the time, but by reading *FM* I had become a "Monster Kid," a subgroup that boasts such luminaries as Stephen King, Steven Spielberg, Alice Cooper, Peter Jackson, and countless others. Through the pages of the magazine, I learned more and more about the history of horror movies, and in bits and pieces I picked up information about the history of fandom itself thanks to the commentary of Forrest J Ackerman, the creator of *FM* and himself a prominent editor, agent, and collector of "sci fi" (a term he claimed to have invented). An interest in history in general soon dovetailed with my interest in fandom, and eventually the twain met. To this day, I remain fascinated with the origins of fandom and interested in how it continues to develop.

Exactly what constitutes the Big Bang of fandom is debatable, but there is no doubt that a major step in its development took place in the late 1920s when Hugo Gernsback, founder of the seminal science fiction magazine *Amazing Stories* and other pulps, began printing letters from readers in his publications. Because Gernsback included readers' addresses with the printed letters, he encouraged both personal and professional connections among science-fiction enthusiasts. Many of these relationships remained purely epistolary in nature — for example, the noted fantasist H. P. Lovecraft, whose Cthulhu Mythos tales have spawned one of the most fervent cult followings, never met many of his correspondents, including a teenaged Robert Bloch, later the author of *Psycho*—but the friendships grew and the hobby prospered as more and more fans turned to amateur and professional creative endeavors. During this time, young Forry Ackerman began lifelong friendships with Ray Bradbury and Ray Harryhausen, both of whom would go on to distinguish themselves as legendary figures in science fiction and fantasy media; Ackerman would even serve for a time as Bradbury's literary agent. Many other creative types got their start in the pages of amateur press associations, or APAs, the models for the so-called "fanzines" of a later generation.

It is generally acknowledged that the first science-fiction convention took place in 1939, when the first World Science Fiction Convention took place in New York. Pulp artist Frank R. Paul was the first Guest of Honor, and attendees included such luminaries in the field as Issac Asimov, Jack Williamson, Frederik Pohl, Bradbury, and Ackerman, who wore a home-made costume and thus is credited with starting one of the most popular elements of the convention experience. Now known as Worldcon, the World Science Fiction Convention has been held regularly for more than 70 years (though World War II interrupted the tradition for a few years) and remains the primary model for fan gatherings everywhere. Similarly, the attendees at that first convention count as representatives of "First Fandom," the first organized science-fiction fan community.

Fandom grew, albeit slowly, over the next few decades. There seems little indication that serious aficionados had much of an influence on science fiction (except perhaps in its literary form) until the late 1960s when a letter-writing campaign spearheaded by John and Bjo Trimble of Los Angeles helped convince NBC to reconsider its decision to cancel *Star Trek*. By this time, editors such as Julius Schwartz at National Periodical Publications (known today as DC Comics) and Stan Lee at Marvel Comics had revived Hugo Gernsback's custom of printing readers' addresses in the letter pages of their comic books, contributing mightily to the growth of comic-book fandom as a distinct offshoot of general science-fiction fandom. In the wake of *Star Wars*, interest in organized fandom grew at a much faster rate, and the number of fan conventions increased rapidly. The proliferation of these gatherings meant that fans could gather almost every single weekend of the year, and the areas of interest at such "cons" became increasingly diverse.

The early conventions focused almost exclusively on literary science fiction, but in time other aspects of fantasy were celebrated, including science fiction in other media, horror in various media, comic books, and gaming. These variations were not always welcomed by the traditional science-fiction audience, who began making distinctions between the "hard" science fiction they loved and the "soft" forms generally associated with movies and television. Eventually, specialized fan gatherings became common; conventions devoted exclusively to comic books came first, and *Star Trek* conventions set the standard for specialized media conventions, but events focused on horror, gaming, anime, and other areas grew in both size and sophistication. Some conventions have grown to proportions that even the most visionary attendees of the first World Con could not conceive, such as DragonCon, held in Atlanta every Labor Day weekend, and the San Diego Comic-Con, which has emerged as the leading fan gathering in the country. Comic-Con now draws 100,000 fans a year and is supported by publishing companies, movie studios, and game producers; the convention is so popular and influential that it is now extensively covered by the mainstream news media.

There is no way to underestimate the impact of technology on the growth of fandom. Indeed, practically every technical innovation of the last 40 years has directly or indirectly contributed to the development of the fan community. The emergence of consumer video recording has made easy access to the vast majority of movie and television projects an everyday occurrence. Improvements in computers have led to improvements in computer games, which in turn have become one of the pillars of fandom. However, it is the rise of the Internet that has had the greatest impact on the growth of fan culture. Instant communication between fans from all over the world is now possible, and blogs, podcasts, and other online activities have expanded opportunities to express interest in the various aspects of the hobby — and to promote various properties.

Because computers and the Internet have become so integral to contemporary life in the industrialized world, the term "geek," once used so pejoratively, has lost much of its sting. While many older sci-fi readers and "Monster Kids" recall being ridiculed and bullied for their preferences by both children and adults ("that stuff will rot your brain," or so many parents and teachers claimed), younger fans are far less likely to report such prejudice. Even the stereotypical high school "jock" of the 21st century is computer literate and likely plays video games; for that matter, the Internet has given rise to "fantasy football" and other hypothetical sports games that strike me as far weirder pastimes than collecting action figures or learning the Klingon language could ever be. In short, we are all online, all following something religiously, all collecting something obsessively — we are all of us geeks.

This diversity of fan interests mirrors the growing diversity of fandom itself. Traditional fandom consisted largely of white males — the "fanboys" so often mocked by *Saturday Night Live, The Simpsons, Family Guy,* and countless other TV shows (these jokes are often conceived by fans who have themselves become professionals). However, a growing number of "fangirls" now take part in the hobby, as do more and more non-white fans. Perhaps the most notable characteristic of fan culture is how it welcomes fans regardless of political persuasion, sexual orientation, social class, or national origin. Not all fans exemplify inclusiveness, of course; political, racial, and sexual prejudice exists even in fandom. Furthermore, bitter feuds among factions can be traced back to the first Worldcon and to the pages of the pulps before that. There is no way to tell how many friendships have ended because one person's admiration of Captain Kirk was as passionate as another's esteem for Captain Picard, but ultimately the world would do well to note the model of inclusion and acceptance that fan culture has long established.

As fandom grows and diversifies, and as technical innovation increases access, it would seem logical that all of the various subcategories of interest would benefit. However, I am not convinced this is the case. The farther we get from the era of pulp magazines and radio dramas, the fewer the fans. I am particularly concerned about the diminishing presence of Classic Horror Fandom, which has largely been replaced with (for lack of a better phrase) "regular" horror. In a sense, this is to be expected; after all, the actors, writers, directors, and other creators of the original Universal horror films (the hallmarks of the Golden Age of Horror Cinema) are dead, as are most of the creators associated with what can be considered the Silver Age of Horror Cinema — the period that included the masterworks of Vincent Price and director Roger Corman at American International Pictures and the re-imaginings of Gothic terror initiated by England's Hammer Films, which usually involved Christopher Lee and/or Peter Cushing. It is strange to think that so few younger fright addicts seem interested in exploring the origins of the nightmares they profess to enjoy. Perhaps this trend demonstrates how perishable popular culture really is, or maybe it simply represents how a world with infinite options means some options will not be chosen.

Ultimately, though, I must conclude that the plethora of options is a good thing. Knowing how cyclical popular culture has always been, I assume that everything comes around again as a matter of course. Sooner or later, the professional scholar and the casual fan will wonder where the texts they devour come from; they will be captivated and excited by the journey to the wellspring of all wonders. The new works and areas of interest cannot exist without their forebears, as the innate desire for enlightenment and edification will verify.

In terms of fan scholarship, where do we go from here? While Kris and I are very pleased with the topics covered in this volume, we are acutely aware that there are more areas to cover. For example, we are intrigued by the powerful devotion viewers of the AMC TV show *The Walking Dead* continue to demonstrate, a devotion that has led many of them to show up on location in Georgia hoping to be cast as undead extras. We are interested in Lady Gaga's "little monsters," followers who seem to represent a force for social change, particularly in the area of gay rights. We note with satisfaction the revival of Hammer Horror as the long-dormant company has recently returned to film production and has released several impressive pictures, most notably the international box office hit *The Woman in Black* (2012), which has provided Harry Potter star Daniel Radcliffe with his first major "adult" film role. We see an almost endless realm of possibilities for explorations into the worlds of *Star Wars*, *Star Trek*, *Twilight*, and other fantasy franchises; we also think there is much to say about more "mundane" areas such as cult music ("Bieber fever"), literature (the *Fifty Shades of Grey* phenomenon), and sports (legendary NASCAR driver Dale Earnhardt). These and many other topics are worthy of further exploration and explication, and with any luck they will be included in a future edition of *Fan CULTure*.

About the Contributors

Kent **Aardse** is a PhD candidate at the University of Waterloo. He studies the relationship between media and narrative, particularly how digital media and social networking challenge longstanding narrative forms such as novels and film. His research focuses on all forms of digital textuality, from electronic literature to computer games to alternate reality games (ARGs).

Kristin M. **Barton** earned a PhD from Florida State University and is an associate professor of communication at Dalton State College. His research has explored the effects of watching reality television programming, and he has published articles on this topic in the *Journal of Broadcasting & Electronic Media* and *Communication Quarterly*. He wrote *The Big Damn* Firefly *& Serenity* Trivia Book (Bear Manor, 2012) and contributed to *Joss Whedon: The Complete Companion* (Titan, 2012) and *Investigating* Heroes (McFarland, 2011).

Jennifer C. **Garlen** is an independent scholar and writer in Huntsville, Alabama. She is the co-editor with Anissa M. Graham of two books about Jim Henson, *Kermit Culture* (2009) and *The Wider Worlds of Jim Henson* (2013; both McFarland), and the author of *Beyond Casablanca: 100 Classic Movies Worth Watching* (Westview Press, 2012). She teaches courses on literature, film and popular culture for LearningQUEST and the Osher Lifelong Learning Institute.

Anissa M. **Graham** teaches composition and literature in the English department at the University of North Alabama. She pursued an interest in 18th and 19th century British fiction at Georgia Southern University and Auburn University where she received her degrees. She is the co-editor with Jennifer C. Garlen of *Kermit Culture* (2009) and *The Wider Worlds of Jim Henson* (2013; both McFarland).

Michael **Graves** received a PhD from the University of Kansas and is a lecturer in KU's Department of Film and Media Studies. His research focuses on the media industry's use of transmedia storytelling and participatory strategies to engage with audiences.

Owain **Gwynne** is a PhD student in the Department of Media, Film & Communication at the University of Otago, New Zealand. His research interests include media fandom, new media, and video games. His doctoral thesis is on the online activities of fans during the pre-release period of Peter Jackson's *The Hobbit* movies.

Bethan **Jones** is a PhD candidate at Aberystwyth University's Department of Theatre, Film and Television Studies. She has written about gender in *Buffy the Vampire Slayer* and the Twilight Saga, fanmixes as fan-adopted paratexts, Harry Potter and social media, and *The X-Files* fan activism. Her work has been published in the *Journal of Creative Writing, Participations,* and *Transformative Works and Cultures.*

Meyrav **Koren-Kuik**'s research interests include narrative theory and the intersection between the visual arts, literature, and space. She contributed essays to the edited collections *Camelot on the Small Screen* (Boydell & Brewer, 2013) and *Film and Literary Modernism* (Cambridge Scholars, 2013). She has presented papers in conferences both in Israel and the United Kingdom and has taught basic academic composition classes at Tel Aviv University.

Jonathan Malcolm **Lampley** is an assistant professor of English at Dalton State College. He is the author of *Women in the Horror Films of Vincent Price* (McFarland, 2011) and is co-author (with Ken Beck and Jim Clark) of *The Amazing Colossal Book of Horror Trivia* (Cumberland House, 1999). His articles have appeared in many magazines and journals, and he frequently presents academic papers on classic horror and other topics at various conferences.

Susan **Orenstein** has a PhD from New York University and has been a teacher for the New York City school system, an instructor at Middlesex, Mercer and Ivy Tech community colleges, and a staff member at Lehigh and Bloomsburg universities. She is also a reader for ETS and a creator of content for the Learning House in Kentucky, a purveyor of online curriculum programs.

Jeff **Thompson** is an associate professor of English at Tennessee State University in Nashville. He is the Rondo Award–nominated author of *The Television Horrors of Dan Curtis* (McFarland, 2009) and *House of Dan Curtis* (Westview, 2010). He has written about *Dark Shadows* for fanzines, books, magazines, websites, slide shows, and academic presentations, and he has served as the emcee of many Dark Shadows Festivals.

Don **Tresca** is a graduate of California State University, Sacramento, and has written extensively on film and television for a variety of print and online publications. He is also interested in found-footage horror films.

Kathleen **Williams** is a PhD candidate in the Journalism and Media Research Centre at the University of New South Wales, Australia. Her research is concerned with the negotiation of cinematic culture into networked online spaces such as YouTube through the vehicle of the recut trailer. She has published in *Transformative Works and Cultures, Media/Culture Journal,* and *September 11 in Popular Culture* (Greenwood, 2010).

Index